Civil War

Civil War

Taylor Downing & Maggie Millman

A Juliet Gardiner Book

PARKGATE
BOOKS

First published by Collins & Brown Ltd, 1991
This edition published in 1998 by

Parkgate Books Ltd
Kiln House
210 New Kings Road
London
SW6 4NZ
Great Britain

1 3 5 7 9 8 6 4 2

British Library Cataloguing in Publication Data:
A catalogue record for this book is available
from the British Library

ISBN 1 85585 575 5

Art Editor Ruth Prentice
Designer Alison Shackleton

Contents

Dunrobin Castle

Aberdeen
Dunottar Castle

ATLANTIC OCEAN

SCOTLAND   Scone

NORTH SEA

Dunbar ▲
Edinburgh   Berwick
Glasgow
R. Tweed

Firth of Clyde

Newcastle
Carlisle   *R. Tyne*
R. Tees

Scarborough

Marston Moor ▲ York

ULSTER   *IRISH SEA*   ▲ **Preston**   Leeds
Belfast   Hull
                                    ENGLAND
▲ **Drogheda**   Manchester   *R. Humber*

CONNAUGHT
Galway   Liverpool

Dublin   Lincoln

R. Shannon   Newark
LEINSTER   *R. Trent*   Nottingham

Shrewsbury   Norwich
WALES   Birmingham
IRELAND   Stratford upon   *R. Avon* ▲ **Naseby** Huntington
MUNSTER   Avon   Warwick   Northampton   Cambridge
                Wexford ▲   **Worcester**   ▲ **Cropredy Bridge**
Cork   Hereford   *R. Severn*   **Edgehill** Banbury   Colchester
                                    Burford
Bantry   Monmouth   Gloucester   Oxford
Bay   Abingdon   *R. Thames* ▲ London
                                    Cardiff   Bristol   Windsor   **Turnham**
                                          Bath   **Roundway**   **Green**   Canterbury
                                          ▲ **Down**   Basingstoke
0   50   100 Miles   **Basing House**   Dover
                                    Bridgwater   Salisbury   ▲ **Cheriton**
                                          Sherborne   Southampton
                                    Exeter   Dorchester   Portsmouth

Plymouth   *ENGLISH CHANNEL*

Acknowledgment

We have written this book whilst making the television series of the same name produced by Flashback Television for Channel Four and first shown in 1991. We would like first of all to thank all those with whom we have also worked on the series. Many of the ideas in both series and book have developed in long conversations during the year of production. We owe a special debt to the two series directors, David Edgar and Richard Broad. Also central to the production was Caroline Jackson who acted as researcher for part of the series and Sian Williams, the Production Manager. The crew who shot and recorded the programmes over the course of the year consisted of Gerry Pinches, Simon Priestman and Bob Webber. The programmes were edited by Safi Ferrah and John White. Programme making is an essentially collective process whereas writing a book is more insular. However, we are the first to acknowledge that every member of the production team has played an important part in talking through and working out the ideas included on the following pages.

During the making of CIVIL WAR we have met with, talked to and interviewed scores of people. Our discussions with historians whom we have asked to describe impossibly complex ideas in tantalisingly brief answers have been enormously important to us. Our conversations with specialists who have contributed specific knowledge and expertise on many occasions have been invaluable. We are grateful to them all for the time they have given us and for the interest they have shown in our project. It would be impossible to try to list them all but we have included a bibliography of all the main books and pamphlets we have found useful in researching and in trying to understand this period.

The book has itself been a collaborative venture with David Souden writing the boxes and the additional material, and Celia Jones researching the illustrations. We are indebted to Celia for the superb quality of the pictures over the following pages. The range of information and evidence in the boxes illustrates the depth of David's knowledge of this period and adds greatly to the scope of the book.

Neither the series nor the book would have happened without the support of Gwynn Pritchard at Channel Four who commissioned the programmes, based on the original proposal by Taylor Downing of Flashback Television. From the first discussions about the idea, Gwynn saw potential in what was being proposed. We would also like to thank Juliet Gardiner our editor and publisher at Collins and Brown, whose enthusiasm largely brought the book about. But, of course, ultimately we must take responsibility as authors for what follows and for any errors or follies contained therein.

Taylor Downing and Maggie Millman
Flashback Television

Introduction

Every year on 3 September, a small group gathers outside the Houses of Parliament. A few hymns are sung, a brief speech is made and a bugler pipes the Last Post. A wreath is laid. Puzzled passers-by look as they hurry through Parliament Square or, if the House is in session, as they queue for seats in the Visitors Gallery. They would be forgiven for not realizing that this ceremony is one of the few formal ways in which the events of 1640-60 are commemorated in Britain today. The event is the annual gathering of the Cromwell Association at the statue of Oliver Cromwell which stands awkwardly, now surrounded by a security fence, outside Parliament. The day on which Cromwell died in 1658 was 3 September, also the day of two of his greatest victories at the battles of Dunbar in 1650 and Worcester in 1651. Other nations remember their revolutions with vast military parades, with Independence Days, with the singing of songs, the closing of schools, factories and offices. The French have their 14 July when the Champs Elysées is decked out with Tricolours. The Russians have their military parade every October in Red Square. In the United States of America, Independence Day is one of the major public holidays, an opportunity for fireworks and celebrations. But in England only a handful of enthusiasts gather beneath the statue that was erected in the 1890s after a fierce debate about whether or not it should be there at all.

It is uniquely British that the events in our history that come nearest to being classed as a 'revolution' go almost entirely unmarked. The years of turbulence and fighting that made up the Civil Wars were followed by the period of Commonwealth and Protectorate, when the British Isles were united for the first time in their history under a republican government in London. Events of these years completely laid waste the political map of the nation. Few institutions survived without change and some were swept away forever. The monarchy, the House of Lords, the House of Commons, the Church of England, the law, the armed forces were all affected. But the years of conflict and change were followed by the restoration of Charles II and of many features of the 'old world' in 1660. This has meant that these decades are now too often seen as an aberration, as a sort of cul-de-sac of history. Once the nation rejoined the right route, continuity could be restored and the onward march of progress towards the present day was possible.

Fortunately few people still perceive the past in this way, but some of these attitudes prevail when it comes to assessing the Civil War and its aftermath. The very words that are used are loaded. Do the events amount to a 'revolution', the like of which has never been repeated in British history? Or do they amount to a 'rebellion', of which there are many scattered throughout the pages of history? When an MP recently went to the library of the House of Commons to see a copy of the Act of Parliament which abolished the House of Lords from the time of the Commonwealth in 1649, the librarian looked puzzled: What did he mean by the Commonwealth? The only statutes from this time are listed under the 'Interregnum'. The word suggested that the period didn't really exist, that it was no more than a missing decade between lawful reigns. Moreover, civil wars often tend to be the most bloody of conflicts, ones that societies try to forget as soon as possible. Perhaps, therefore, it is not so surprising that we fail to mark these events with a special day.

There are some ways, however, in which these tumultuous years are remembered. Like a genie in the lamp, the abolition of all forms of censorship brought a fantastic outpouring of radical ideas in the 1640s and 50s. When the lamp was rubbed again at the Restoration the radicals disappeared inside once more. But their ideas lived on and emerged again and again to influence the likes of the American revolutionaries, the Chartists and later the Socialist movement itself. The Left has recently come to realise the importance of the radical debate that was unleashed by the Civil War and the Levellers, the Diggers and the Ranters have all been much studied and invoked. A few years ago a plaque was placed on the wall of Burford Church in Oxfordshire where three Levellers were executed by the army high command in 1649. In recent years a celebration has been held each May to mark the occasion. The Levellers Day event in and around Burford churchyard is perhaps the most overtly political commemoration of the years of civil war and popular agitation.

Others recall the wars in different ways by dressing up and re-enacting battles from the Civil War. There are now thousands of people who give up not only weekends to take part in these vivid reconstructions but devote many hours to the painstaking re-creation of the costumes and research into the lifestyle of the mid-seventeenth century. But their memory is again a partial one, and it would be strange for a nation to remember its political history only through the staging of shows at fairs and open days on weekends through the summer months.

Perhaps we should look elsewhere for signs that recall these years. Almost every town has a pub called the 'Royal Oak'. Many of these were established, it is often claimed, by Royalist soldiers who were compensated after 1661. Pubs called the 'King's Head', perhaps recall another phase of the struggle between Crown and Parliament. In the eighteenth century Charles II's escape after the battle of Worcester when he hid in an oak tree at Boscobel in Shropshire was commemorated annually by Oak Apple Day on 29 May. Today this tradition has almost completely died out except for its last vestige in the oak leaves worn by Chelsea Pensioners on this day as they remember their royal founder. Again, a foreigner would be forgiven for being perplexed by the memory of a revolution that is only to be found on pub signs and on the uniforms of war pensioners.

In one sense, the principal and most important way in which the years of Civil War are remembered is in schools and colleges throughout the world where the story of these years is taught. Few periods of British history have been so extensively written about and are so widely debated as the great political, religious and military conflict in the middle of the seventeenth century.

Ever since Christopher Hill set the metaphorical cat amongst the pigeons fifty years ago when he wrote about these events, calling them the 'English Revolution', they have been the central battleground of British historical writing. By the 1960s and early 70s the school of history that believed in the vast, underlying forces that shape history seemed to have won the day. People no longer talked about the 'Puritan revolution' but about 'preconditions', 'disequilibrium', 'trends' and 'triggers'. But in the late 1970s and 80s there was a swing against this view and the revisionists stress the minutiae of the breakdown from 1640 to 1642. These historians believe that civil war was certainly not inevitable and could have been avoided right up to the last minute, by rational men sitting around a table. More recently historians have seen the Civil War in the wider dimension of the 'war in three kingdoms' between England, Scotland and Ireland; others have come back to an emphasis on religious factors, seeing the Civil Wars as the British 'wars of religion'. There is now a rich and lively mixture of interpretations for the reader to choose from to guide him or her through the labyrinth of seventeenth-century history.

It is not the purpose of this book to take one view or the other. In both the book and the television series on which it is based, we have assiduously tried to present different views rather than to offer a single interpretation of events. There are plenty of single volume histories of this period written by the leading exponents of one view of history or another. Many of these can lay claim to being both comprehensive and authoritative. We do not pretend to be either. There are plenty of military histories of the Civil War. This book is certainly not that. There are fine accounts of each stage of the story of the Commonwealth and the Protectorate. Again, we cannot claim to present this. Rather, the book attempts to convey some of the significance of these years to the general, well-informed but nonspecialist reader, and to give an impression of what it might have been like to live through these tumultuous years.

Each chapter is based upon a programme in the series of the same name and is an attempt at an essay around a single theme. The story does not unfold in a straightforward chronology. There are overlaps between some of the chapters, especially between Chapter Two, 'Taking Sides', and Chapter Three, 'Battle'. Both chapters record events of the same years but from a different perspective. Similarly, the end of Chapter Four, 'Liberty', overlaps with the beginning of Chapter Five, 'Execution'. We make no apologies for this, in the hope that the reader will see each chapter as a separate and distinct theme in the story of civil war and revolution.

Each chapter is supplemented by the use of material that picks out specific topics or refers at greater length to primary documents. It is hoped that some of the colour of these years will be conveyed in the boxes and that the main arguments will unfold in the text. The boxes are intended to be read alongside the text rather than separately from it and the two are intended to work together. In both the book and the television programmes we have tried to convey the extraordinary nature of these times when father fought son and when brother took up arms against brother, when communities were divided down the middle and when it became impossible for men and women to sit on the fence and watch events pass them by. For most people in Britain choices had to be made and often they were painful ones. Contemporaries who lived through the years 1640-60 found them remarkable. As was said by many at the time, the world seemed to have been truly 'turned upside down'. It is hoped that in this book and in the television series we can evoke some of the extraordinary nature of these times of civil war and revolution.

Taylor Downing and Maggie Millman

Agitators. Representatives from the *New Model Army* elected in April 1647 to confer with officers over grievances.

Agreement of the People. Constitutional proposal of 28 October 1647 drafted by *Levellers* and *Agents* in the Army. Lilburne and others issued a moderated version in May 1649.

Arminianism. School of theological thought that emphasized free will over predestination, usually used as synonymous with *Laudianism* of High Church group headed by Archbishop Laud.

Attainder. Act of Parliament condemning a person convicted of high treason to forfeiture of property and goods, used against Strafford in 1641.

Billeting, Free Quarter. Placing of soldiers in civilian households, often supposedly to be paid for later.

Bishops' Wars. The conflict between England and Scotland 1639-41, caused by Scottish antagonism to the new Prayer Book, and ending in Scotland's favour, necessitating the recall of the *Long Parliament*.

Clubmen. Armed resisters to the armies on both sides, active from late 1644.

Convocation. Assembly of the clergy, in the two archdioceses of Canterbury and York. Voted money to Charles to fight the Scots in 1640.

Council of Officers. Body of the *New Model Army*, formed in August 1647 to negotiate with the King.

Council of State. Executive arm of the *Rump Parliament*.

County Associations. Formed by both sides in the Civil War overcoming localist tendencies. Most effective was the Eastern Association, crucial to the Parliamentary effort, formed in 1642 from all the counties of East Anglia.

Covenant, Scottish National. Drawn up in 1638 to unify Scottish resistance to the new Prayer Book.

Diggers. Popular name for communist group of 'true *Levellers*' led by Gerrard Winstanley in 1649.

Excise. Tax upon luxury goods and alcohol first introduced by Parliament in July 1643 to raise finance.

Fifth Monarchists. Sect of the 1650s who believed in using violence to help bring about the imminent Fifth Monarchy of Christ.

Five Members. Leading MPs whom Charles I tried to arrest from the *House of Commons* on 4 January 1642, which was seen as a gross attack on privileges.

Grand Remonstrance. The demands put to the King by Parliament on 1 December 1641, and subsequently rejected, which rehearsed grievances and recent reforms and demanded further concessions. Its passing by a narrow margin alienated many waverers.

Heads of the Proposals. Relatively generous peace propositions of the *New Model Army* presented to the King on 23 July 1647, and summarily rejected by him.

High Commission. Senior church court used by Laud to coerce opponents of his reforms in the 1630s, and abolished in 1641.

High Court of Justice. Commissioners appointed by the Rump Parliament after 4 January 1649 to try the King for levying war against his people and for high treason.

House of Commons. Lower house of Parliament, whose Committees guided the war effort.

House of Lords. Upper house of Parliament, much depleted from 1642 and abolished on 19 March 1649.

Humble Petition. *Leveller* document of 11 September 1648 appealing for constitutional change.

Humble Remonstrance. Army's assertion of its constitutional role, which was ignored by the *House of Commons* and precipitated the Army's occupation of London in December 1647.

Iconoclasm. Defacing of effigies and furnishings in churches, usually done from religious fervour.

Impeachment. Arraignment of persons charged with serious offences against the state – Strafford and Laud were prime cases – before Parliament.

Independents. Many sects, which all rejected state-regulated worship in favour of autonomous congregations.

Interregnum. One of the terms for the period between the execution of Charles I and the Restoration of Charles II, embracing the Commonwealth of 19 May 1649 to 16 December 1653, and the Protectorate that followed. The term Commonwealth is often used for the entire period.

Laudianism. Religious policies led by Archbishop Laud in the 1630s, often inspired by *Arminianism*, that promoted uniformity in worship and discipline and a promotion of ritual and ceremonial.

Levellers. Radical political group active 1647-9, who had considerable support within the *New Model Army*. Their programme included an extension of the franchise, religious toleration, and the *House of Lords'* abolition.

Long Parliament. Met 3 November 1640 and sat, without being dissolved, until 16 March 1660. After 1648 and *Pride's Purge* it became known as the *Rump Parliament*, which Cromwell expelled in 1653 and which reconvened in 1659.

New Model Army. Parliamentary fighting force established after 17 February 1645, based largely upon the Eastern *Association* and under Fairfax's command, and crucial to Parliament's ultimate success. It became imbued with radicalism and *Leveller* ideas.

Nineteen Propositions. Ultimatum sent to the King by Parliament on 1 June 1642.

Ordinances. Legislation passing through Parliament but lacking royal assent, therefore technically not Acts and so dependent upon their enforceability.

Oxford Parliament. Alternative body of MPs and peers loyal to the King, which met at Oxford from January 1644 until dissolved by Charles in March 1645 after it proposed compromise.

Personal Rule. Period during which Charles I ruled without recourse to Parliament, but with many expedients for raising revenues, from March 1629 until the meeting of the *Short Parliament* in April 1640.

Petition of Right. Grievances presented to the King by Parliament in 1629, which was soon followed by the dissolution of Parliament and the eleven years of the *Personal Rule*.

Presbyterianism. Church government by presbyters of equal rank, without bishops. It was the main form of church government in Scotland; the attempts to introduce it in England in 1647 following the intentions expressed in the *Solemn League and Covenant* were crushed by the *Independents*.

Pride's Purge. Exclusion from the *Long Parliament* of 140 MPs considered antagonistic to the Army in December 1648, by a group under Colonel Thomas Pride. The residue became known as the *Rump Parliament*.

Puritanism. A blanket term for more extreme Protestants. Strictly speaking, puritanism (with a small p) was the accepted condition of religion before the advent of Laudianism, with little emphasis upon ritual and special emphasis on preaching. The term Puritan (with upper case P) became a particular form of abuse in the early years of Civil War.

Putney Debates. Debates, especially involving soldiers and officers of the *New Model Army*, that were held in Putney church, Surrey in October and November 1647 to discuss *Leveller* ideas and the issues of the *Agreement of the People*.

Root and Branch. Pressure for the abolition of bishops, vigorously expressed in the Root and Branch Petition of the clergy of London sent to Parliament in December 1640.

Rump Parliament. Remaining membership of the *House of Commons* following *Pride's Purge* in 1648, usually around 80 in number. They were ejected by Cromwell in 1653 and recalled in 1659.

Self-Denying Ordinance. Measure of 3 April 1645 paving the way for the establishment of the *New Model Army*, preventing MPs or peers from holding military office (although excluding Cromwell).

Sequestration. Parliamentary process of seizing estates of Royalists, and the diversion of the revenues to the war effort, following an *ordinance* of 27 March 1643.

Ship Money. Contentious form of raising revenue ostensibly for maritime defence used by Charles I during the period of *Personal Rule*, and levied on all counties rather than coastal areas after 1635. The case against John Hampden for non-payment helped focus opposition. The *Long Parliament* abolished the tax on 5 July 1641.

Short Parliament. Following the *Bishops' Wars* Charles I was forced to recall Parliament to raise finance. Meeting on 13 April 1640, it was dissolved on 5 May when it resisted the royal will.

Solemn Engagement. A military covenant of the *New Model Army*, that preceded the establishment of the Army's General Council.

Solemn League and Covenant. Alliance between Parliament and the Scottish *Covenanters* of September 1643, promising to enforce *Presbyterianism* in England. From 5 February 1644 all those holding command under Parliament were forced to take the Covenant, but its meaures were never enforced.

Star Chamber. Court of law at Westminster used for speedy action, and seen as an instrument of royal oppression during the period of the *Personal Rule* and so abolished by the *Long Parliament* in 1640.

Thomason Tracts. Unique and voluminous collection of publications during the Civil War years and the lapsing of censorship, collected by London bookseller George Thomason and now in the British Library.

Trained bands. Citizens under arms organized on a county or urban basis, and extensively used in the early days of the Civil War.

1637 Case of Burton, Bastwick and Prynne. Ship Money case against Hampden et al. Introduction of new Prayer Book in Scotland, met armed resistance.

1638 Scottish National Covenant.

1639 First Bishops' War.

1640 Short Parliament. Second Bishops' War. King forced to concede to the Scots and call Long Parliament. Root and Branch Petition. Strafford and Laud impeached.

1641 Strafford's trial and execution. Army Plots. King leaves for Scotland. Abolition of Star Chamber and High Commission. Militia Bill. Censorship breaks down. Irish rebellion. Grand Remonstrance.

1642 Attempt to seize the Five Members. Militia Ordinance. King leaves London and denied entry to Hull. Nineteen Propositions. King raises Standard at Nottingham. Battle of Edgehill. Battle at Turnham Green. King sets up Headquarters in Oxford. Closing of theatres. Suspension of bishops.

1643 Oxford negotiations. Waller's Plot. Battles of Lansdown and Roundway Down. Excise introduced. Fall of Bristol. Relief of Gloucester. First Battle of Newbury. Pym and Hampden die. Solemn League and Covenant.

1644 Scots army enters England. Oxford Parliament. Committee of Both Kingdoms set up. York besieged. Battles of Cropredy Bridge and Marston Moor. Surrender of York. Battle of Tippermuir. Battle of Lostwithiel. Second Battle of Newbury. Henrietta Maria leaves England.

1645 Execution of Laud. Uxbridge negotiations. New Model Army and Self-Denying Ordinances. Battles of Leicester and Naseby. Battles of Langport and Bridgwater. Bristol retaken. Battles of Kilsyth and Philiphaugh. Battle of Rowton Heath. Glamorgan enters into treaties with Irish confederates.

1646 Prince of Wales leaves. King flees to the Scots, who surrender him to Parliament. Surrender of Newark and Oxford. Newcastle Propositions (Parliament's peace proposals). Abolition of episcopacy and passing of Blasphemy Ordinance. Earl of Essex dies.

1647 King taken at Holdenby. Proposals for reducing the Army. Saffron Walden meetings. Growth of Leveller movement, appointment of Agitators. Indemnity ordinances. Charges against the Eleven MPs. Army peace Heads of Proposals. Putney Debates. King's escape to Isle of Wight. Engagement with Scots.

1648 Second Civil War. Battle of Maidstone. Colchester rising and siege. Battle of St Neots. Surrender of Pembroke. Battles of Preston and Warrington. Surrender of Colchester. Levellers' Humble Petition. Cromwell leaves Scotland. Pride's Purge.

1649 Rule of Rump Parliament. King's trial. King executed. Lords abolished. Commonwealth established. Arrest of Leveller leaders; Digger experiments begin. Mutinies, Burford executions. Lilburne's first trial for treason. Sack of Drogheda and Wexford, Cromwell's Irish campaign.

1650 Charles II makes treaty with Scots. Cromwell made Lord-General. Battle of Dunbar. Blake destroys Prince Rupert's ships.

1651 Charles II crowned at Scone. Battles of Inverkeithing and capture of Perth. Battle of Worcester. Charles II flees. Navigation Act.

1652 Proceedings against Lilburne. First sea battles with Dutch in Channel. Settlement of Ireland. Increasing recognition of Commonwealth, by colonies and foreign powers.

1653 Cromwell dissolves the Rump. Barebones or convention Parliament. Dutch wars continue. Instrument of Government. Cromwell made Lord Protector.

1654 Engagement repealed. Sealed Knot formed. Dutch peace. Western Design initiated. Protectorate Parliament opens.

1655 Arrests of dissidents. Parliament dissolved. Penruddock's Rising. Landing in Jamaica. Major-Generals appointed. War with Spain.

1656 Second Protectorate Parliament. Nayler's Case. Rule of the Major-Generals in localities.

1657 Remonstrance to Parliament. Humble Petition and Advice. Cromwell refuses the crown. Attempted Fifth Monarchist rising. Death of Lilburne.

1658 Parliament dissolved. Anglo-French victory over Spain. Death of Cromwell, succeeded by son Richard.

1659 Parliament recalled. Richard Cromwell resigns. Recall of the Rump Parliament. Act of Pardon and Indemnity. Booth's rising in Cheshire. Army dismiss and again recall the Rump. General Monck marches from Scotland. New Council of State.

1660 Army remodelled by Rump Parliament. Monck enters London. Parliamentary elections. Declaration of Breda. Convention Parliament. Charles II recalled. Restoration of the Monarchy.

CHAPTER ONE

Crisis

For ten years from 1641 to 1651 the British Isles were engulfed in some of the most bloody fighting ever known on British soil. This was followed by a decade in which for the only time in modern British history the country was run as a republic. Following the deaths of tens of thousands of men and women as a direct consequence of the fighting or from the disease and disruption that followed in the wake of travelling armies, the surviving members of the purged Long Parliament gathered at Westminster again in December 1659. One of the many subjects they discussed was the causes of the conflict that had divided the nation. For several days the remaining members of the Parliament that had first been called in the autumn of 1640 debated the causes of the great and tumultuous events that they had all lived through. Not surprisingly perhaps, they could not agree as to what the causes of the troubles had been. Some argued that the cause had been primarily the great constitutional crisis between Crown and Parliament, others maintained that the religious divide in the nation had been the starting point, others again claimed that the great economic changes of the last hundred years had been at the root of the nation's distemper.

Daniel Mytens' classic regal portrait of Charles I in 1631.

A militia man exercising in Charles I's reign, with his musket and rest.

If contemporaries who had lived through these troubled times could not agree as to the causes of events, perhaps it is not remarkable that modern historians looking back across the centuries are not able to say with certainty what caused the divisions of the 1640s and 1650s. Indeed, before even trying to assess the events of the twenty years 1640-60, we must distinguish between the different types of causes that prompt such momentous events. Some causes were deep-seated and had their origins in the changes that had been going on for generations before men took up arms against one another. But it is rare for what T.S. Eliot called 'the vast impersonal forces' of history to be the spark of violent events. So in addition to these underlying causes there are bound to be more immediate factors, or triggers, that set off the final conflagration.

Nobody would deny that the assassination of the Archduke Franz Ferdinand by a Serbian nationalist during his visit to Sarajevo on 28 June 1914 started the cycle of events that led to the outbreak of the First World War. But only the most superficial observer would say that the killing of the Austro-Hungarian aristocrat *caused* the First World War. The long-standing tensions and rivalries between the Great Powers, the build-up of alliances that turned Europe into hostile armed camps, the ambitions of the recently united Germany denied its imperial place on the world stage, these are all the more fundamental factors that can be said to be the causes of the Great War. The metaphor of the bonfire is appropriate here. For a bonfire to burn there must be an accumulation of dry timber. But this alone will not cause a fire. There is still the need for a spark to set alight the timber for the fire to blaze.

Of the underlying, long-term factors that relate to the Civil War or Revolution of the seventeenth century, none is more significant than the great growth of population in the period before the civil wars. As society emerged in the early sixteenth century from the era of dynastic squabbling known as the Wars of the Roses into the long period of stability ushered in by the Tudors, the population of England and Wales amounted to something between 2.5 and 3 million. For well over a century before this date the population level had stagnated or even declined slightly. But the century and a half between 1500 and 1650 saw a dramatic growth in numbers. By the time of the civil wars the best estimates put the population of England and Wales at about 5.5 million, roughly double what it had been a century and a half earlier. Historians can only guess as to the reasons for this growth but a careful study of the parish registers in parishes where records are complete suggests that there was an increase in births over deaths. In the language of the demographer, the sixteenth century saw a rise in fertility levels over mortality. Men and women seem to have got married at a younger age and therefore had more years of child-bearing, producing more babies, more of whom survived than before. Although this population growth was uneven and could easily be disturbed by factors like a series of bad harvests or an attack of plague or typhus epidemics in a region, the growth was continuous and considerable.

As the experience of any third world or underdeveloped country today will bear witness, doubling the population over a few generations puts immense strain on that society's resources. In early seventeenth-century England, rapid population growth produced an ever-growing class of landless labourers who were compelled to buy rather than produce their own food themselves. It was impossible to increase supplies of food sufficiently to meet this new demand as the productivity of the land could not be quickly made more efficient. There were no chemical fertilizers that could rapidly increase yields. It was difficult to find new land to bring under cultivation without long-term projects for draining marshes and fens or reclaiming wastelands. Similarly, to clear woodlands or to turn the great forests that covered much of the country into cultivatable land also took time. The process of 'enclosing' common land had been going on for over a century and in areas adjoining market towns this did succeed in increasing production and had created the surplus that could feed the growing urban population. But enclosing land had by and large been an unpopular process and was frequently met with resistance from those who felt that their common rights were threatened. Food production was, in the jargon of the economist, 'inelastic' in that it could not respond rapidly to changes in demand.

One of the consequences of the increase in population was the constant migration of people in search of work or land. Just as in many third world countries today, England witnessed a dramatic drift of population away from the countryside and into the towns which became swollen with the numbers of new arrivals. By the mid-seventeenth century at least 8,000 people a year were forced by a shortage of land or employment to move into London, attracted by the great variety of both legitimate and criminal opportunities that the capital had to offer. Contemporaries were fully aware of these changes that were going on around them. In the late sixteenth century the bureaucrats of the Tudor regime tried to tackle the problems caused by the increasing numbers of paupers and vagabonds in the cities and the villages of England with new legislation. None of this, however, had any effect on the root causes of the changes that were underway in the economy of the time.

The other dramatic consequence of this population growth which was equally worrying to contemporaries, was the tremendous rise in prices brought about, at least in part, by the growth of demand over supply. From the beginning of the sixteenth to the middle of the seventeenth century food prices in England rose approximately seven-fold and the prices of manufacturing products went up roughly three-fold. There were indeed many other factors that contributed to the price inflation of the sixteenth and early seventeenth centuries, one being the influx of gold and silver bullion from the Americas into western Europe. This influx helped to increase the supply of money and coins in circulation which added to inflation. However, in England at least, this was probably not as major a factor in prompting price rises as the growth of demand. This rise in prices was aggravated by harvest failures in the 1550s, the 1590s and the 1630s, or was occasionally alleviated by good harvests as in the early 1560s. But the long-term trend was a gradual and continuous increase in prices which, although mild by comparison with the standards of the twentieth century, was alarming to the citizens of seventeenth-century Britain.

Another worrying feature of these economic changes was that prices rose faster than average wages which were held down by the existence of a large pool of surplus labour in both the towns and the countryside. This was to affect different parts of the community in different ways. The changes brought about by 150 years of severe inflation were complex but, roughly speaking, anyone who could produce goods above the needs of his own and his family's subsistence

Population

The group portrait of the Saltonstall family from Chipping Warden, Oxfordshire, painted by David des Granges around 1636, is a charming puzzle. Sir Richard Saltonstall holds his two children Richard and Ann, while pulling back the bed curtain to reveal their dead mother. She died in 1630, and the children are shown at the age they were when Lady Saltonstall died. Seated on the right, and looked upon with undoubted tenderness by Sir Richard, is Mary, his second wife, with their infant son Philip. The ever-present threat of an early death, the chances of survival for children, and the frequent remarriage of widowers, are touchingly expressed in the painting. The Saltonstall portrait shows love and family continuity, birth and death, combined, with a sense of time and setting that is different from ours today.

MVSEVM
BRITAN
NICVM

Parliament sitting in 1629, before its dismissal by the King who embarked on his eleven-year period of personal rule – or, some said, tyranny.

could in theory prosper by being able to sell those goods at a price that was continuously rising. For instance, farmers who held their land on the secure tenure of a freehold with fixed rents were going to prosper as they could take advantage of rising prices for their products. In addition, manufacturers with access to capital could invest and expand their production to meet increasing demand. This would lead to larger profits as their income would increase more quickly than their outgoings at a time when wages were going up more slowly than prices.

On the other hand, anyone with a fixed income would suffer from the price increases and the large labouring workforce often found that their wages were not increasing enough to keep up with prices. But also some of the great landowning families could find that their outgoings exceeded their income if they were unlucky or if they were guilty of bad management. The de Vere family, the Earls of Oxford, nearly went bankrupt in the early seventeenth century whereas the Herbert and Percy families who efficiently reorganized their estates prospered. Any farmer near an expanding town or city who produced a surplus was bound to profit. The Russells who held land just outside London grew wealthy on the income derived from selling their produce in the vast market of the capital. London's consumption of corn more than doubled between 1605 and 1661 and demand from the city led to an enormous growth in market and dairy farming in the Home Counties. In many villages the smaller landowners did well, often coming from the ranks of the more successful yeomen who had been able to acquire two or more farms and who over a few generations had benefited by being able to produce a surplus at a time of rising prices.

As could be expected, these economic changes meant that some groups of people were prospering and wanted a society in which wealth could develop further. Others were having a hard time and some even faced ruin. Contemporaries were certainly troubled by these changes and wrote a great deal about one particular development at the time which was the emergence of men of the 'middling sort', whom today we would class as gentlemen or businessmen of modest means but whose income from either agriculture, trade or industry was keeping well ahead of their outgoings. It was this group that was best represented in the House of Commons, and it is significant that in 1628 a peer observed in disapproving terms that the Lower House could buy the Upper House three times over.

These demographic and economic changes were having a dramatic effect on just about every section of British society. Although most people believed in the need for a strict order and hierarchy, there was a considerable degree of movement within pre-industrial British society. In the century before the Civil War there was both geographic mobility between town and countryside and between one part of the country and another, and social mobility upwards and downwards on the class scale. This context of change within society is an essential factor in understanding the background to the great struggle of the mid-seventeenth century.

One of the most crucial effects of the inflation was on the Crown itself. Although the King was the largest landowner in the country, the revenues from the crown estates were no longer sufficient to finance the work of government. Elizabeth I had sold off vast amounts of crown lands to raise cash in the short term and the Stuart kings were to do the same, but of course the net result of this was to diminish the long-term ability of the crown to raise money, perhaps by as much as 25 per cent. This meant that the crown became more and more reliant upon Parliament to vote the necessary taxes, known as subsidies, to govern. Throughout the Middle Ages, the King had ruled with Parliament whose members had jealously guarded their right to approve taxation. The old cry of 'No taxation without redress [of grievances]' had summed up the relationship between Crown and Parliament. Although the meetings of Parliament were infrequent and they could be dispensed with altogether for short periods, the Tudors had always worked closely with Parliament and had understood the need to manage and manipulate the members of the House of Commons. Price inflation meant that all the costs of government administration increased and the cost of declaring war or sending a military expedition abroad became almost prohibitive. These changes profoundly affected the balance in government between Crown and Parliament requiring the sovereign to be prudent and careful in his relationship with the powerful groups of landowners represented in Parliament.

Another of the great sources of change was that caused by the religious transformations of the period. In the sixteenth and seventeenth centuries when we talk of the Church we are not describing the sort of institution on the margins of most peoples' lives which the church represents in the late twentieth century. The Church was at the centre of the life, the culture and the

The unfinished Queen's House by Inigo Jones, set in the sprawling Tudor palace at Greenwich (opposite), with the King, Queen, and their courtiers in the Park.

experience of almost every Briton at this time. Politically, the parish was the basic administrative unit of the country and through the parish priest the government could issue statements, proclamations about peace and war and demand the reading of sermons or homilies – the most famous ones being homilies on obedience. Attendance at church in your parish each Sunday was compulsory and anyone caught not attending could be fined. Moreover, church courts 'policed' the spiritual and moral life of the nation and it is in the records of the church courts that historians find stories of disorderly behaviour, of drunkenness, of adultery, of abandoned babies and jilted wives. Church punishments of excommunication and public penance remained a controversial issue throughout this period.

On another level, in an age when the scientific rules by which nature was governed were barely understood, the church provided solace and comfort. To anyone living in the seventeenth century life could be unpredictable, brutal and unjust. Disease could strike at anyone in any walk of life at any time leaving a family without its breadwinner, without a mother to look after the children or parents without children to care for them in their old age. Even amongst the nobility the expectation of life of boys born between 1650 and 1675 averaged only 29.6 years (today it is nearly 70 years). The food supply was always precarious and the harvest seems to have failed on average about once every six years. Chronic under-nourishment and a lack of vitamins made for regular medical complaints like 'sore eyes' (lack of vitamin A) or 'rickets' (lack of vitamin D). Plague was only the worst of many epidemics and indeed disease was almost endemic in many areas for much of the seventeenth century. Medical knowledge was elementary and also costly. Most people would have relied upon a local herbalist or wise-woman rather than a physician. Sudden disaster by fire was another common fate in this era. Closely constructed wooden houses without any sort of fire prevention made for countless disasters. The Great Fire of London in 1666, in which over 13,000 houses were destroyed and more than 100,000 people were left homeless, was the worst of many catastrophes. Livelihoods could be destroyed, fortunes lost all at the apparent whim of fate.

In this context the Church provided not only a system of explanation but also a source of relief and an opportunity for ceremony and ritual to sustain grief. The Church marked all the phases of life – baptism, confirmation, marriage, churching (the purifying of women after childbirth) and death. The Church

Bring out your dead – the cry that echoed in the streets when bubonic plague struck London.

Carts full of dead to bury.

The Great Chain of Being

'Almighty God hath created and appointed all things in heaven, earth and waters in a most excellent and perfect order. In heaven he hath appointed distinct orders and states of archangels and angels. In the earth he has assigned kings, princes, with other governors under them, all in good and necessary order.'

The words of the great Tudor 'Homily on Disobedience', ordered to be read from pulpits throughout the land on many occasions, were underwritten by the concept of the Great Chain of Being. In heaven the orders of angels were ranked below God. The sun ruled over the planets. In the animal kingdom, the lion was supreme. So it was in the political order: the king ruled with a descending hierarchy of order and authority below him, stretching through councillors

and magistrates to village constables. The concept even extended to the human body, where the head ruled, arms had authority over legs, the liver over the spleen. Order always equalled hierarchy.

Man held prime position in this universal order. Having a soul placed him between the angels and the beasts, and his political order was an earthly version of the divine hierarchy. This idea did not, however, give kings absolute power to do as they wished – since they might upset the carefully-balanced order on which authority rested. Charles I's actions were seen by many as just such an upset. The political theories that were lasting legacies of the Civil War years ensured that the idea of the Great Chain of Being could never again be used to hold society in a rigid bond.

calendar recorded all the agricultural cycles of the year – from mid-winter celebrations at Christmas, through spring fertility ceremonies like May Day, to harvest festivities in the autumn. The Church provided a sense of community, of belonging to the broader unit of social organization beyond the family. But, perhaps most fundamentally of all, the Church provided a sense of order and harmony. Belief in a divinely ordained social order, linking the entire universe from inanimate matter to God himself provided every individual with a natural place. 'The powers that be are ordained of God' proclaims the Book of Romans and in understanding this there developed a belief in a social hierarchy starting with God, descending through the angels to the king and lords, through the squire and the parson, the gentlemen and the aldermen, to the humblest of mankind and down through the animal kingdom to the soil, the stones and the earth itself. At the heart of this philosophy was the patriarchal family with husbands ruling wives, parents ruling children, masters overseeing servants, and so on. This was all backed by a belief in the after-life and a conviction that through obedience to the Church and its rituals an individual would earn eternal salvation but failure to obey could bring hellfire and damnation. To challenge any of this was to invite confusion, anarchy and social collapse.

The relationship between master and servant was integral to society.

Order was maintained not only by a belief in the social hierarchy but also by the fact that English people lived in communities, in towns and villages, which had their own local hierarchy from the gentry or aldermen at the top to the landless poor at the bottom. Again the Church not only sustained this but also endorsed it by the fact that the seating arrangements in every parish church reflected the local order, with village dignitaries seated at the front and servants and the poor at the back, with men and women often segregated within their own social order. The Church, therefore, was central to the life of the nation and every

Sunday the community would gather in what for most people was the largest building they would ever enter, called by church bells making the loudest sound they would ever hear, for a ceremony that would both remind everyone of their place in the hierarchy and affirm the role of each individual in the life of the community. Little wonder that when men and women spoke and wrote in the mid-seventeenth century their language was dominated by the phrases, the imagery and the way of thinking that they had learned in church, sustained by the vast edifice of ecclesiastical control.

Although the reality of daily life might have been different from the ideal, changes or challenges to the Church could be guaranteed to excite great passion. Under Henry VIII the English Church had thrown off its subjugation to Rome and had taken sides with the Protestant Reformation that was shaking Europe like seismic waves after a major earthquake. The monasteries had been dissolved, bringing the largest amount of land on to the market for centuries and those who acquired this land now had a vested interest in not seeing the Reformation reversed. But the exact theology of the English Church was still a matter for argument.

Under Elizabeth's long reign the new Church of England extended its roots deep into the life of the nation. Anglicanism came to represent a broad church of interests, generally reflected in the High Church of those who stressed priestly powers and the magic of the sacrament, and a Low Church in which personal communion with God was emphasized as the principal route to salvation. Queen Elizabeth had recognized the need for the Anglican Church to represent the national identity but realized that it was futile to interfere too closely in the precise workings of religious devotion or, as she put it herself, not 'to open windows into men's souls'. The Stuarts, however, held different views, and the monarchy slowly grew out of alignment with the wishes and the views of a growing mass of the population.

By the early seventeenth century Protestantism had become indelibly associated with patriotism. Fears of Catholic agents and subversives were undoubtedly exaggerated but in the public mind the St Bartholomew's Day Massacre and the Gunpowder Plot added to the popular demonology of Catholicism. England's identity and mission became bound up with an anti-Catholic fervour that was never far below the surface of seventeenth-century society and was to emerge many times through the story of the Civil Wars. Elizabeth had ensured that her foreign policy reflected England's role as a Protestant nation. The defeat of the Spanish Armada in 1588 had been the occasion for genuine and heart-felt rejoicing throughout the land. But the Stuarts, who succeeded in 1603, pursued a foreign policy that failed to live up to the expectations of many Englishmen.

From 1618 onwards, what is now Germany and much of central Europe was torn apart by what historians have called the 'Thirty Years' War'. This was a critical life-and-death struggle between Catholicism and Protestantism, in which the Habsburg rulers of Spain and the Empire of central Europe were trying to reverse the effects of the Reformation. In the minds of contemporaries this was as significant as, say, the struggle between capitalism and communism in the forty years of cold war following the end of the Second World War. Britain stayed out of the great continental conflict partly because James I was inclined

Thirty Years' War

The horrors of war were brought home to Europe in the Thirty Years' War, as shown in Vrancx's portrayal of a village being pillaged (above) or Callot's graphic view (below) of the Miseries of war and its reprisals.

Callot inv. et fec.

A la fin ces Voleurs infames et perdus ,   Monstrent bien que le crime (horrible et noire engeance)   Et que cest le Destin des hommes vicieux
Comme fruits malheureux a cet arbre pendus   Est luy mesme instrument de honte et de vengeance ,   Desprouuer tost ou tard la iustice des Cieux . 13

In 1643, when conflict had begun in England between King and Parliament, one MP informed the House of Commons that 'These are days of shaking and this shaking is universal: the Palatinate, Bohemia, Germania, Catalonia, Portugal, Ireland-England.' In the first half of the seventeenth century there was barely a single year without war being waged in some part of Europe, and there were periods in which virtually the whole of the continent seemed to be fighting. 'Religion and liberty stand and fall together' was the fighting phrase: Catholic fought Protestant, Habsburg Spain fought with France and the Dutch Republic, Sweden and Poland were bitter rivals, and drew Denmark and Russia into their conflicts to the ruin of both. There were revolts in many countries, often against excess taxation and the autocratic control of the favourites who ran their nations for their kings: Cardinal Richelieu in France, the Count-Duke of Olivares in Spain. The Holy Roman Emperor was confronted by the rulers of the estates of his hereditary provinces, both on the grounds of religion and as a challenge to his waning imperial power. Europe was armed, in a conflict which ran for thirty long years.

Everything had begun with an open window in Bohemia in 1618, out of which armed and angry Protestant members of Bohemia's parliament were hurled on the orders of the Catholic council of regents. (They landed on piles of rubbish, and survived.) The tragedy-cum-farce of the 'Defenestration of Prague' precipitated the Protestant revolt which, although initially crushed by the Emperor, ushered in the long series of conflicts which were not resolved until 1648. Although England did not get actively involved, James I's daughter Elizabeth was the wife of the Elector Palatine and there was English pressure to come to their rescue in 1619. Certainly in that conflict and then later in the Low Countries in the 1630s, English and Scottish soldiers and gentlemen gained experience of war, siege and battle which they were to use in the conflict at home. The English Civil War did not come in an age which had little experience of war, nor were the English ignorant of what atrocities were committed by armies or what hunger and waste they produced.

Voltaire, in the Age of Reason, believed that the causes of the Thirty Years' War were simply 'The three things that exercise a constant influence over the minds of men: climate, government, and religion.' The reality was lengthy and bloody.

Le Sueur's magnificent bronze bust of Charles I exemplifying the high artistic standards and innovative taste of the King and his Court.

Court style

Charles I and Henrietta Maria, in the sort of classical and formal setting that was the style of their Court.

At one time, any vaguely classical seventeenth-century house in England would be attributed to Inigo Jones, so dominant was his memory and influence. In fact, there is very little that survives which may be attributed to this incomparable Renaissance man, the first to import the fruits of Italian classical architecture. His influence was severely restricted to a small body of influential people surrounding the courts of James I and Charles I; and what he designed illustrates the division between Court and Country that bedevilled England in the 1630s.

One of Charles I's abiding characteristics was that he was happiest with a small group of intimates and connoisseurs, who joined him in collecting on the grandest scale, employing Inigo Jones, and taking part in the lavish court entertainments. Charles clearly abhorred public display, reserving himself for private occasions. At his coronation he refused to have the triumphal arches erected that were traditional in the City of London. Instead, such arches were to be part of the stage scenery Jones designed

for the Court masques that glorified Charles and his reign. Designs for many of them survive, along with the costumes. The last of the Court masques was *Salmacida Spolia*, performed in a temporary theatre attached to the Banqueting House in Whitehall in January 1640. The King appeared as Philogenes, the lover of his people, a divine king who had secret wisdom which quelled the forces of disaster. Among the final scenes was a tableau set 'among craggy rocks and inaccessible mountains... sitting in the Throne of Honour, His Majesty highest in a seat of gold and the rest of the lords about him'. If Charles did possess secret wisdom, it never became apparent.

When the aged Earl of Newcastle set down in 1659 his *Advice* to Charles II on the eve of his restoration, one thing he felt needed to be stated urgently. 'Ceremony, though it is nothing in itself, yet it does everything – for what's a king more than a subject, but for ceremony and order? When that fails him, he is ruined.' The new king could be in no doubt about the pointedness of the remarks.

to peace but also because he could ill afford a costly continental expedition. But the failure to support the Protestant cause was a source of great annoyance to many proud Englishmen who had grown up under Elizabeth with a sense of England's Protestant mission. In the Parliament of 1621 voices called for a war with Spain before James dissolved it refusing to allow Parliament to discuss foreign policy. Further calls in the Parliament of 1624 led to the planning of an expedition to help protect James's son-in-law, one of the leading German Protestant princes, Elector Frederick Palatinate. To many in a nation that was beginning to trade with distant, often Spanish, ports in the Americas and in the East, a war with Spain, the great Catholic power in Europe, was an opportunity to combine religious and strategic objectives. Sir Edward Coke, the prominent lawyer and Parliamentarian commented that England 'never throve so well as when at war with Spain'.

At this point, amidst the full clamour of war, James I died and it is the character of his son Charles I who succeeded him that provides the key to understanding the course of the drama that was played out over the next few years. Charles had many characteristics that were admirable, he was austere and self-disciplined by contrast to his father who was slovenly, talkative and often drunken. But Charles was also reserved and rather cold. He suffered from a stammer which inhibited him in conversation both public and private and this helped to make him a poor communicator, reliant upon a small circle of friends. This would have been less important if the King had not had the unnerving knack of picking the wrong people as friends and advisers.

Charles inherited the close friendship of George Villiers, the Duke of Buckingham, who rose effortlessly through the ranks of the nobility at James's court where the King, in his latter years, had become besotted with him. George Villiers came from a minor gentry family in Leicestershire and was made earl, marquess and finally, in 1623, duke. Not only had he won favour with the old king but he had also become the closest friend of the heir and for a decade Villiers dominated royal policy. England became entangled in a series of expensive foreign adventures that necessitated the calling of Parliament to raise taxes. Because the adventures proved disastrous, Buckingham became a deeply distrusted and unpopular figure and the Crown's relationship with Parliament suffered major damage. Buckingham was blamed for the fiasco of the expedition in the Palatinate in the early stages of the Thirty Years' War which fell apart in disarray before even reaching its objective and for the failure of a naval expedition against Cadiz which collapsed due to every form of incompetence. These failures and Charles' marriage to a French Catholic princess, Henrietta Maria, greatly humiliated and annoyed many patriotic English Protestants.

There was strong opposition to these policies which was voiced in the first Parliament of Charles's reign. It was dissolved before voting for any taxes including the usual customs dues, known as tunnage and poundage, which were normally voted to every sovereign for life at the beginning of his reign. This was an omen of things to come between King and Parliament. Charles, however, continued to collect the customs dues and levied forced loans on the nobility and gentry, imprisoning without trial those who refused to pay.

As the pendulum swung against the Protestant cause on the continent, Charles had no option but to call another Parliament in 1628. Immediately the members began to discuss a Petition of Right which prohibited the levying of any taxes without Parliamentary authority and declared illegal any form of arbitrary imprisonment– calling for the confirmation of ancient liberties. In August, Buckingham was assassinated by an unhinged ex-officer but his death failed to bring any lasting reconciliation. In March 1629, in an unprecedented act, some MPs barred the door to Black Rod and held down the Speaker (who was then the Crown's representative in the Commons). Charles dissolved Parliament in a fit of rage, imprisoned the ringleaders and announced that he would not call another Parliament. There then began what Whig historians used to call the 'Eleven Year Tyranny' governing without Parliament.

In fact, this period of personal rule began well. Peace was signed with both France (against whom another ill-fated expedition had been sent to La Rochelle) and Spain. Slowly, without the vast expenditure of war, the Crown's financial position improved. This was partly due to an increased income from customs following a rapid improvement in trade. Charles also found other devices by which he demanded money from his subjects. The 'distraint of knighthood' was a medieval custom which Charles revived by fining gentlemen with an income above £40 who had not assumed the honour of knighthood, raising £150,000 over two years from this. He fined landowners who had encroached upon the medieval hunting grounds designated as Royal Forests. He issued fines against enclosures and sold off offices and peerages. With the prodigious efforts of his Lord Treasurer, Sir Richard Weston, Charles finally managed to balance his budgets in 1635. It was in this year that he felt sufficiently confident to commission Rubens to paint the magnificent ceiling of the Banqueting House in Whitehall.

Van Dyck's death portrait of the Duke of Buckingham.

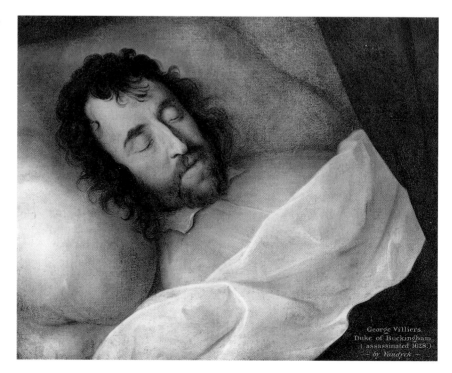

The Banqueting House Ceiling

*James I, crowned with wreaths and attended by the
Virtues, is seated at the centre of Rubens' magnificent
ceiling painting for the Whitehall Banqueting House.*

In 1619, Inigo Jones built one of the very earliest wholly classical buildings in England: the Banqueting House in Whitehall, the first stage of a projected but unbuilt magnificent new palace. Two grand storeys rise from a rusticated basement while the great chamber within is a perfect double cube. Remarkable to contemporaries was the ceiling, composed of nine large panels rather than the myriad of small interlocking shapes which filled other plaster ceilings of the day. By 1635 these blanks had been filled with what is the greatest surviving monument to the artistic splendour and expenditure of Charles I's court, Sir Peter Paul Rubens' baroque paintings on the theme of the Apotheosis of James I. Rubens had come to England as a diplomat in 1629, and left with a commission to paint the ceiling. For his pains, he received the enormous sum of £34,000 plus a gold chain and medal, indicative of how much Charles I despite his straitened finances was willing to invest in his greatest love, art. Rubens depicted James I surrounded by Justice, Zeal, Religion, Honour, and Victory; in the south panel Peace and Honour embrace before the late king and, ironically, Minerva is shown banishing Rebellion to Hell, while in one of the corner ovals, Government tramples upon Rebellion. It was to be from this room that, fourteen years after the ceiling paintings were installed, Charles I stepped on to the balcony to meet his executioner.

Mr. Burton, Dr. Bastwick, & Mr. Prinne, triumphantly from perpetuall captivity, those 3 famous wittnesses of Truth, return home to London, attended with thousands of horse and foot,

Celebrations at the final release of the three religious radicals tried and mutilated by the Court of Star Chamber.

Many of these methods to raise funds failed to provoke much opposition but the one device that did cause widespread agitation was the levying of 'Ship Money', an annual charge which kings had used since the Middle Ages to raise ships (or their equivalent in money) from certain ports. In 1635 the King extended Ship Money to the whole country, arguing that it was only fair for everyone to be involved in raising money for national defence. Certainly the need to protect English shipping from privateers was widely recognized and in the early years the yield from Ship Money was a remarkable 90-95 per cent. But gradually men began to fear that Ship Money would become a regular tax which the King could collect without Parliament's consent. So, in 1637, John Hampden and Lord Saye and Sele (who had been holding secret meetings of a nascent Parliamentary opposition in Broughton Castle in Oxfordshire) refused on principle to pay a one pound claim for Ship Money. At court the bench was heavily pressured by the Crown and the decision came out against the protesters. There was outrage at the verdict. Sir Simonds d'Ewes wrote, 'What shall freeman differ from the ancient bondsmen and villeins of England if their estates be subject to arbitrary taxes?' Almost the entire propertied classes united in opposition to the payment of Ship Money which was stored up as one of the major grievances against Charles.

However, the greatest resentment against Charles was provoked by his attitude towards the church. The principal architect of Charles's religious policy was William Laud who in 1629, as Bishop of London, enjoyed a complete monopoly of ecclesiastical appointments. Laud declared that the Church of England was perfect as it then stood and there should be no further reform. He was thus destined to come into conflict with the great momentum generated by the Puritans who wanted the church to be more godly than it then was.

In the mid-seventeenth century, England was going through what today would be called a fundamentalist revival as the forces unleashed by the Reformation continued to work themselves out. The essence of the Protestant doctrine was

---

Difficulties in collecting the Ship Money

'Matthew Stevenson and Roger Reynolds, two chief constables of Blofield Hundred (Norfolk) have not collected and paid unto me one penny of the ship rate imposed upon that hundred. And I am informed and do believe that they have been very backward and cold in calling upon the petty constable to demand or gather the same within their several parishes, albeit I have by frequent and most pressing letters and warrants urged upon them (even as I have upon others) the levying of ship money, and have appointed them divers several days for the payment thereof unto me at all which days and times they have failed to pay anything...

'I am informed that Edmond Holt of Hemblington in Walsham Hundred and Edward Hilton of Lin-wood in Blofield Hundred, being attorneys at the law, have not paid their ship rates and that many others are encouraged by them to stand out...

'There may be more in the country to be complained of. I have thought it best to certify these few, not desiring to draw up multitudes before their lordships. And I have not hitherto troubled their lordships with any. If their lordships be pleased to afford some assistance to my work, I have good hope that all or very near all the shipping monies of that county will be paid in. But by the power which is only in my hands, I cannot presume upon the levying of much more in the county.'

Francis Asteley (Sheriff of Norfolk)   *1 May 1638*

'justication by faith alone', a belief that man could be saved by his own faith and actions and not by the intercession of some priestly intermediary. This doctrine put great emphasis on the individual and his inner faith and less on the outward, sacramental forms of worship. Puritanism took this a stage further and emphasised a doctrine of spiritual equality. All men were equal in the eyes of God and if men honestly studied their bibles and searched their consciences they would find salvation. Moreover, the Puritans believed in a doctrine of pre-destination. They believed that the elect, those who were pre-destined for salvation, were likely to be evident in this world before reaching the next, that they would excel in temporal life as well as the spiritual. Those who through hard work, thrift and industry were successful were going to be those who were pre-destined for salvation. This became an ideology for success, a justification for works. As Thomas Taylor, the Puritan lecturer, said 'We teach that only Doers shall be saved'. Men who worked hard for themselves and for their community were helping to serve God.

The Puritans had tried to capture the church since the age of Elizabeth and whilst outwardly conforming to the modest Anglican requirements the zealots set about canvassing their views and developing the structure of a church almost within the church. The Puritans rejected anything that hinted of the old Catholic ways like the wearing of vestments that separated the priest from his congregation, or kneeling at the communion table, or the observation of saints' days. In Puritan ceremonies great emphasis was put on the sermon and Puritan churches were organized around the pulpit, where the emphasis was on understanding the word of God not on the mysteries of the sacrament. For generations there had been arguments within the church about the role of prayer as against preaching, about the need for Bible-reading against traditional Sunday sports, and about the nature of the sacrament and the rituals associated with it. It was these arguments that Laud now set himself to resolve knowing that behind him he had the complete support of Charles. One of the main

Three opponents of the King

Die Sabbathii, 14° Ianuarii, 1642.

IT is this day Ordered by the COMMONS now Assembled in Parliament, That Mr. *Pym* be desired to publish in Print, what yesterday he did by order of both Houses at the Common-Hall: And that none do presume to Print or re-print it, but such as *Iohn Hinde* shall appoint.

H. Elsynge, Cler: Parl: D: Com.

I appoint *Peter Cole* to Print this Copy:

JOHN HINDE.

John Pym became one of the leading voices in the war of words and printed pamphlets that preceded the start of hostilities.

Opposition to Charles I crystallized around men who came to great prominence at the end of the 1630s. Their resistance to the impositions being made by the King without recourse to Parliament set the agenda for the confrontation when Charles was forced to recall Parliament in 1640.

The setting for the planning and discontent against the King was Broughton Castle, near Banbury in Oxfordshire, home of William Fiennes, 1st Viscount Saye and Sele, one of the staunchest Presbyterian aristocrats, in an area renowned for religious strictness. Saye and Sele – 'Old Subtlety' as he came to be known – gathered many dissident voices. Those who met there were engaged upon schemes of colonization, first Providence Island in the West Indies and then Saybrook, in modern Connecticut. The Earls of Warwick, Lincoln, and Bedford, Lord Brooke, John Pym, and John Hampden were among those who discussed colonization schemes, even considered emigrating themselves, and orchestrated their reaction to the King.

Saye and Sele was one of those who tried to force a test case for non-payment of Ship Money, but Charles chose to make an example of the Buckinghamshire gentleman and MP John Hampden. Hampden's 1637 trial became one of the great *causes célèbres*: the judges were divided about the legality of Ship Money, and mass campaigns of non-payment resulted, cutting revenues by two-thirds. Hampden had emerged from obscurity to become a focus of opposition. He was a member of the Parliamentary Committee sent to keep a watchful eye on Charles' activities in Scotland late in 1641 after the first outbreak of hostilities, and then was one of the Five Members whom the King tried to arrest on 4 January 1642. He was later to raise a troop of horse, and the revered Hampden became a martyr to the moderate Parliamentary cause when he died fighting in 1643.

John Pym had had a career of opposition to Charles; his rise to attention had come in Parliamentary attacks on the Duke of Buckingham in 1626, and as Secretary of the Providence Island Company he was part of the rumbling discontent during the Personal Rule. His great hour came as Leader of the House of Commons during the early days of conflict: he revealed, in melodramatic style, the first Army Plot of 1641 to support Charles against Parliament, he steered the first measures to try to persuade Charles to come to terms, and then was one of the MPs Charles tried to arrest. Pym then led the group who were moving towards armed conflict: he might want peace, but if a war was inevitable then it should be fought to be won. His became the dominant voice in the prosecution of the early part of the war – the 'reign of King Pym' people were to call it – and he died in 1643 having steered the Solemn League and Covenant through the Long Parliament.

Of these three leading lights of early opposition, only Lord Saye and Sele survived the war. He was disgusted at democratic proposals for a new upper house in 1648, refusing to 'sit alongside brewers and draymen' and he retired to Lundy Island in the Bristol Channel for the duration of the Commonwealth.

THE NORTH-EAST VIEW OF BROUGHTON-CASTLE, IN THE COUNTY OF OXFORD.

This Castle near Banbury, was the Manour House & Estate of Sr. Wm. Wickham Kt. who gave it in Dower with his Daughter Margaret. in marriage to Sr. Willm. Fiennes, or Fines, Lord Say & Sele; who had summons to Parliamt. from ye 20. H.6. to ye 9th. of Edw.4th. He was Heir to Sr. James Fines Baron Say & Sele, & Lord high Treasurer of England; who was cruelly beheaded by a rebelious Rabble in ye reign of K.H:6th. It continued the Seat of this Family for 300 years, and afterwards in ye 1st. of K.James ye 1st. the Stile & Title of Baron Say & Sele was confirm'd & re-cognized to Sr. Richd. Fines & his Heirs; who was lineally descended from ye above sd. Sr. James. This Estate is now in ye possesion of Col. Twisselden.

S. & N. Buck Delin: et Sculp: 1729.

William Fiennes,
Viscount Saye and
Sele (right), who was
one of the Crown's
leading opponents.

Broughton Castle,
near Banbury
(above), Lord Saye
and Sele's home,
where oppositionists
met in secret.

demands of the Puritans was the abolition of the episcopate but Royalists saw in this the inevitable undermining not only of the Church but of the whole hierarchy on which social order was built. The Puritan slogan 'No Bishop, No King', was both apt and accurate, and Charles knew it.

During Charles's personal reign, Laud played a major role in the King's councils. In 1633 he was appointed to the top ecclesiastical post in the country, the Archbishopric of Canterbury. A further sign of his influence was when his faithful and like-minded supporter William Juxon, Bishop of London, took over from Weston as Lord Treasurer in 1635. Laud believed fervently in the 'beauty of holiness' in stark contrast to the Puritans for whom ritual and ceremony smacked of popish superstition. He sent out commissioners to visit almost every parish in the land with the task of bringing every church service into line and to stamp out the evil ways of the Puritans. The main change Laud called for was to move the wooden communion table from the nave to the east end of the chancel and to rail it in. This apparently minor rearrangement of parish furniture provoked outrage. With the communion table in the nave the priest

Laudian Churches

In some English parish churches today it is still possible to see the legacy of the 1630s when 'Laudianism' was pre-eminent in the Anglican Church. Although a fixed altar, communion rails around it, and coloured vestments are usually the result of Victorian medieval revivalism, occasionally they are stray survivals from the 1630s. The Church of England as established in Elizabeth's reign was what we have come to know as 'Puritan', in which liturgy and outward displays were limited and emphasis was placed on sermons, the Bible, and in more radical quarters a Calvinist theology of pre-destination. A movable wooden communion table replaced the medieval stone altar; communicants were often seated around the table; vestments were frowned upon. The Puritans represented the church; posed against them, with the full backing of the King, was the vigorous campaign for change led by William Laud, Archbishop of Canterbury from 1633, to render the interior of the church and its worship more seemly. Many said, more Catholic.

Few new churches were built in the 1630s. The largest was in the City of London, St Katherine Cree, completed in 1631 when Laud was Bishop of London, in a stately hybrid of Gothic and classical forms. It survived the Great Fire, and the communion table stands against the east wall, but lacks the variety of carved and painted screens and rails adorning the untouched interior of St John's church

Iconoclasts wrecked altars, images and rails in their attacks on Laudian churches.

in Leeds, built in 1635. Across the country, the most common innovations and arguments were over the Laudian orders to place rails around a fixed communion table. Perhaps those from Isleham in Cambridgeshire survive because of their unique decorativeness, with pointed railings like bold stalactites and stalagmites. At Lyddington in Rutland, where the communion rails also survive from the 1630s, they surround the altar which is placed near, but not at, the east end-a compromise between Laudian and Puritan ways which satisfied the authorities.

The Wren family were one of the great supporters of Laud. Matthew Wren, Bishop of Ely and Master of Peterhouse, Cambridge, built a new chapel in

had to come forward to the congregation to administer the sacraments, thus emphasizing the Puritan view of the equality between the priesthood and the laity. But to put the table at the end of the chancel behind railings was to separate the priest from the congregation, the pastor from his flock, in a way that seemed designed to give the priest once again a privileged status. Milton described the railed-off altar as 'a table of separation'. For most men and women the change was positively Romish. Over the following years when soldiers got drunk, they would often pull down altar railings, a sign of the deep offence that this change had provoked.

Laud also tried to remove Puritan lecturers from their posts. The Puritan demand for a preaching clergy had led to the appointment of lecturers outside the established church. They were often appointed and paid for by wealthy merchants or town corporations and so were especially numerous in the cities. These lecturers were central to an alternative view of the church, often preaching quite a different message on Sunday afternoon or market day to that of the established priest on Sunday morning. Appointed by the congregation

One of the plaster panels installed by Christopher Wren at East Knoyle, Wiltshire.

Peterhouse in 1632, while his brother Christopher (father of Sir Christopher Wren) decorated his parish church in the Wiltshire village of East Knoyle with plasterwork pictures in the chancel, showing Jacob's Dream, a pious man kneeling in prayer below a dove, and other scenes and mottoes which were regarded as scandalous and crypto-Catholic, and for which he was later to be tried.

A re-emphasis on the sacraments also brought the baptismal font back into prominence. The church of Terrington St Clement in Norfolk has an extraordinary canopied font cover, with doors opening to reveal painted landscapes and scenes of the Baptism of Christ.

Some of the best-known examples of new religious sensibilities are in Huntingdonshire. Nicholas Ferrar, like Laud a follower of the Dutch theologian Arminius, used family wealth to set up a religious community at Little Gidding in 1624, whose mystical brand of religion attracted visits from Charles I on a number of occasions (including sheltering him on his flight during the Civil War). Ferrar remodelled the dilapidated church, elements of which still remain, while in the nearby parish of Leighton Bromswold, the mystical poet and cleric George Herbert rebuilt much of the decaying church when he moved to the parish in 1626, refurnishing it with desks and stalls. These survivals managed to escape the onslaught in the changed religious climate in and after the Civil War, as testimony to the often firmly-resisted new broom that Laud was trying to sweep through the Church of England.

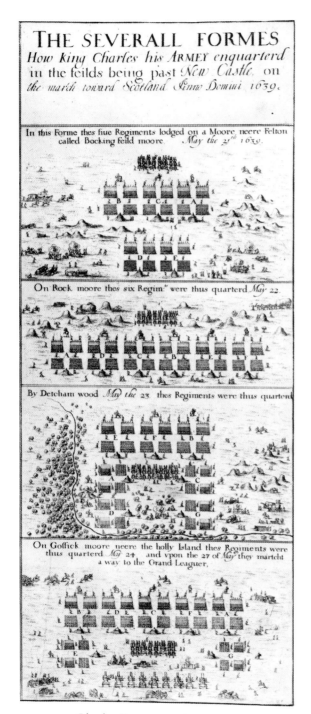

THE SEVERALL FORMES
How King Charles his ARMEY enquarterd in the feilds being past New Castle, on the march toward Scotland Anno Domini 1639.

In this Forme thes fiue Regiments lodged on a Moore, neere Felton called Bocking feild moore. May the 21th 1639.

On Rock moore thes six Regim.ts were thus quarterd May 22.

By Detcham wood May the 23 thes Regiments were thus quarterd

On Goslick moore neere the holly Island thes Regiments were thus quarterd Maij 24 and vpon the 27 of Maij they marcht a way to the Grand Leaguer,

Charles I's army on its route to humiliation by the Scots.

Leaving England

On 22 March 1630 a small fleet of ships carrying 700 passengers, 240 cows, and 60 horses, waited at Southampton to sail across the Atlantic to New England. It was one of many contingents of settlers to the Americas in the years before the Civil War, when perhaps 21,000 people went to New England, as well as many others to Virginia. Leading this band of new colonists was John Winthrop, a lawyer and gentleman from Groton in Suffolk, who like many emigrating to New England was inspired by deep religious zeal.

The story of the expedition began nine months earlier when Winthrop rode into Lincolnshire, to visit Tattershall Castle. On the way, Winthrop was thrown from his horse, but took his safety as God shielding him and his mission from harm. At Tattershall he was met by the Earl of Lincoln's household: Bridget, Countess of Lincoln, the Earl's sister Lady Arbella Johnson, the steward Thomas Dudley, his daughter Anne Bradstreet and her husband Simon (steward to the Countess of Warwick). They were part of a great inter-locking group of families and friends inspired with puritan godly zeal, and disheartened at the prospects for religious life in a Laudian England. The Countess of Lincoln was the Viscount Saye and Sele's daughter. Simon Bradstreet, Isaac Johnson (Lady Arbella's husband), Winthrop's and the Viscount's sons had all been educated at the puritan stronghold Emmanuel College, Cambridge. Winthrop convinced the group of the potential for settling a new colony, under the Massachusetts Bay Company formed with a royal charter to provide investment in the enterprise, and naming Winthrop to be the colony's first governor.

When the fleet was prepared, the puritan divine John Cotton came from Lincolnshire to preach, his text 'Moreover I will plant a place for my people Israel, and I will plant them that they may dwell in a place of their own and move no more.' The passengers included many people from Winthrop's native Groton, and Lady Arbella, the Bradstreets, and Dudley. The voyage was a long agony of storms, overcrowding and sea-sickness. Winthrop prepared his fellow-passengers for their new life, exhorting them to regard themselves as a covenanted company knit together by love, 'a city upon a hill, the eyes of all people are upon us.' They reached the other side after a gruelling sixty-six days. Winthrop recorded,

'We now had fair sunshine weather... and there came a smell off the shore like the smell of a garden.'

All was not sweet in the garden. The harvest had failed, and a thousand new colonists had to be fed and housed. The Massachusetts colony almost died at its inception for everyone was starving and cold, the main source of heat being constant religious argument. Two hundred newcomers died by the end of the year, including Lady Arbella, another two hundred returned to England, many of them disillusioned. Trade with the Indians, new supplies from England, and a successful harvest saved the colony, and emigration continued. By 1640 there were about 14,000 people living in the New England colonies, communicating with those they had left behind, exhorting more to follow them.

Emigrants, like those (above) who left for religious reasons, often went in groups like that organized from meetings at Tattershall Castle, Lincolnshire (right).

who paid his salary, the lecturer was outside the control of the bishops who appointed ministers to cure souls. Their significance is shown by the claim that Hull, the first city to oppose Charles, had been 'corrupted' by its lecturers.

Laud was largely successful in putting down the lecturers, especially in the city of London. Several lecturers were driven to emigrate, often taking their congregations with them. Laud used High Commission and the Court of Star Chamber to punish adversaries and the severity of their actions added to the view that the court was being taken over by Catholic influences. Popery and arbitrary power were indelibly linked in the minds of Englishmen and by the end of the 1630s, the era of Charles's personal rule without Parliament seemed to provide many examples of a drift to popish ways whilst the great international crisis of Protestantism was being fought out on the continent.

In this context, the decision by Charles and Laud to impose a modified version of the English Prayer Book on the Presbyterian Church of Scotland was disastrous. Fears of centralized rule from London and of the introduction of popish ways provoked spontaneous riots in Edinburgh in 1637 which spread rapidly. A National Covenant pledging resistance to church reform was signed by a large number of Scottish noblemen and ministers at Greyfriars Kirk in Edinburgh in February 1638. A year later Charles himself set out to lead an army against the rebellious Scots. He mobilized the trained bands of Yorkshire, Durham and Northumberland, counties that usually were only too willing to take up arms against the Scots, but Charles had not enough money to pay or equip them. When the Scots themselves took the initiative by marching south, Charles decided to negotiate a truce, the Pacification of Berwick. On the advice of Sir Thomas Wentworth, the Lord Deputy of Ireland, who had enjoyed great success in quelling rebellion in that troubled island, the King decided to recall Parliament who met on 13 April 1640. Wentworth was confident that Parliament would rally with great patriotism to the national crisis and indeed at first Parliament offered Charles twelve separate subsidies. But it refused to grant any of these taxes until the many grievances, accumulated over the previous eleven years of personal rule, had been settled. After a mere three weeks the King dissolved what has gone down in history as the Short Parliament.

Charles was now in desperate need of funds but the city of London refused to grant him a loan. The King made secret overtures to Spain asking for financial support. The Queen even appealed to the pope. But all was in vain and although the King was offered £20,000 from the Church this was not enough. Events now began to move at speed. When Charles tried to raise an army in the south to march north the Scots again ventured over the border. Their army of 25,000 men crossed the Tweed on 20 August 1640, arrived at the Tyne on 27 and on 30 August took the city and fortress of Newcastle. In desperation, Charles summoned a Great Council of the peerage to York in September hoping to bypass the Commons altogether. But the peers almost unanimously advised him to make peace with the Scots and to call another Parliament. This time he had no choice. By the Treaty of Ripon signed in October the Scots army occupied Durham and Northumberland and were to be paid £850 a day maintenance until a final settlement was reached. The Scots knew that by this they were forcing Charles into calling another Parliament. The Long Parliament assembled in London on 3 November 1640. It was to sit off and on for twenty years.

The sun of glory shines upon the capital.

Edinburgh riots

According to tradition, Jenny Geddes was the first to pick up her stool in St. Giles' Kirk in Edinburgh on 23 July 1637 and hurl it at the preacher, to be followed by a mass riot and 'assaults with crickets, stools, sticks and stones'. Jenny is probably a mythical figure, but there was no doubting the vehemence of the reaction on that day to the new Prayer Book.

The Scots were accustomed to controlling their own church affairs, with a modified form of episcopal government and their own liturgy, with variant forms that expressed the deep divisions between the episcopalian and the increasingly presbyterian branches of the Kirk. Many Scots were already alarmed at what they saw as Papist tendencies south of the border, and they were outraged when Charles I introduced a modified version of the English Prayer Book, by royal proclamation. There were deep theological reactions to the Prayer Book, which provocatively included only one of the two forms of communion. There were also political objections. If a king could introduce this by proclamation, then he could arbitrarily impose whatever he chose.

The Prayer Book galvanized the hitherto divided Scots into action. Presbyterian ministers, and disillusioned and usually anti-clerical peers, were united in their opposition. The Marquis of Montrose for one called the new Prayer Book 'the brood of the bowels of the whore of Babel'. After the disturbances of July 1637, when women, and apprentices dressed as women, protested in the streets of Edinburgh, petitions poured in. Charles was obdurate that he would not give in to rioters. Meanwhile the Bishop of Brechin was conducting services from the new liturgy holding a pair of loaded pistols.

By February 1637 the Scots had mobilized resistance in the National Covenant, which called for a return to the previous, moderate episcopalian church – and also appealed to the primacy of parliamentary authority. The first signatures were inscribed by the leading noblemen in Greyfriars Kirk in Edinburgh on 28 February 1637, pledging mutual defence 'to the utmost of that power which God hath put into our hands'. In July 1637 the Scots had been hurling stools; within a year they were preparing for battle.

Scottish reaction to the new Prayer Book.

CHAPTER TWO

Taking Sides

The Long Parliament met in November 1640 in a climate of hostility and mistrust. The eleven years when Charles I had ruled without Parliament had fermented numerous grievances against him and particularly against his advisers towards whom most antipathy was directed. Disaffection was openly expressed with two of Charles' key advisers, Archbishop Laud and Thomas Wentworth, Earl of Strafford, who had become objects of hate as well as obstacles in the path of any negotiable settlement with the King. Other unpopular ministers, churchmen and judges also came under criticism and some fled abroad, fearing for their safety.

Within a week of the opening session of the Long Parliament, the Commons impeached Strafford for treason. Although these charges were dropped, Strafford was eventually brought to trial under the Act of Attainder. Parliament was divided over taking such a measure but in the intervening months of preparation of the case against Strafford, his fate had extended beyond the confines of the House of Commons and House of Lords. Angry crowds of demonstrators massed in the streets of London, petitioning Parliament and calling for justice – and the execution of Strafford. The London mob, inspired by religious radicals, had expressed their discontent so forcefully that their King now feared for his own and his family's safety. On 10 May 1641, in an act for which he would always reproach himself, Charles signed the death warrant and Strafford was duly executed on 12 May. Five years later, after a long imprisonment, Archbishop Laud suffered the same ignominious death.

Colonel Thomas St Aubyn, prepared for fighting (opposite),
wearing a finely decorated pikeman's neckpiece.

The authority of Charles had been severely undermined and his position was extremely tenuous. His Parliament had rebelled against him and his closest advisers; the people of London had taken to the streets in their thousands in acts of defiance parallelling earlier disturbances amongst his Scottish subjects and discontent was widespread in the provinces. Suddenly the King faced revolts against his policies on all fronts – constitutional, economic and religious. Yet, in spite of all this evident disaffection, there remained the notion, deeply embedded in the seventeenth-century mind, that the King was divinely appointed and to oppose him was to oppose God's anointed. Therefore attention was directed instead towards the King's councillors; identified as evil, they provided a ready alternative to direct confrontation with the King himself. If they were removed, then some form of compromise and negotiation with Charles would be possible. However the Scots had already learned that their King could not be trusted in any negotiations; it remained for his English subjects to discover the unpalatable truth about their monarch.

With the challenge to royal authority and evident divisions among the ruling classes, there was a pressing need for some form of reconciliation, some restoration of political and social control. The initiatives to settle the grievances against the King and shift the balance of power in the country to Parliament had been seized by some members of the House of Commons, notably John Pym and John Hampden. With a series of legislative measures designed to sweep away the abuses of the years of Charles' 'personal rule', they sought to end once and for all government by arbitrary rule of the monarch. In order to ensure that Parliament could not be dissolved purely on the whim of the King, the Triennial Act was passed in February 1641, which made provision for the holding of Parliament every three years. In the summer of the same year the deeply unpopular Star Chamber and High Commission were abolished, ship money was declared illegal and knighthood fines and the extension of the forests were ended. The impact was to restrict the royal prerogative considerably and diminish the power of the King. Some of these measures remained permanent features of the constitutional changes of the seventeenth century, not least the recognition of the place of Parliament in the political process.

While these measures achieved a degree of unanimity, others were to prove much more divisive. Not only was there widespread fear of popery and Catholic plots and Laudian innovations in the church were condemned in many quarters, but there were also differences between the moderates who simply wanted to return to the religious practices of former times and those radical Puritans who saw the opportunity for a wholesale reformation in the church and church government. 'No Bishops' was the rallying cry of the 15,000 Londoners who signed the 'root and branch' petition calling for the abolition of the episcopacy. Elsewhere in the country, protests against the authority of the bishops caused disruption in church services. The removal of bishops from the House of Lords and from secular office was not unwelcome but many wanted to retain a limited form of episcopacy in church government. For them, the attempt to dismantle the church hierarchy was threatening the stability of the social order and therefore pushing reform into dangerous territory. The Commons remained deeply divided over the issue while, not surprisingly, the House of Lords refused to consider the measure at all.

Strafford

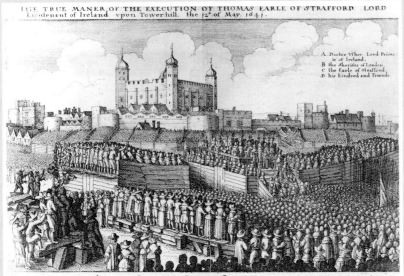

THE TRUE MANER OF THE EXECUTION OF THOMAS EARLE OF STRAFFORD. LORD Lieutenant of Ireland vpon Tower-hill. the 12ᵗ of May. 1641.

A. Doctor Vsher, Lord Primate of Ireland
B. the Sherifes of London
C. the Earle of Strafford
D. his kindred and Friends

Execution des Grafen Thomæ von Strafford Stathalter in Irland auf der Tawers platz in Londen 12 Maj 1641
A. Doct. Vsher Primat in Irland.
B. Rahts Herren von Londen.
C. Der Graf von Stafford.
D. Seine anverwanten vnd freunde.

Great crowds witness Strafford's execution at the Tower of London.

After the Petition of Right of 1628, Thomas Wentworth had uttered the fateful words, 'Whoever ravels forth into questions the right of a king and of a people shall never be able to wrap them up again into the comeliness and order he found them in.' Although he had supported the Petition, in following years 'sweetened by the rewards of office' he became one of the King's most devoted servants; and his shadow stalked the early years of the Civil War.

In 1633 he was despatched to govern Ireland, where he mixed reform with peculation; the legacy of his rule was the Irish revolt. Although Charles did not entirely trust him, he recalled Wentworth, whom he created Viscount Strafford, to advise on the war with the Scots. Strafford promised to bring Charles Irish troops in return for an earldom and the recall of Parliament, which could then be brought to heel; in the event, Parliament refused to vote Charles taxes and, against Strafford's advice, the Short Parliament was dissolved. Yet when Charles had sent the Parliament packing, Strafford shifted to match the King's opinion and urged Charles to 'go on with a vigorous war as you first designed...loosed and absolved from all rules of government. Being reduced to extreme necessity, everything is to be done that power might admit, and that you are to

do. They refusing, you are acquitted towards God and man.'

Strafford, as Commander-in-Chief of the King's army, went north to 'go on with a vigorous war' and face the Scots, only to see his cavalry routed. It was an expensive humiliation since Charles' strained resources now had to pay the expenses of the Scottish army. As one of the most prominent advisors, who clearly both reinforced the King's absolutist principles and formed new extremes of royal opinion, Strafford became the target for the pent-up anger of the recalled Commons. On 22 March 1641 a Bill of Impeachment was entered against this 'evil counsellor'. Soon it was changed to a Bill of Attainder, condemning him as a traitor for severing the ancient harmony between King and Parliament. Oliver St John was of the opinion that 'it was never accounted either cruelty or foul play to knock foxes and wolves on the head...because they be beasts of prey', and as a wave of public outrage against Strafford swept through London, both Houses of Parliament passed the Bill of Attainder, against the express wish of the King. On 10 May Charles disowned Strafford by signing the Bill and, although he immediately regretted his action, Strafford was brought to the scaffold two days later.

Thomas Wentworth,
Earl of Strafford, with
his secretary, in a
portrait after van Dyck.

In the midst of turmoil, another event occurred which fanned the flames of rebellion even more strongly. In October 1641 a revolt by Ulster Catholics against Protestant settlers erupted. It was the events in Ireland which proved to be the catalyst for the outbreak of civil war in England.

Ireland's identity, language and culture were different from those of England, based in part on its own distinctive tradition of Catholicism. It had also emerged from the influences of the various settlers and adventurers who had colonized Ireland since the Middle Ages. Some, for example the community of 'Old' English of whom many were Catholic, were well integrated into Irish life and politics. However, this was not the case with the most recent settlers from England and Scotland whom the Irish Catholics bitterly resented. Their presence in Ireland was due to the strategy adopted by James 1 to exert power over the rebellious regions of Ireland. To this end, Protestant settlers had been

The tears of Ireland

'Mr Ford's house rifled, and to make her confess where her money lay, they took hot tongs clapping them to the soles of her feet and to the palms of her hand, so tormented her with the pain thereof that she died.

'At one Mr Atkin's house, seven Papists broke in and beat out his brains, then ripped up his wife with child after they had ravished her, and Nero-like viewed Nature's bed of conception, then took the child and sacrificed it in the fire.

'English Protestants stripped naked and turned into the mountains in the frost and snow, whereof many hundreds perished to death, and many lying dead in ditches and savages upbraided them saying, "Now are ye wild Irish as well as we".'

Rumour flourished in the immediate wake of the 1641 rising in Ireland, and the most gruesome and ghoulish stories and tracts circulated. These accounts were published in early 1642 by James Cranford, a Presbyterian with as virulent anti-Catholic feeling as any, in *The Tears of Ireland… Reported by Gentlemen of good credit living there, but forced to fly for their lives…*

Anger against the Protestant settlers was fuelled by the difficulties in England in late 1641 with the occasion to be turned into violence, and the Catholic population took bloody retribution. The stories of atrocity, exaggerated as they were, served to intensify the siege mentality of the English and the Protestants in Ireland.

The tales and images of atrocities that circulated after 1641 underwrote strong anti-Irish feeling.

'planted' on land taken from the indigenous Irish. In 1609, a vast and carefully organized Plantation of Ulster was prepared and by 1641 the English and Scottish settlers numbered between 50,000 and 100,000. Antagonism to the settlers' Protestantism and what was perceived as ever closer links between Dublin and the English parliament had bred deep resentment amongst Irish Catholics. Meanwhile, the events in England, where the King was in conflict with his Parliament, threatened the beleaguered Irish with fears of further religious discrimination and settlement. They seized the opportunity to rebel openly and in October 1641 the Irish Catholics of Dungannon, Charlemont and Newry rose against the Protestants. The rising spread rapidly, and it was the impact of this news as it reached England that had such devastating results.

Undoubtedly, as in any violent uprising, atrocities were committed but historians are agreed that the scale of them was exaggerated at the time. Lurid

The Grand Remonstrance, 1 December 1641

'Most Gracious Sovereign,

'Your Majesty's most humble and faithful subjects the Commons in this present Parliament assembled, do with much thankfulness and joy acknowledge the great mercy and favour of God, in giving your Majesty a safe and peaceable return out of Scotland into your kingdom of England, where the pressing dangers and distempers of the State have caused us with much earnestness to desire the comfort of your gracious presence...The duty which we owe to your Majesty and our country, cannot but make us very sensible and apprehensive, that the multiplicity, sharpness, and malignity of those evils under which we have for many years suffered, are fomented and cherished by a corrupt and ill-affected party...

'The root of all this mischief we find to be a malignant and pernicious design of subverting the fundamental laws and principles of government, upon which the religion and justice of this kingdom are firmly established. The actors and promoters hereof have been:

'1. The Jesuited Papists, who hate the laws...

'2. The Bishops and the corrupt part of the clergy, who cherish formality and superstition...

'3. Such Councillors and Courtiers as for private ends have engaged themselves to further the interests of some foreign princes or states...The common principles by which they moulded and governed all their particular counsels and actions were...to maintain continual differences and discontents between the King and his people...to suppress the purity and power of religion...to conjoin those parties of the kingdom which were most propitious to their own ends, and to divide those who were most opposite... to disaffect the King to Parliaments by slander and false imputations, and by putting him upon other ways of supply...

'188. They have strained to blast our proceedings in Parliament, by wresting the interpretations of our orders from their genuine intention.

'189. They tell the people that our meddling with the power of episcopacy hath caused sectaries and conventicles, when idolatrous and Popish ceremonies, introduced into the Church by the command of the bishops, have not only debarred the people from thence, but expelled them from the kingdom...

'197. That His Majesty be humbly petitioned by both Houses to employ such councillors, ambassadors and other ministers, to maintain his business at home and abroad as the Parliament may have cause to confide in, without which we cannot give his Majesty such supplies for support of his own estate, nor such support to the Protestant party beyond the sea, as is desired...

'204. That His Majesty may have cause to be in love with good counsel and good men...to see happiness, wealth, peace and safety derived to his own kingdom, and procured to his allies by the influence of his own power and government.'

propaganda portraying Catholics massacring thousands of Protestants fuelled the ever-present hatred of Catholics and fear of popery amongst the English. Once more, the spectre of an international popish conspiracy was raised and Charles was again implicated. Fear of an Irish Catholic invasion of England, perhaps with the aid of a foreign army, made the matter of national security urgent. Troops were needed to bring an immediate end to brutalities and to put down the Catholic insurrection for good. In an atmosphere of deep distrust of the sincerity of the King's commitment to the cause of Protestantism and fear that he might use force against his enemies in his own kingdom, the question of who should command the armed forces was crucial.

The events in Ireland exacerbated rifts between Charles and his Parliament and indeed within Parliament itself. News of the Irish uprising coincided with the passing in November 1641 of the Grand Remonstrance, a bitter indictment of the government of Charles from the beginning of his reign listing all the accumulated grievances against him. It was passed by a majority of only eleven members, an indication of the divisiveness of the measure. It was then proposed that the Remonstrance should be printed – and therefore available for anyone to read. The outrage was so great that swords were drawn in Parliament for the first time. Sir Edward Dering protested, 'When I first heard of a Remonstrance... I thought to represent unto the King the wicked counsels of pernicious Councillors...I did not dream that we should remonstrate downwards, tell stories to the people and talk of the King as of a third person.' For some members, like Dering, the challenge to the King was in danger of being carried too far.

Although the Grand Remonstrance had been divisive, the challenge to the traditional authority of the King continued in the disputes over control of the armies in Ireland. Pym and others pressed further in attempts to bring the Trained Bands and the militia under Parliamentary control. The matter was urgent as rumours were circulating that the Queen, Henrietta Maria, was attempting to raise troops and finance from abroad. Alarmed by the threat to his wife, Charles entered Parliament by force with the purpose of arresting five members for treason. The five fled to the City where they prepared for armed resistance. Charles' action played into the hands of his enemies; the attack on Parliament and its elected members incited the people of London and put the City of London and the corporation firmly behind Pym and the other parliamentary leaders. It had been a disastrous move which succeeded only in weakening the King's position further. The political blunder left him yet again fearful for his safety and on 10 January 1642 Charles left Whitehall. Hopes of a return to political harmony faded.

The narrative of events so far has concentrated on London. London as the capital city was of course where the major conflicts were played out between the King and his Parliament with the citizens of London making a decisive contribution. But it would be wrong to see the conflict confined to the metropolis. In the 1990s our view of government policies is determined by our experiences of how they affect our daily lives, whichever part of the country we live in. This was no less true of the seventeenth century: indeed there has been considerable debate among historians over the relative importance of local communities defined by county, compared with allegiances to national politics

The Five Members

Charles I depicted surveying the scene in the Commons when his birds had flown, one of the most celebrated episodes in the history of Parliamentary privilege.

and the nation state. This debate is not a matter of purely academic interest, but is crucial to our understanding of why and how people all over the country made choices about which side to support when civil war finally broke out, and what factors determined those choices.

In the seventeenth century the county was an important unit in the government of England and as such had a great deal of autonomy. Local government was in the hands of local dignitaries. The gentry, the mass of landowners, were responsible often as Justices of the Peace for the administration of local government as well as sitting in Parliament as members

On 4 January 1642 the King came to Parliament in a foolish attempt to arrest MPs and one peer who were among his most consistent opponents: Pym, Hampden, Arthur Haselrige, Denzil Holles, William Strode, and Lord Kimbolton (or Mandeville). Here, it seemed, was Charles' true intention to break Parliament's privileges. Some members committed what they saw to paper.

'The five gentlemen which were to be accused came into the House, and there was information that they should be taken away by force. Upon this, the House sent to the Lord Mayor, Aldermen and Common Council to let them know how their privileges were likely to be broken, and the City put into danger...

'It was moved, considering there was an intention to take these five men away by force, to avoid all tumult, let them be commanded to absent themselves...A little after, the King came in, with all his guard...The Speaker was commanded to sit still, with the mace lying before him...Then the King came upwards, towards the chair, with his hat off, and the Speaker stepped out to meet him. Then the King stepped up to his place and stood upon the step, but sat not down in his chair. And, after he had looked a great deal, he told us, he would not break our privileges, but treason had no privilege. He came for those five gentlemen...Then he asked the Speaker if they were here, or where they were. Upon that the Speaker fell on his knees and desired his excuse, for he was a servant to the House and had neither eyes nor tongue to see or say anything but what they commanded him. Then the King told him, he thought his own eyes were as good as his, and then said, his birds were flown, but he did expect the House would send them to him, and if they did not he would seek them himself, for their treason was foul and such as they would thank him to discover. Then he assured us they should have a fair trial, and so went out, putting off his hat until he came to the door.'

The royal warrant for the Five Members and Lord Mandeville.

of the House of Commons. The wealth and influence of the local gentry remains visible today in parts of England wßhere fine seventeenth-century manor houses still exist. The gentry in many localities had felt particularly aggrieved during the years of Charles' personal rule. The increasing interference by central government into local affairs was seen by them as an erosion of their traditional rights and duties. For, although Justices of the Peace were unpaid, the post had other attractions. It affirmed a gentleman's social standing among the county elite and also brought local power. Alongside the aristocracy, the gentry wielded considerable economic and political power and, because they controlled the local militias, they were also militarily powerful. Control over armed forces was crucial when the country was plunged into war. Below the gentry were the yeomen freeholders and farmers who attended to local administrative duties as high and petty constables. The high constables were responsible for apportioning rates and reporting local abuses and grievances. The petty constables had the unenviable tasks of maintaining social control over many areas of people's lives and social activities such as alehouses and village festivities. The parson and the squire also performed the traditional role of maintaining social order and discipline.

The structure of towns was also hierarchical, run by merchant oligarchies some of which were extremely rich, especially in London. Here the wealthy Merchant Adventurers and other large companies held monopolies in their trade giving them sole rights over specified markets. Their power was deeply resented by the smaller merchants who were less powerful and affluent and excluded from the tight cliques of wealthy merchants. The small provincial merchants also disliked the domination of London over the export trade and supported Parliament's attempts to break the monopolies which had existed so forcefully during the years of Charles' personal rule. The main bulk of the urban workforce was made up of artisans and craftsmen who also resented the domination and exploitation of the wealthy merchants. They also had grievances against the middlemen who supplied them with raw materials, and so sought remedies for their economic problems in the political sphere. They organized and agitated for more democratic forms of government in which their interests would be represented and protected. The burden of taxation both by the state and by the Church in the form of tithes fell heavily on this 'middling' group, a grievance the craftsmen shared with yeomen farmers in the rural areas. They therefore identified their interests with Parliament's attempts to curb the powers of the King, the House of Lords and the bishops. The events of 1640 and 1641, particularly although not exclusively in London, increased the political awareness of many of the craftsmen and artisans and, when the revolution occurred, they were at the centre of the most radical groups like the Levellers.

Strong cultural traditions existed both in towns and the rural areas but this does not necessarily suggest that the counties were homogeneous. Somerset is a good example of a county which some historians see as divided by its traditions rather than unified. In North Somerset, Puritanism had spread very widely during the 1620s and 30s and many of the traditional festivals like church ales and village sports had been largely, although not completely, suppressed. On the other hand, such festivities were very much part of the rural life of South Somerset. The same was true of differences between the towns; Taunton with its clothing industry was staunchly Parliamentarian while Sherborne in nearby Dorset was subject to the very strong influence of the aristocratic family, the Digbys who became strongly Royalist. As the conflict between the King and Parliament worsened the cultural and religious differences which already existed in the country became more open as people were forced to declare support for one or the other.

When Charles abandoned his capital in January 1642 and began making his journey northwards his intention to raise support was clear. Queen Henrietta Maria had set sail for Holland with the object of securing arms and financial aid;

Queen Henrietta Maria
in a setting typical
of the portraits of the
Caroline Court.

Old London Bridge (above), the only dry route across the River Thames.

Fortifying London

'Reasons for fortifying the City of London by dykes, earthen wall, and bulwarks.

'**1st,** That it will best secure the City etc., and defend it from any furious and grand assault by day, but especially by night, when bulwarks, unless united by dyke and earthen wall, will not serve, but may be used against us.

'**2nd,** That it will be a very great advantage and profit to the City...It will not only discourage the enemies of the City from warlike and violent approaches, but will encourage our friends to frequent her, and come with their estates to inhabit in her by multitudes, whereby she will grow mighty, famous, and rich even in time of war, instance the Low Countries, besides the aid of strangers by weekly contributions and the increase of trading...'

London remained true to Parliament's cause, through the conflict, and no assault was ever made upon it.

London fortified (right), in a ring of walls and forts.

Raising the King's Standard at Nottingham

The King's standard, raised at Nottingham.

On 22 August 1642, Charles I raised his standard on the Castle Hill at Nottingham in front of a small band of followers, but with the ceremony appropriate to the occasion. The standard itself needed twenty supporters, it was 'much of the fashion of the City streamers used at the Lord Mayor's Show', one observer wrote, 'and on the top of it hung a flag, the King's Arms quartered, with a hand pointing to the crown, with this motto: Give Caesar His Due.' With characteristic indecision, the King made last-minute changes to the proclamation of the causes of his raising the standard; and it was later taken as an ill omen that the wind blew the standard over, which 'could not be fixed again in a day or two, till the tempest was allayed.'

Nottinghamshire was to remain a county controlled by the Royalists through the war. But the city of Nottingham itself, which Charles left in mid-September, stayed firmly in the hands of Parliament, largely due to the untiring efforts of Colonel John Hutchinson, whose exploits were proudly recorded by his wife Lucy. Coming from a local landowning family, Hutchinson took control almost by right, but like many in the early years of struggle he had little or no military training or expertise.

Hutchinson organized Nottingham's defence with only the training given him as a schoolboy by 'an old Low Country soldier' who taught him 'military postures and in assaults and defences'. He became Governor of Nottingham Castle, although he fought almost as much with the intransigence of those on his own side as he did with the enemy, which included many in his own family, especially his Biron cousins.

When the King's forces came near to taking Nottingham in September 1643, and the Hutchinsons found themselves face to face with Sir Richard Biron, the order was nevertheless given to 'take him or shoot him...and not let him escape though they cut his legs off.' When the enemy returned in January 1644, Hutchinson rallied the town, and 'stirred them up to such a generous shame', that they beat the Royalists back, who 'left a great track of blood, which froze as it fell upon the snow.'

Later in the wars, Hutchinson was elected to Parliament, and signed the death warrant of Charles I. Caesar, he felt, had been given his due.

the implication that the King was seeking military support against his enemies was now apparent. For its part, Parliament had capitalized on Charles' departure from London which had left the way clear to seize the country's major arsenal kept in the Tower of London. Since there was no standing army which the King could readily call on to coerce his rebellious Parliament and the resources of the Tower of London were now in his opponents' hands, he was obliged to find support where he could. In the meantime, Parliament responded by passing the Militia Bill which would place all Trained Bands in the counties under its control. This represented a major challenge to the King and a fundamental attack on royal prerogative. At the same time, Parliament passed an act excluding all bishops from the House of Lords and the clergy from all secular offices. While Charles assented to the latter, he refused to approve the Militia Bill. In reply, he issued the Commissions of Array, an archaic device whereby individual commissioners were appointed to take control of their local militia. The issue was decisive – who should be obeyed, King or Parliament? It also brought the nation one step closer to war. Curbing the King's powers, ridding him of his evil advisers and putting obstacles in the way of his perceived attempts at absolutism may have been acceptable so far, but to some moderates it seemed that Parliamentary privilege was being pushed too far. Was royal tyranny to be replaced by the greater menace of 'King' Pym and his allies? Openly to oppose the King himself and take up arms against him was to raise the stakes too high.

But it was the King himself who had turned the crisis into a conflict and now both sides were setting about raising troops. Charles attempted to occupy Hull and seize the large magazine of arms there. In a humiliating defeat he was

AFBEELDING van de VISITE van Haare MAJESTEYT van GROOT BRITTANIE HENRIETTA MARIA, met haare Neef PRINS WILLEM van NASSAU, Gegeven aan den HEERE ADRIANUS PAAUW, Heere van HEEMSTEDE-OP 'T SLOT te HEEMSTEDE den agtsten September 1644.

Henrietta Maria arrives in Holland in 1644 to raise arms for the King.

Charles at Oxford

The dashing Cavalier John, Lord Byron, with his scar, who sat to Dobson at Oxford (right).

The army encamped before the fortified city of Oxford (below).

*Endymion Porter,
one of Charles'
leading negotiators,
who was also painted
by Dobson.*

After Edgehill the King rode in triumph into Oxford where his wartime court was established. He stayed there until April 1646, and the city became a new quasi-capital, with the panoply of royalty run on a shoestring. William Dobson, who had absorbed the art of van Dyck's portraiture, became the court painter and left many pictures of the swaggering Royalists. Some had come fresh from battle, and bore their wounds proudly; others stayed firmly behind the city walls. The city was defended, the King and Queen and their leading courtiers were housed in the colleges – Charles at Christ Church, Henrietta Maria at Merton – and everyone else had to make do where they might. Lady Fanshawe was one of the aristocrats to whom conditions in Oxford came as a rude and unwelcome shock.

'We that had till that hour lived in great plenty and great order found ourselves like fishes out of water... [They had come] to a baker's house in an obscure street, and from rooms well furnished to lie in a very bad bed in a garret; to one dish of meat, and that not the best ordered; no money, for we were poor as Job; nor clothes more than a man or two brought in their cloak bags. We had the perpetual discourse of losing and gaining towns and men; at the windows the sad spectacle of war, sometimes plague, sometimes sickness of other kinds...always want; yet I must needs say that most bore it with a martyr-like cheerfulness.'

refused entry to the town by Sir John Hotham, Governor of Hull and was forced to withdraw to York where he continued to rally support and from where he organized his recruiting campaigns. The nucleus of a Royalist party began to form round him in York; some members of both the Lords and Commons had gone north to join their King and he was gaining support in northern counties, Cumberland, Westmoreland, Lancashire among them, and further west in Herefordshire and Wales.

When Charles left London, he effectively left it in the control of Parliament and it was from among the citizens of London that the Parliamentary army was initially drawn. The London Trained Bands provided the core under the command of Major-General Phillip Skippon. These citizen soldiers had received training from professional soldiers in regular training sessions held in Artillery Garden in Bishopsgate, for example. The City of London also provided considerable financial backing to the Parliamentary army. Under the overall command of the Earl of Essex, leading Parliamentarian gentry raised troops from their own localities; John Hampden, for example, a Buckinghamshire gentleman made famous by his resistance to ship money, led a regiment and Oliver Cromwell raised a troop of cavalry from his constituency in Cambridge.

Most historians agree that those who actively took sides at this stage represented a committed minority but there is a difference of opinion over what the basis of these convictions was. For some historians, religion was the divisive and decisive issue and it was religious zeal, particularly on the Parliamentary side which motivated the people to take up arms. Anti-Catholicism, heightened by events in Ireland, fired many Parliamentarians to declare themselves ready for the fight in the providential struggle for God's cause against the Antichrist. The underlying fear of popish plots, of a king corrupted by popish advisors and under the influence of his Catholic wife, were very real to the extreme Puritans in the Parliamentary ranks. On the other side, the King's supporters also claimed to be fighting for the true Protestant religion and for the necessity of defending it against the subversion of the Puritan extremists. We have seen how the House of Commons was split into factions over religious reforms with some wanting to

The King is humiliated, refused entry to Hull.

Sir John Hotham,
Governor of Hull, who
closed the town gates
on the King in 1642.

seize the opportunity for a wholesale reform of the church and its government whilst others wanted to return to the traditions of Elizabethan times.

While the significance of religion in determining allegiance to King or Parliament cannot be over-estimated, political and constitutional divisions also contributed to the formation of two opposing sides. Royalists supported the status quo as well as having a loyalty to the concept of kingship and to traditional notions of an ordered, hierarchical society. Indeed, in the early stages of the conflict, some Royalists were as much concerned with maintaining social order as they were with supporting their King. It is perhaps not surprising then that some of the nobility and the wealthiest gentry eventually sided with the King, although many felt personally aggrieved by Charles' treatment of them and more generally by his policies. Choosing between the King and Parliament could be an anguished decision; Sir Edmund Verney wrote:

'I have eaten his bread and served him near thirty years, and will not do so base a thing as to forsake him; and choose rather to lose my life (which I am sure to do) to preserve and defend these things which are against my conscience to preserve and defend.'

In his case, honour and loyalty eventually outweighed religious convictions. All sectors of society were faced with painful choices and were divided between themselves as to which side to support. Local and social allegiances often played a strong part in determining choices, but in many instances taking sides could be unpredictable and vary with circumstances. Propaganda from both sides confused the issues further. But if only the minority were clear in their commitment to one side or the other, what was the attitude of the vast majority?

The overwhelming mood amongst the population was for the preservation of peace and the wish of individuals and communities to stay neutral and keep out of the conflict altogether. War was looked on with dread and there was a spate of petitions from the counties to the King, expressing growing disquiet and fear of civil war. Petitioning was one of the traditional ways in which grievances were expressed; these petitions strongly reflected the desire to remain neutral.

A family divided

Sir Edmund Verney, Standard-Bearer to the King, who fell at Edgehill.

In the Civil War, temperament and ideology were to set father against son, brother against brother. Among those split by the actions and necessities of war was the upper-gentry Verney family, from Claydon House in Buckinghamshire. The head of the family, Sir Edmund Verney, had carefully managed his estates, trying to extract more revenue from them in a time of inflation, and he had sought preferment at court and the financial advantage that accrued. He held the office of the King's Knight Marshal, which gave him opportunity to line his pocket. He obtained patents for licensing hackney coaches, invested in the lucrative alnage wool trade control, and received Crown pensions. Verney was one of the courtier profiteers against whom the mounting anger of the country was directed.

Verney had other problems. He lent money to Charles, which the King 'had often promised to pay him' but never did. And he had ten children to provide for. Were it not for the Civil War, Sir Edmund would have managed comfortably, but allegiance took him into battle, when the King required Verney's services as Knight Marshal in 1639 in the war against the Scots. He went despite his son Ralph's pleas that 'your years, your charge, your distracted fortunes, your former life were privilege enough to keep you back without the least stain to your reputation.' Sir Edmund was now in serious debt, while the difficulties of war compounded the problem. As the royal standard-bearer, Verney was in the centre of action, and he died in the battle of Edgehill in 1642 (only his severed hand was ever found) with suspicions that his bravery was suicidal.

Ralph had been told Sir Edmund was 'infinitely melancholy, for many other things I believe, besides the difference betwixt you.' The rift between father and son came because Ralph, the MP for Aylesbury, supported Parliament. Lady Sussex wrote to him, 'These distracted times put us in great disorder...I pray God bless you with safety; your Parliament flies high; truly it is a happy thing, I think, they have so much courage to stand to maintain their right.' The Solemn League and Covenant, 'a sword to divide', proved the breaking-point for Sir Ralph. His family and friends were Royalist in the main, and yet he had kept firm for the Parliamentary cause, but his conscience did not extend to signing. He was ousted from the Commons – and lost his immunity for the debts he had inherited. 'I have resolved', he wrote, 'to take a journey and for a while to retire to some such place, where I may have leisure enough to inform my judgement in such things wherein I am doubting... whatever reports are raised or however I may suffer by them, I shall always honour and pray for the Parliament.'

Verney retired to France, under the assumed name of Smith, with his wife and children. From there he watched as his estate was sequestrated. He extended a helping hand to his brother Edmund who was steadfast in the Royalist service to the end, dying at Drogheda in 1649. By that time the sequestration had been lifted, partly through the intervention of friends, and in 1653 Sir Ralph was able to return to

SACRED
To the Memory of the
Euer Honored
S.ʳ EDMVND VERNEY who was
K.ᵗ Marshall 16 yeares
And Standard Bearer to Charles y.ᵉ first
In that memorable Battayle
of Edge Hill.
where he was Slayne.
on the 23 of October
1642.
Beinge then in the two and
Fifteth yeare of his Age.
AND
in Honour of
Dame MARGARET his wife
Eldest Daughter of S.ʳ Thomas
Denton of Hellesdon K.ᵗ
by whome Hee had
Six Sonnes and Six Daughters.
She Dyed at London
on y.ᵉ 5.ᵗ and was buried here on y.ᵉ 7.ᵗ
of Aprill 1641.
In the 47 yeare of
Her Age.

The Verney family monument in the church at Middle Claydon, Buckinghamshire.

England and settle his affairs. Settlement involved retrenchment: the accumulated debts, and the loss of revenue from estates that were sited in one of the most fought-over areas of the country, led to the sale of all the outlying areas of the estate between 1648 and 1664. Sir Ralph lived quietly. although he was imprisoned briefly in 1655 as a suspected Royalist; and he died in 1696, an aged and somewhat embittered man, although the estates had fallen on much better times by then. One of his first actions on his return from exile had been to commission a huge family memorial for the church at Middle Claydon next to the Verney Buckinghamshire home, to the memory of his father, his wife who had died in exile in 1650, and his brother. Their busts stare out together, where once they were divided.

Sould by Tho: Ienner at the Ex: — W Hollar fecit 1640.

For a nation which had been at peace for several decades, the reluctance to engage in war is understandable both in terms of the perceived disruption of normal life but also in the horror of the idea of Englishman taking up arms against Englishman. The grim experience of the Thirty Years' War being fought out in Europe and the subsequent devastation was not something to be replicated on English soil.

When Charles raised his standard at Nottingham on 22 August 1642, making in effect a formal declaration of war, it remained little more than a symbolic gesture. In spite of such exhortations to the people as 'Your religion, your liberties, your laws are at stake. The concurrence and affection of my people with God's blessing will supply and recover all', Charles failed to rally much active support. One of the reasons for this was the fear that Charles was raising a papist army. Certainly some of his active supporters were Catholics but the extent of their support was exaggerated. More significantly, as the evidence from private correspondence and the local petitions shows, was the basic impetus to stop the war and negotiate a settlement. Francis Newport's letter written from London to his uncle, Sir Richard Leveson was typical of a general feeling:

'As the face of public affairs now looks, there is nothing to be seen in it but ruin and desolation unless we speedily incline all hearts to some good accommodation...God grant that which is sour destroy not that which is sweet and that a happy agreement betwixt king and parliament may speedily prevent our ruin and destruction.'

The personal correspondence exchanged between individuals and families of the gentry gives us some insight into how news of the imminent war spread throughout the country. With the collapse of Charles' government, the strict censorship which had existed also broke down giving rise to a plethora of printed news, debate and discussion which was widely available and eagerly read. Literacy levels in this period were higher than might be supposed and even if a large number of the population were unable to read for themselves, pamphlets and newsletters were read aloud in pubs and taverns where they would have been discussed. The other major source of information was the pulpit controlled by the local parsons. In an age when attendance at church on Sundays was obligatory, the church performed all the functions of the mass media today. It was from the pulpit that national and local news would be heard and public declarations read. The pulpit too was the site of conflict over religious practices and observances, therefore every parish would have been only too aware of the frightening developments in the nation. As the war progressed, its impact would also have been felt even in the parishes where no actual fighting was taking place. There is a well-known anecdote relating to a husbandman ploughing his fields near Marston Moor when the armies arrived for battle. He was supposedly happily unaware of the conflict even though it was taking place in his immediate vicinity; an obvious impossibility. The research of historians today indicates that the Civil War and its impact touched all parts of the country; even in remote areas such as Caernarvonshire the gentry received news from London which was read and disseminated avidly. For most of the population the war was a terrible and traumatic experience which bitterly divided the nation.

The equestrian portrait (opposite) became an icon of the Civil War years, and leaders on both sides, like Essex here, were depicted in this grandest of martial poses.

Unlike many wars, it is difficult to pinpoint exactly when and where the Civil War broke out. It was a messy and chaotic affair right up to the major battle at Edgehill in October 1642 when the two armies confronted each other for the first time. We have seen that support for the initial war efforts of both sides came from within small committed minorities with the majority campaigning and petitioning for peace. In the first year of the war many counties signed or attempted to sign pacts of neutrality. As the situation worsened and both sides struggled for control of the militia, polarization increased and passive neutralism became harder to sustain. In most civil wars the issues around which individuals and communities forge allegiances are to some extent clearly defined ; for example a political divide, class conflict or different religious or tribal groupings account for the divisions in a society. The Civil War of the seventeenth century presents a more complex picture of a divided nation since there is no clear-cut interpretation of the divisions in social, religious, geographical or economic terms. The decision to take sides divided families and friends as the famous letter which Sir William Waller wrote to his friend Sir Ralph Hopton so poignantly demonstrates. In some families, fathers and brothers found themselves on opposing sides, perhaps following the dictates of their conscience or more cynically for the assurance of the survival of the family estates.

Many people had to examine their own consciences as they were exhorted by both sides to take up God's cause. On the other hand, people also made choices based on pragmatism rather than principle. For some, particularly of course the unemployed, joining either army offered the opportunity of work with pay, for others it opened up possibilities of excitement and adventure. For some, the turmoil of war provided the chance to settle local grievances as well as drawing

The alehouse was seen by authority as the seat of sedition, and as the 'nursery of naughtiness'.

Bristol

Few in Bristol wanted a civil war. Theirs was a merchant city, and war was bad for business. Many of the matters of religious and constitutional principle which had roused other men and places to anger passed Bristol by. Yet the city was to be the setting for some of the most dramatic actions of the war. Like other large centres of population – Bristol was the third largest city in England, after London and Norwich – it had its trained bands, three foot companies 'besides a voluntary company of genteel, proper, martial, disciplined men', but nevertheless the hope was that the city would remain neutral.

By November 1642, Bristol was under great pressure to commit itself to the Parliamentary cause, especially since the surrounding countryside was already heavily committed. Earthworks were constructed for defence, and by early December after some resistance Parliament's soldiers were admitted. It was reported that a large deputation of women appealed for it since otherwise 'the effusion of blood would be great' and the city would be starved out.

The soldiers proved unpopular, especially under the rapacious command of Colonel Essex, replaced the following February by Colonel Nathaniel Fiennes. A month later a Royalist plot to admit Prince Rupert was intercepted; but by late July 1643 Prince Rupert's troops lay in wait. In storming the city on the 26th, one small band of troops broke through the outer line of defence and eventually, despite a valiant attempt by a strong group of women to barricade the Frome Gate, Prince Rupert took the city. The two sides agreed terms, and the Parliamentary force was allowed to withdraw.

For two years thereafter, Bristol was to be held for the King, and was groomed as a counterweight to London's mercantile power. The townspeople seem to have accepted their new masters as amiably as they did the old, until August 1645. The tide of war had turned, and Parliamentary forces laid siege to Bristol again. The city was prepared, and had laid in supplies, although an outbreak of bubonic plague weakened the population. Sir Thomas Fairfax's opinion was, 'as for the sickness, let us trust God with the army, who will be ready to protect us in the siege from infection, as in the field from the bullet.' On 10 September the city was stormed for the second time, and Prince Rupert capitulated, to the great wrath of the King. Many had lost their lives in the fighting, but few of them were the people of Bristol who only occasionally – like the women who were prepared to 'dead the bullets' with their bodies and those of their children in 1643 – took sides.

ordinary people into political action. In normal times, deference to landlords from tenants would be expected and loyalty to social superiors may have determined choices as well as safeguarding livelihoods. Nevertheless in the abnormal circumstances of the war these social relationships could be disrupted. One such example can be seen in the letter written to William Davenport, a Cheshire Royalist, by a group of his tenants. While showing due deference, they assert very firmly that they felt obliged to support Parliament which was their representative body. Davenport was outraged, 'they not waiting for my answer nor much caring for it either, enrol themselves on the Sabbath day too in the army of Captain Leigh who was for Parliament'. The dislocation of war inevitably disturbs the patterns of daily life and opens up new horizons and new political awareness; this was as much the case in the experience of the seventeenth-century Civil War as in the two World Wars of this century.

As the war progressed, it became increasingly difficult to remain neutral and to be unaffected by the consequences of a civil war. An immediate impact was of armies on the march through towns and villages and the subsequent need for quarter and supplies in the form of food, money or horses. In many instances payments were not forthcoming in cash but by promissory notes as the records of local accounts committees testify. In some cases, payment or compensation was

The Clubmen

The largest popular movement of the entire Civil War period was neither support for the side of the King nor for Parliament, but a third force which was tired of the fighting and the cost in lives, crops, and money. The Clubmen emerged in 1645, notably in southern, south-western and Welsh border counties. They were aggressively neutralist, in some places vigilante groups harassed troops, and one of the surprising things about them was how they united all levels of local society, from the clergy and minor gentry to poor farmers and labourers. Like many of the popular risings occuring almost simultaneously in France, they were intensely localist in their appeal to ancient traditions.

Some just wanted, as Dorset clubmen did in May 1645, 'to preserve ourselves from plunder and all other unlawful violence.' Others like the men of Sussex had deeper-seated motives, appealing to the authority of Magna Carta and the traditions of good rule which were the touchstone of political rhetoric, condemning 'some particular persons crept into authority who have delegated their power to men of sordid condition whose wills have been laws ...by which they have overthrown all our English liberties'.

It hardly mattered whether those 'particular persons' were for King or for Parliament. One of their abiding wishes was for the war to end; some of the starkest confrontations were to come in the West Country, as Fairfax's army marched to victory in July 1645, culminating in Cromwell's assault on the Dorset men assembled on Hambledon hill.

The Clubmen are an expression of one of the enduring aspects of the Civil War conflict: local resistance and localist neutralism. Their protests were both backward-looking, to the 1630s and the reaction to the Personal Rule and antagonism to the court, and forward-looking to the 1650s and resistance to the county committees and the rule of the Major-Generals. For every person caught up in the fervour of conflict and King or Parliament, there were always many more who wanted it all to stop.

virtually non-existent or took years to be settled. Hardship was widespread and the effects on the economy of some localities devastating. Everyone suffered from the unprecedented levels of taxation; in 1643 a weekly assessment tax was levied by Parliament in order to finance the war effort. The estates of Royalists and Catholics were sequestered and the revenues used for the Parliamentary armies. Landowners suffered from taxation as well as a reduction in their income from rents as many tenants were unable to pay. Large estates and houses also suffered when they came under siege from armed forces; there were a number of heroic incidents of women of the gentry defending their property while their menfolk were away fighting but such episodes cannot disguise the real horrors and traumas suffered by the civilian population. Throughout the course of the war it was not uncommon for people to change sides; and as the struggle for territory gained momentum, the population of towns found themselves under siege and under the control of different forces, perhaps contrary to those which they had supported initially.

For many of the gentry, the economic hardship caused by the war was temporary but among the lower ranks of society the disruption of the war was permanent and it was a situation from which they did not recover. For a small farmer to lose his corn or his animals, particularly his horse – horses were in great demand for the cavalry – could mean ruin. It is not difficult to imagine the additional hardship caused to families who were already struggling financially by the sudden arrival of hungry soldiers in their village in need of food and quarter. Lacking the discipline of trained armies, troops of both sides plundered, almost inevitably in siege conditions or when their own pay was not forthcoming. In these circumstances, taking sides was less often a positive choice but more a means of ensuring survival.

By 1644 there were signs of growing war weariness as the conflict was taking its toll not only on the economy but also of human lives. In 1644 and 1645 many communities felt tried beyond endurance and men from some localities banded together to try to end the war by a compromise. Known as the Clubmen, they demonstrated their rejection of the war by raising armies of their own to oppose both Parliamentary and Royalist armies invading their territory. They operated at first mainly in the south east and west of the country, from Sussex through to Somerset and Devon. In their manifestoes they argued for a settlement between the King and Parliament with a return to just powers and privileges for both sides. However, although the attitude was of 'plague on both your houses' and a real desire to see the end of the war, the Clubmen were not always wholly neutral and showed preferences for one side against the other. In spite of their efforts in raising large forces to keep the armies out of their localities, the war continued. In 1645, the King was defeated at the battle of Naseby and hopes for a settlement were raised. Instead, the war dragged on bringing in its wake increasing bitterness and brutality.

The conflict between Charles and his Parliament which reached crisis proportions in the years between 1640-42 had escalated into a full-blown civil war. For the people of England it was an atrocious and bewildering experience. Gradually every community was affected not only by physical hardship but by the overturning of religious and political institutions and the deep divisions this created within the whole fabric of society.

Cap.ᵗ Hen: Ireton 1642

Coll: Lambert 1642

Cap.ᵗ Ruſſell 1642

Deo Duce Nil Desperandum

Soyes Ferme

Tam Gladio Quam Trula.

Sanguis Cæmentium Facit

Cap.ᵗ Sheffield

Sʳ Willᵐ Conſtable Kᵗ & Barᵗ Coll. 1642

Cap.ᵗ Reeve 1642

Patria Poscente Paratum

Per Bellum ad Pacem

Cave adſum

Cap.ᵗ Barnard

Lord Grey

Majʳ Guntier

Gladius Jehova et Gideonis

Contra Impios

For Re-formation

CHAPTER THREE

Battle

As the events of 1642 gathered momentum it looked increasingly unlikely that a political solution could be found to resolve the conflict between the King and Parliament. Once both sides took up arms, the descent into war became inevitable. People were forced, however reluctantly, to choose sides and even those who tried steadfastly to remain neutral found themselves dragged into the conflict. Even for the committed minorities on both sides, taking the final steps towards a military solution was almost unthinkable. After all, England had been at peace for over one hundred years, unlike its European neighbours who had fairly constantly experienced the ravages of war. Germany and central Europe were at this time embroiled in what has come to be known as the Thirty Years' War which had begun in 1618 and brought in its wake appalling brutalities and atrocities. In the twentieth century, the experience of wars in Spain, Nigeria and Lebanon, for example, bear witness to the horrific realities of civil wars and the evidence from photographs, film, newspaper and personal accounts is a constant reminder of the tragic consequences of a country embroiled in internal conflicts and fighting. With more recent examples in mind, it is perfectly understandable why the English, three hundred years ago, recoiled from the prospect of civil war.

War and its consequences were too horrible to contemplate. The prospect of civil war perhaps invoked stories of the bloody battle on Bosworth field in 1485 the culmination of the War of the Roses when England was last caught up in civil strife.

Civil war is qualitatively different from a war against a foreign force where the enemy is clearly identifiable as an outsider. The devastating impact on the nation, the possible savagery and reprisals following in the wake of the English waging war against each other was foreseen at the time. For instance, Henry Slingsby , a Yorkshire landowner, a member of the Long Parliament and Royalist recorded his reflections and misgivings in his diary:

'These are strange, strange spectacles to this nation in this age, that have lived thus long peaceably, without noise of shot or drum and after we have stood neutrals and in peace when all the world besides has been in arms, and wasted with it; it is I say a thing most horrible that we should engage ourself in war with another, and with our own venom gnaw and consume ourself.'

Banners and standards (opposite) of Parliamentary leaders in the Civil War,
behind which their soldiers rallied in battle.

If England was unprepared psychologically for war it was even less well prepared militarily. Because of the long period of peace, England was effectively demilitarized with a population largely lacking any military knowledge or expertise. There was no standing army to provide either side with trained troops and equipment and so both sides initially had to capitalize on and compete for what small resources of trained men and arms were available, and after that they had to resort to improvisation and innovation.

The country was of course not totally without military resources. Every county had its own local militia units known as Trained Bands who served only within their own counties. Generally the little training they had consisted of drilling for a few days each year. A major exception were the London Trained Bands who were commanded by career soldiers and were therefore the nearest equivalent to a professional army. In the autumn of 1642 they numbered 6,000 men organised in six regiments. All the Trained Bands had their own magazines and there were many private arsenals which provided arms. Many noblemen and the richer gentry had their own private armouries with weapons and armour. Some of this was decorative or outdated but at time of crisis could be adapted; for example, most gentlemen carried swords as part of their everyday dress and as a symbol of their status. These civilian swords were easily turned into weapons of war. The major national arsenals in the Tower of London and at Hull had been seized by the Parliamentary forces who also controlled the main areas of arms production in London and the Weald of Kent where there were blast furnaces and ironworks for the production of cannon and artillery. Since Parliament had virtually all the major sources of armaments under its control, Royalist areas such as Oxford were obliged to set up their own arms production to keep their soldiers supplied during the course of the war. There was also an appreciation of the need for imported foreign weapons: at a very early stage Queen Henrietta Maria had left England taking with her the royal jewels. She sailed to Holland with the objective of pawning the jewels in order to raise the finance to purchase supplies for the King's war effort. Holland had the advantage of being both the centre for arms dealing as well as the chief market for diamonds and precious stones. However, the purchase of foreign weaponry could be a hazardous business since, as the evidence from Royalist ordnance officers shows, some countries used the opportunity to dump deteriorating powder supplies and odd assortments of ammunition on the English. The consequences for soldiers on the battlefield could be dire; for a man, probably untrained, facing the enemy in battle to discover that his supply of musket balls did not fit his weapon or that his gunpowder was defective would have been a terrifying experience.

Professional military personnel was also in short supply although there was a pool of officers and men with military experience. Their experience had been gained abroad in Holland, Spain and France where they would have learnt the newest military arts, particularly the Swedish techniques of Gustavus Adolphus. Prince Rupert, the King's nephew, was one of the outstanding officers who returned from abroad with the necessary experience and expertise to take command in battle. A flamboyant figure and a superb horseman, Prince Rupert was in charge of the King's cavalry. On the other side, the cavalry was led by the Earl of Bedford, a nobleman completely lacking any military experience. His inexperience was offset by other officers with professional training and both

Call to arms.

Occupation and pillage

Bulstrode Whitelock (1605-76).

A senior lawyer and MP in the forefront of Parliament's move to war, Bulstrode Whitelock was not quite clear himself how it had come about. 'It is strange to note how we have insensibly slid into this beginning of a civil war, by one unexpected accident after another', he said in 1642. When he went home to Buckinghamshire, he 'found the country much affrighted...and in most places they began to arm and to provide for their own defence.' His household soon found that their efforts were in vain.

'...a regiment under Sir John Byron quartered at Whitelock's house at Fawley Court, whereof his tenant William Cooke and his servants having some notice, they threw into the moat their brass, pewter and iron things, and removed to some of his tenants' houses and into the woods some of his books, linen and household stuff, as much as the short warning would permit. Sir John Byron and his brothers commanded the horse quartered there to commit no insolence, nor to plunder Whitelock's goods, but 1000 of them being in and about his house, there was no insolence or outrage which such guests commit upon an enemy but these brutish soldiers did at Fawley Court.

'There they had their whores, they spent and consumed in one night 100 loads of corn and hay, littered their horses with good wheat sheaves, gave them all sorts of corn in the straw, made great fires in the closes, and William Cooke telling them that there were billets and faggots nearer to them than the plough timber which they burned, they threatened to burn him...They ate and drank up all the house could afford...Whatsoever they could lay their hands on they carried away or spoiled, and did all that malice and rapine could provoke barbarous mercenaries to commit, and so they left William Cooke and his company in the highest affright and detestation of them, that lewdness and damage could persuade him unto.

'[Bulstrode Whitelock's] small children at William Cooke's had better usage, there Sir Thomas Byron quartered...they confessed they were Whitelock's children and prayed they might have no hurt done them. Sir Thomas said it were a barbarous thing to hurt those pretty innocent children, and kissed and made much of them, and showed great generosity towards Whitelock whom they reputed their enemy.'

sides were served by foreign professionals and mercenaries. Captain Carlo Fantom, a Croatian, and Hans Behre, a Dutch mercenary, fought for the Parliamentarians while the Royalists had the support of the engineer Bernard de Gomme and the explosives expert Bartholomew La Roche. There was little to choose between the two sides in terms of social status; the Parliamentary army included many peers amongst its colonels of regiments. Apart from the Trained Bands, the majority of the rank and file were volunteers (conscription would come later) and totally inexperienced. The local nobility and gentry raised troops in the area from among their tenants and therefore the discipline and

One parish in the wars

'Sir Paul Harris sent out warrants requiring or commanding all men...between the ages of 16 and three score to appear on a certain day upon Myddle Hill. I was then a youth of about 8 or 9 years of age, and I went to see this great show. And there I saw a multitude of men, and upon the highest bank of the hill I saw this Robert More standing, with a paper in his hand, and three or four soldier's pikes stuck upright in the ground by him; and there he made a proclamation, that if any person would serve the King, as a soldier in the wars, he should have 14 groats [4s. 8d. or 23p] a week for his pay.'

In 1701 Richard Gough wrote a remarkable history of his native parish, Myddle in Shropshire, which is a few miles to the north of Shrewsbury. He based his work around the properties and families of Myddle, and his book is filled with antiquarian titbits, anecdotes and personal reminiscences. Although he was a boy during the Civil Wars, his narrative suggests how that period both seared itself on his memory and affected many of the families of his neighbours.

Myddle is a parish composed of scattered hamlets in what were then woodland clearings, and at the time it would have had perhaps 350 inhabitants. 'Out of these three towns' (the main hamlets in the parish), 'there went no less than twenty men, of which number thirteen were killed in the wars' who enlisted for the King, and a few for Parliament. Some of those who enlisted were clearly desperadoes: Nathaniel Owen's 'common practice was to come by night with a party of horse to some neighbour's house and break open the doors, take what they pleased, and if the man of the house was found, they carried him to prison, from whence he could not be released without a ransom in money...' Owen died in the siege of Bridgnorth, when the Royalist army set fire to their garrison as they fled. Only one armed skirmish took place within Myddle itself, when a Royalist raiding party which pillaged the village houses on a regular basis was surprised by a band of Parliamentary horsemen, and a bloody fight ensued, 'part of which I saw, while I was a school boy at Myddle, under Mr Richard Roderick, who commanded us boys to come into the church.'

The most prominent changes the parish witnessed were in the church: the newly-installed rails around the communion table 'were taken down, and the

The church at Myddle, with the seating plan (opposite) from Richard Gough's History.

chancel floor was made level, and the communion table placed in the middle of it', and a prominent new pulpit was erected. Meanwhile, the rector had fled to London at the outbreak of the troubles, and 'during his absence his places were slenderly and seldom served'. Mr More was refused leave to return to his incumbency in 1646, and in his place, Joshua Richardson took the rectory. Gough was himself ever a Royalist, but he remembered Richardson with affection as 'an able and laborious [i.e. hard-working] minister' whose 'whole employment was about the concerns of his ministry.'

The ramifications of the unrest were felt in most households. 'There were several gentlemen in our neighbourhood', Gough remembered, 'that were forced to fly from their houses in the wars, and to shelter themselves in garrisons.' Families lost their menfolk into the armies, young women married soldiers they met in Shrewsbury. Gough's own cousin was a deserter from the King's army; 'his father cast him off, but my sister sent him into Wales to some of his father's relations, and gave him money...'

Myddle was just one small settlement, off the main road and away from the main seats of the action. Yet Myddle was caught up in the unrest, like almost every village and town in the land. The memories and the legacy lingered for generations.

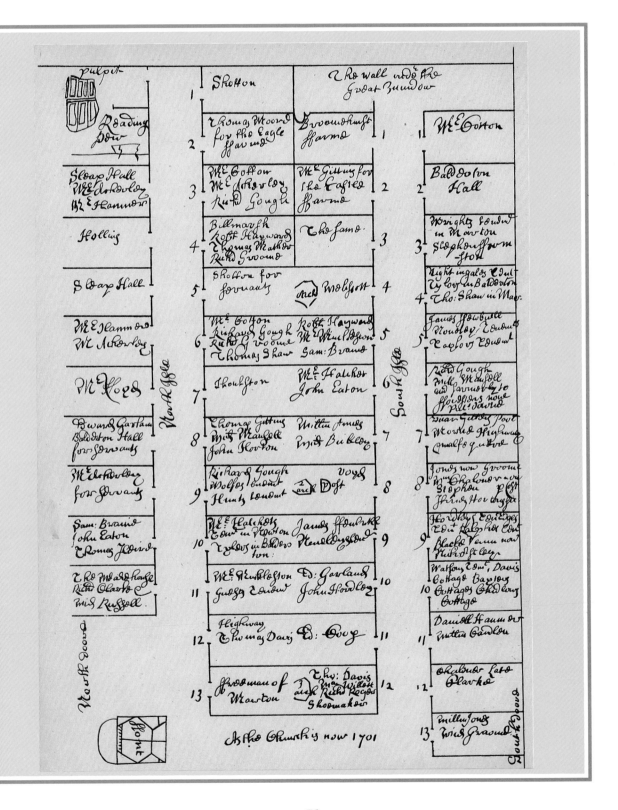

enthusiasm with which these men went off to fight would have been contingent on the esteem – or lack of it – in which the officers were held. As the war went on, officers and men learned through experience and some, like Cromwell for example, who began the war with no military expertise, became good and effective soldiers. However, when the two armies faced each other on the field of battle at Edgehill in Warwickshire in October 1642 for the first engagement of the Civil War, inexperience far outweighed professionalism.

After leaving London, Charles had set about raising an army from his base in York. From there he had travelled westwards recruiting in Derbyshire as he made his way to Shrewsbury. Shrewsbury was the gateway to Wales and it was from the areas of North Wales and Denbighshire as well as Cheshire and Lancashire that many rallied to the King's support. In the meantime, the Parliamentary army, commanded by the Earl of Essex, was also on the move with the objective of preventing the King from advancing on London. At the rendezvous in Northampton, they were joined by contingents from the Midlands and the Eastern counties. One of the problems facing Essex, and one which recurred throughout the war on both sides, was the inability to pay the soldiers their full wages. At this early stage, this lowered morale amongst the men who were also suffering from their lack of training. Morale was higher on the King's side although his army was smaller in numbers and it was reinforced by the first serious action between the two armies.

This took place at Powicke Bridge outside Worcester. The Earl of Essex had marched on the Royalist town of Worcester and Charles had despatched Prince Rupert to the aid of the town. In the action which followed, Rupert's cavalry successfully routed the opposition and established his own reputation in the process. As Clarendon wrote, 'it gave his troops great courage and rendered the name of Prince Rupert very terrible indeed.' Although this was a relatively small skirmish and similar to the many that would take place during the course of the war, it was the first encounter and therefore significant to the morale of both sides. It was imperative for Essex to prevent the King's advance on London. By mid-October, the two armies were on the move towards London but poor reconnaissance meant that neither army knew the whereabouts of the other. In fact both armies had quartered for the night in the small villages north of Banbury. By accident, the situation was reversed and the King's army was now positioned between Essex's army and London occupying the ridge of Edgehill, between Kineton and Banbury. Edgehill was the rendevous chosen by the Royalists and at daybreak on 23 October 1642 as Rupert arrived with his cavalry, the scene was set for the first major battle of the Civil War.

The King's forces consisted of about 24,000 men while the Parliamentary side numbered slightly fewer. For several hours, contingents of Royalist foot and horse arrived. During the delay, inevitable as troops came in from varying distances, the Royalist commanders quarrelled amongst themselves over how the infantry should be drawn up, whether on the Dutch or Swedish pattern. Argument about major tactics at such a juncture indicates the state of unpreparedness, chaos and lack of discipline even among the officers which existed at the outset of military hostilities. Meanwhile, Essex was still awaiting the arrival of his artillery and some of his infantry. The start of a seventeenth-century battle necessitated the participants waiting, perhaps for hours, as both

Prince Rupert

At the outbreak of Civil War, Prince Rupert was a young man whose entire existence was framed by war and battle. He was the son of the Elector Palatine Frederick and Elizabeth of Bohemia, the Winter Queen, Charles I's sister, around whom the early conflict of the Thirty Years War had crystallized. At the age of only nineteen Rupert had distinguished himself in fighting at the Siege of Breda, where many later combatants in England had a foretaste of battle; and within a couple of years he was at his uncle's side in the gathering days of war in England.

In 1642 he joined Charles' cause as General of the Horse, and distinguished himself by his fearlessness and by the devastation which his cavalry wrought, first clearly seen in the Battle of Powicke Bridge on 22 September 1642 and then at Edgehill a month later. Prince Rupert's tendency to take his horsemen thundering away in pursuit of fleeing troops, as happened at Edgehill, was ultimately to be his undoing, but for a while his military exploits were sufficiently daring and successful to command awe. At Cirencester, which he took on 2 February 1643, at the Battle of Chalgrove Field where John Hampden fell on 18 June, at Bristol which succumbed on 26 July, and at Newark which he relieved nine months later, Rupert acquired a reputation of being almost invincible. His innovations in fighting included mining against besieged towns and fortifications, which aided his success. The fear in which Parliamentary commanders held him helps explain Rupert's relatively easy march north, when many of the enemy were cruelly slain in attacks on towns and the relief of besieged houses, to relieve the city of York on 30 June 1644.

It was after that string of successes that Rupert began to fail. The Battle of Marston Moor on 2 July was the turning point, when Rupert and the forces of the King were defeated; Cromwell reported that the Royalists had broken rank and fled, and 'God made them as stubble to our swords.' The Prince then seemed to lose heart – he was reluctant to fight at Naseby, he urged the King to sue for peace, and he was cashiered after Bristol was retaken by Parliament in September 1645. Contributing to his decline, it was widely believed, was the loss at Marston Moor (*below*) of his pet white poodle, Boy, of which he was inordinately fond. Some believed that Boy had super-canine powers, others that his loss threw the Prince into melancholy. Charles dismissed his nephew, who finally left England after the fall of Oxford in July 1646. His later career was at sea, leading the naval fight against Cromwell until final defeat in 1650, running piracy campaigns against English shipping during his exile with Charles II in the 1650s, during which he was of greater nuisance value than strategic, and returning as an admiral at the Restoration.

armies assembled and positioned their troops often within close range of each other. In effect, a war of nerves existed prior to the actual fighting with each side watching the preparations of the other and waiting for the orders to begin the fighting – and the killing.

At Edgehill, the battle proper began with an exchange of artillery fire, which was followed by a charge by Rupert's cavalry. They started on the trot, increased their speed to a canter and finally at the gallop discharged their pistols into enemy lines; it was no wonder that the Parliamentarian cavalry fled in fright. It was notoriously difficult to control horses on the battlefield and, although Rupert's action was effective as a shock tactic, it was a far from successful manoeuvre. Moving the cavalry at the gallop made control of them even more difficult than usual. Prince Rupert's cavalry, having dispersed some of the enemy, continued in pursuit, leaving the field of battle altogether. They swept on to the village of Kineton where they plundered colours and equipment from the Parliamentary camp but by then both men and horses were too exhausted to fight effectively again. The fighting continued between regiments of foot,

Charles I with his secretary Edmund Walker, and a military engagement in the background.

pikemen and musketeers. Following an exchange of fire, the pikemen standing shoulder to shoulder in tight formation brought their pikes up into the 'charge' position and moved forward to 'push of pike'. Resembling a huge rugby scrum, this was the moment in battle when men were locked in close physical contact with their opponents; with very limited vision they were also in danger from the unwieldy pikes of their own side, from the pike butt of the soldier in front and the pike point of the soldier behind. A charge towards the Royalist gun positions resulted in the capture of the King's standard and the death of Sir Edmund Verney who bore the Royal standard. It was eventually recaptured by Captain John Smith was knighted for his efforts. Night was now approaching and although some of the Royalist cavalry had returned to the battlefield, they and their horses were too exhausted to engage in further combat. The night was spent on or near the battlefield, both sides exhausted, cold and hungry and when they faced each other the following morning, neither wanted to resume the conflict. Essex retreated to Warwick and the King's forces headed for Banbury and then Oxford, where Charles felt support for him was unequivocally loyal.

Earl of Essex

In Robert Devereux, 3rd Earl of Essex, Parliament had a glittering Commander-in-Chief for its army whose cult of personality disguised his incompetence. After twoyears in which the best result he had achieved in battle was an honourable draw,Oliver Cromwell's pressure for more vigorous prosecution of the war at the end of 1644 and the Self-Denying Ordinance in the wake of the second Battleof Newbury led to Essex's removal from command.

Scouting for news

News travelled fast in the aftermath of battle. The problem was usually to make sure that it was the right news. Poor communications as well as inadequate maps and unfamiliar terrain often meant that military operations were difficult indeed, and the need for proper intelligence was vital both on and off the battle field. Each army had a scout-master-general, whose scouts and spies were sent out gathering whatever information they could glean. After Edgehill, for example, Buckinghamshire Paliamentarians sent out 'scouts to enquire of the King's march and of the general', and heard it reported first that the King's army had routed the Parliament's. 'Other scouts brought intelligence quite contrary, and much more welcome, that Essex had routed the King's army and gained a full victory.' So the gentlemen 'sent for news from London...to know the certain, and were answered that the two armies had fought at Edgehill, many thousands were slain, and that the Parliament's forces had a great deliverance, and a little victory, which was a true description of it.'

As the war progressed and scouts were better trained, fanning out to pick up news and watching for signs and events, so intelligence-gathering became easier; but information was still often confused. In June 1643, for example, when Sir Ralph Hopton was marching on Axminster, reports of his whereabouts put him variously as having done battle in Exeter, coming towards Oxford, or else as still being in Cornwall.

Such confusion obviously gave ample opportunity for deliberately falsified reports to circulate. In January 1644, for example, news reached Nottingham that the Royalist forces were planning an attack on the Lincolnshire town of Sleaford. 'The Governor, not trusting that pretence,' his wife recorded, 'commanded all the soldiers and townsmen to sit up that night and expect them; and the next morning... [confirmation came] that the design was against Nottingham. The horse scouts came in with the news of their approach, the enemy's scouts and they having fired upon each other.'

Edgehill was a drawn battle with roughly equal losses on both sides, with about 1,500 soldiers killed. Tactically it left the King with a clear route back to his capital as Essex had failed in the attempt to turn him back. More significantly, because it was an indecisive outcome the battle had not furthered any kind of settlement between King and Parliament. Perhaps a military solution in any case could never be more than an adjunct to some sort of compromise peace. This was to be a continuing dilemma for the Parliamentarians as the Earl of Manchester expressed it, 'If we fight a hundred times and beat him ninety-nine times, he will be King still. But if he beat us but once, or the last time, we shall be hanged, we shall lose our estates and our posterities will be undone.' The uncertain outcome caused gloom among the Parliamentarians in London and pushed the moderates into trying again to open negotiations with Charles. Others, more cynical about their King, looked for aid from the Scots and welcomed the return of Essex to London.

Charles refused the peace settlement offered him and ordered Rupert to attack Brentford, on the outskirts of London which was occupied by two regiments of Essex's army. The sack of Brentford was ruthless and put fear into the hearts of many Londoners, confirming their worst suspicions of Rupert and the Royalist army. In response, the London Trained Bands turned out in force to join other regiments from Essex's army and by the morning of 13 November 24,000 men were assembled at Turnham Green where they successfully blocked the Royalists. Heavily outnumbered, the King withdrew his troops and no battle took place. From then on, the King made Oxford his base, secure in the support of the University and colleges which had consistently backed his religious policies under Archbishop Laud. As winter approached both armies retreated to winter quarters with many officers and men returning to their homes.

The purpose of this chapter is not to provide a detailed military history of the battles and engagements of the Civil War; this has been done excellently elsewhere. It is rather to invoke an impressionistic account of the actual experience of war and the nature of seventeenth-century combat. It is easy perhaps to look back on the Civil War of the seventeenth century with a view refracted by the Victorians. Victorian, and indeed contemporary, paintings put a romantic gloss on military figures and battles with images of dashing cavaliers wearing plumed hats and colourful costumes overlaying the realities of men engaged shoulder to shoulder in combat, 'a dark, stamping, stinking mass' as one military historian has described it. The analogy with a rugby or football match is a more apt description of a seventeenth-century battlefield than any comparison with a modern battle. For a battle to take place there had to be a measure of consent between the opposing factions; like crowds arriving at a stadium, it would take time for both armies to reach the central rendezvous. This was undertaken without the aid of adequate maps, watches or the paraphenalia of communication systems taken for granted and depended on by a modern army. The armies forming up could take hours; a look at a contemporary plan of any of the major Civil War battles indicates the detailed patterns of the initial formations. In the centre were the infantry brigades with the pikemen in the middle of each brigade flanked by the musketeers. On the wings were the cavalry with the heavy artillery, cannon, at the rear. What then ensued resembled a vast rugby scrum but one fought with cumbersome and dangerous weapons.

The confusion of the battlefield at Edgehill (opposite), and the sleekness of the commemorative medal (above).

THE HON.ᴮᴸᴱ COLONEL
NATHANIEL FINES.
MIREVELT. PINX.

*Nathaniel Fiennes,
son of Lord Saye
and Sele, who was
an active soldier in
the early years of
the conflict.*

Stormy weather

The military campaigns were dogged by the bad weather that brought misery to England in the mid- and late-1640s. The fighting was made all the more difficult as men and weapons, and the heavy siege trains, became bogged down in mud and rain; the enormous problems of producing enough food to sustain both ordinary people and the soldiers were intensified by the pillaging and devastation that accompanied war. One Essex clergyman's diary recorded the debilitating effects of the appalling weather, that continued throughout the decade, on the local economy.

'September 15 1646. A marvellous wet season, winter coming on very early. A great hop year; wheat this year was exceedingly smitten and dwindled and lank, especially on strong grounds. All manners of meats excessive dear...

'November 1 1646. This week the wetness of the season continued with little or no intermission and so it hath continued for above two months...

'May 23 1647. This spring was forward. Yet all things considered excessive dear...

'September 26 1647...Things are at that rate as never was in our days: wheat 8 shillings, malt 4 shillings, beef 3 pence, butter 6 pence, cheese 4 pence, candle 7 pence, currants 9 pence, sugar 18 pence, and every other thing whatsoever dear. The soldiers also returning to quarter again with us...

'May 9 1648. Among all the several judgements on this nation, God this spring, in the latter end of April, when rye was earing and eared, sent such terrible frosts that the ear was frozen and so died...

'June 28 1648. The Lord goeth against us in the season, which was wonderful wet, floods every week, hay rotted abroad.'

The pikemen carried pikes topped with steel, measuring between twelve and eighteen feet long, while the musketeers were equipped with matchlock, a slow-firing and inaccurate weapon. Both groups carried swords, useful for cutting through hedges and cutting firewood – although this usually damaged them as battle weapons. One of the prevailing myths about the Civil War is that the Roundheads were so called because of the pot helmets they wore: in fact these were worn by both sides. Identification on the battlefield was a problem since, again unlike popular stereotypes, both sides looked very similar and were only distinguishable by their scarves or sashes, or field signs, such as feathers or oak leaves which were often worn in hats, or by the use of field words, similar to passwords. The fact that both armies looked and dressed similarly and of course spoke the same language made orientation on the battlefield difficult, particularly at the height of battle when the air was thick with smoke and powder and the general mêlée limited visibility. Discipline was a major factor in maintaining control on the battlefield, especially in the initial phase of the war with raw, untrained recruits on both sides. As happened at Edgehill, it proved difficult to re-order and re-group troops after a successful attack; it was not only the cavalry who were difficult to control. No army, however professional and well-trained, can guarantee against fear and panic among its troops at the moment of battle and we can only imagine how a volunteer, a farm worker from a small village for example, inexperienced and untrained, might feel in the midst of battle. In seventeenth-century battle, troops were most vulnerable when the lines of formation broke and it was then that men were most likely to be killed or wounded.

Desertion rates were fairly high on both sides. A number of factors contributed to this; some soldiers simply fled the site of battle and went home. In a predominantly agricultural country as England was at this time, desertion was partly seasonal with soldiers returning home at harvest time to work in the fields. The winter months were the most critical in maintaining army discipline; it was virtually impossible to engage in any military action during the winter when roads, which were more like tracks, became impassable for troops on the march who covered ground slowly even in fine weather conditions. Artillery, supplies and all the impedimenta required by an army on the move were transported by carts which again were rendered useless on roads rutted by frost or awash with rain. Unlike a modern army today, there were no permanent quarters for the troops and in winter soldiers often found themselves in cold, cramped and disease-ridden quarters. The temptation to return home in such circumstances was clearly irresistible. The King's army in Oxford was fortunate in having ready-made quarters in the colleges but controlling soldiers and keeping the army together were not easy tasks.

A pikeman at the ready.

The Royalist armies, like the Parliamentarians, were bedevilled with the problem of soldiers' pay. Provisions, uniforms and equipment were often in short supply but the lack of pay was an obvious source of disaffection, resentment and finally desertion. It also made for indiscipline; after a battle or siege soldiers who had received no pay seized the opportunity to plunder and loot, thus compensating themselves for their lack of renumeration. Rates of pay were established at the beginning of the war but it appears unlikely that either side was able to honour its commitments. For example, in 1644 the cavalry of the

Eastern Association was paid for only 126 days out of 366 and the infantry for 35 weeks out of 52. When conscription became necessary for both sides, arrears of pay became cause for mutiny among the troops.

Both the King and Parliament resorted to a variety of fiscal measures to pay for their war efforts. Voluntary contributions were replaced by taxation and sequestration of estates. Pym introduced compulsory assessments in all parliamentary territory as well as introducing the Excise Ordinance, a purchase tax on commodities such as tea and tobacco. During the course of the war, some villages and communities found themselves paying tax to both sides as control of territory changed hands and they were caught in the middle. For the problem of maintaining armies was not purely a military one; its impact touched the civilian population, even those who saw little actual fighting. The great set piece battles of the Civil War were by no means the sum total of the military actions of the war and their significance can be over-estimated. They were the punctuation marks, so to speak, in the war which was fought more in small-scale battles, skirmishes and sieges of individual properties or whole towns. The struggle for control of territory extended over most of the country changing much of the landscape dramatically as areas were fought over, garrisons sprang up and the fabric and population of towns and villages suffered the onslaught of war.

Recent historical evidence has indicated that the civilian population was profoundly affected as a result of the war. The needs of soldiers – for pay, for quarter, for supplies – and their consequent privations were mirrored by those of the civilian population, what was known in the two World Wars as the home front. Even where armies did not leave a trail of destruction and physical chaos behind them, they often left severe economic disruption in their wake. Crops were trampled and horses were requisitioned. In an era in which horses were not only the basic means of transport but also the source of most power used in agriculture, their loss was a severe blow. In the absence of permanent quarters for the troops, local villagers were faced with demands for 'free quarter' whereby soldiers were lodged and fed by the local population. There were set rates for board and lodging and for fodder for horses: eight old pence a day for troopers, seven pence for dragoons and six pence for foot-soldiers. When money was available, officers or NCOs would pay on the spot. When there was no money they would issue 'vouchers' which supposedly could be redeemed later, although in practice this often proved difficult. The sums of money owing could soon build up. By 1647 the village of Wellow, near Bath, was owed the sum of £1,202. 10s. 8d., an absolute fortune at the time. The population of towns or garrisons under siege suffered miserably and, as in the case of Bristol, might be the victims of both armies undergoing the effects of bombardment, lack of food and probably plundering and looting as well. By far the worst experience for civilians was the ending of a siege by storm rather than surrender, for then military discipline would break down, leaving the inhabitants vulnerable to any excesses of the marauding troops.

Armies on the move and living in insanitary conditions inevitably carry diseases; army fever, a form of typhus, was responsible for many more deaths than those inflicted in the fighting. Moreover, plague often followed in the wake of army-carried disease and further decimated the local population. Local studies into mortality rates in certain counties have suggested that the diseases carried

Under siege

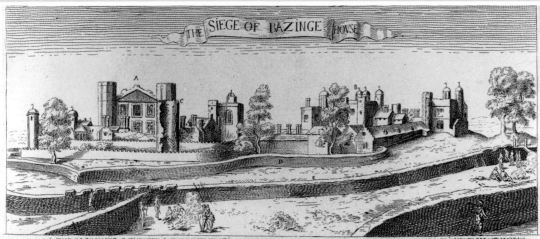

A. THE OLDE HOVSE . B. THE NEW. C. THE TOWER THAT IS HALFE BATTERED DOVNE. D. THE KINGES BREAST WORKS. E. THE PARLIAMENTS BREAST WORKS.

The siege works at Basing House, Hampshire.

Away from the set-pieces of battle, much of the fighting of the Civil War was conducted in small skirmishes and in lengthily drawn-out sieges. The army of one side surrounded a town, like Plymouth, or a fortified household, keeping the opposition penned up inside with the hope of starving them into submission. Basing House in Hampshire, which commanded the main route west to Salisbury, was one of the war's most celebrated sieges, not least because some of the most important men in the Stuart cause were inside.

The Roman Catholic Marquess of Winchester had had Basing House embellished in the 1630s, in the best court, classical style, probably by Inigo Jones. Almost certainly Jones, who fled London, spent the two long years of siege in Basing House, which had become a centre of loyalty to Queen Henrietta Maria. Jones had 'gotten thither for help to the house', by designing fortifications which helped keep the opposing Parliamentary forces at bay. The siege began in November 1643. William Waller's first attack on Basing House had been frustrated by heavy rain, and his second by his disconsolate troops deciding to take themselves back to London, hungry and unpaid. So a Hampshire force laid siege. When, almost a year later, Charles wanted to relieve Basing he found his forces were hopelessly outnumbered as the armies of the Earls of Essex and Manchester, and

the City Regiments, rallied to assist the siege, pitching 19,000 men against his 9,000.

It took Oliver Cromwell and the discipline of his army to resolve the issue and defeat the besieged household. He arrived on 8 October 1645, with great siege guns. The Parliamentary soldiers looted the lead coffins from Basing church to make their bullets, scattering the bones (although stopping long enough to chalk the names of the dead on the wall). Cromwell offered terms of surrender to Winchester, who proudly refused them: Basing was 'Loyalty House' and he would stand firm. Bombardment began. On 13 October the heavy guns breached the walls in two places, and at six the next morning Cromwell's troops swarmed in, strengthened by their hatred of Catholics. Six priests were among the 100 slain, and another 300 prisoners were taken.

Among them was Inigo Jones, symbol of the old Court regime. He was humiliated by the soldiers, stripped, and 'carried away in a blanket' to London. As he departed, Basing House went up in flames. Colonel Hammond treated the vanquished Lord Winchester with great civility, Winchester for his part was unbowed. 'I hope that the King will have his day again.' Cromwell had certainty rather than hope. 'I thank God I can give you a good account of Basing', he wrote to the Commons, as he set off deeper into the West Country.

by the army took an enormous toll on local communities; in 1645, for example, mortality rates increased fivefold in Oxford compared with the years prior to the war. One historian has suggested, on the basis of detailed statistical evidence, that the Civil War claimed as many lives as the First World War, in terms relative to the size of the population. In addition to the economic dislocation and the loss of livelihoods resulting from the military action, the Civil War was indeed devastating.

The tragedy of civil war in terms of the cost to human life was played out all over the country. The battle for control of territory in different areas of the country and in different towns varied with the fortunes of war. During the early part of 1643, the Royalists maintained the initiative, although Parliament had consolidated its hold on most of the south-east, East Anglia and part of the Midlands. Parliament's power base remained in London while the King was established in Oxford but both sides also had separate commanders-in-chiefs of regional armies as well as local forces whose commanders had a significant political as well as military role in the localities.

The summer of 1643 brought gloom to the Parliamentarians. Their unity was fragile, based on an uneasy coalition between the 'win-the-war' faction and the 'peace' faction who were pushing for negotiations with the King; it fell to Pym to ensure Parliament's survival. In the campaigns in the west country, Parliament suffered a severe defeat which was particularly surprising since much of the west of England had a strong Puritan tradition and was therefore strongly Parliamentarian. The campaign was all the more poignant because it was led by two friends who had chosen to support opposing sides. Sir William Waller was one of Parliament's most popular and respected commanders; his friend and now rival was Sir Ralph Hopton. Serving under Hopton were the formidable Cornish Trained Bands numbering 3,000 men. After a series of cat-and-mouse manoeuvres, they encountered each other at Lansdown Hill near Bath. There then followed a disastrous defeat for Waller at Roundway Down where his forces were devastatingly crushed by the Royalists.

The strategic balance of the war was significantly altered by the Scots' entry into the war in support of Parliament. In January 1644 an army of 20,000 crossed the Tweed into England. The Scottish Covenanters had wanted to take up arms earlier in pursuit of their religious goals, the demand for the abolition of episcopacy, but their single-minded pursuit of Presbyterianism made some of even the most Puritan of Parliamentarians uneasy or hostile to the Scottish intervention. In 1643 the Scots negotiated the Solemn League and Covenant with the English Parliamentarians; in return for military help they demanded religious conformity based on Scottish Presbyterianism. While the Scots might see Presbyterianism as the most godly form of church government, many Parliamentarians knew it to be a completely non-negotiable issue with Charles. In the long term, in spite of the military support they had provided, the Scots were to feel betrayed by their English allies since the English failed to honour their side of the treaty and instead treated their former allies with hostility.

The steady advance of the Scots southwards towards York caused consternation to Charles. He summoned Rupert to the aid of the Earl of Newcastle in defending York, already under siege from the allied forces of the English Parliamentarians and the Scots as well as the army of the Eastern

Nehemiah Wharton rides out

Many atrocities were committed by the soldiers on both sides, and the tales magnified for propaganda.

Writing to his former master, George Willingham, merchant, at the Golden Anchor, St Swithin's Lane, London, in the latter months of 1642, Nehemiah Wharton described the life in Parliament's army: a mixture of battles, skirmishes, pillaging, sermons, murders, and iconoclasm. Leaving London, they began in Acton.

'...several of our soldiers sallied out to the house of one Penruddock, a Papist, and being basely affronted by him and his dog, entered his house and pillaged him to the purpose. This day also the soldiers got into the church, defaced the ancient and sacred glazed pictures, and burned the holy rails. Wednesday Mr Love gave us a famous sermon...

'...we came to Wendover, where we refreshed ourselves, burnt the rails; and accidentally one of Capt. Francis' men, forgetting he was charged with a bullet, shot a maid through the head...

'Monday morning we marched into Warwickshire with about 3,000 foot and 400 horse until we came to Southam. On the way we took two cavalier spies. This is a very malignant town, both minister and people. We pillaged the minister...our soldiers cried out to have a breakfast of cavaliers. We strongly barricaded the town, and at every passage placed our ordnance, and watched it all night, our soldiers contented to lie upon hard stones. In the morning...we went to meet our enemies with a few troops of horse

and six field-pieces, and, being on fire to be at them, we marched through the corn and got the hill of them...Their troops wheeling about, took up their dead bodies and fled; but the horses they left behind them, some of them having their guts beaten out on both sides. The number of men slain, as themselves report, was 50...

'This day a whore which had followed our camp from London was taken by the soldiers, and first led about [Coventry], then set in the pillory, after the cage, then ducked in a river, and at the last banished...This morning we are marching off to pursue the rebels...

'Our wounded men they [Prince Rupert's Cavaliers] brought into [Worcester], and stripped and stabbed and slashed their dead bodies in a most barbarous manner, and imbrued their hands in the blood. They also at their return met a young gentleman, a young Parliament man...and stabbed him on horseback with many wounds, and trampled on him, and also most maliciously shot his horse...

'I am persuaded the Lord has given them this small victory, that they may in the day of battle come on more presumptuously to their own destruction; in which battle, though I and many thousands more may be cut off, yet I am confident the Lord of Hosts will in the end triumph gloriously over these horses and their accursed riders.'

Association commanded by the Earl of Manchester with Cromwell at the head of the cavalry. Rupert, following the instructions of the King, left his base in Shrewsbury but instead of advancing directly on York he chose to march via Lancashire to pick up reinforcements. En route, he stormed and plundered Stockton, Bolton and Liverpool. His arrival in the vicinity of York took the Parliamentary armies by surprise, so much so that they called a halt to the siege of the city, marched to Long Marston and prepared to face Rupert and the Royalists in battle. It is generally agreed that the relief of York by Rupert was a masterful operation but the battle of Marston Moor which followed is more contentious. Rupert provoked a battle without the wholehearted support of the other Royalist commanders and with the odds heavily against the Royalists who were outnumbered by 28,000 to 18,000 men. The battle of Marston Moor, which took place on 2 July 1644, was the bloodiest and hardest fought of any in the Civil War. Although the battle lasted only two hours, the numbers of casualties were large; well over 4,000 Royalists were killed and the Earl of Newcastle's regiment, the Whitecoats, was decimated. It was a scene of brutal carnage. In the face of such humiliating defeat, Newcastle went into exile

Friends in a war without an enemy

Sir Ralph Hopton (1596-1651), who found himself in conflict with his friend...

'The experience I have had of your worth, and the happiness I have enjoyed in your friendship are wounding considerations when I look upon this present distance between us. Certainly my affections to you are so unchangeable, that hostility itself cannot violate my friendship in your person, but I must be true to the cause wherein I serve...That great God which is the searcher of my heart knows with what a sad sense I go upon this service, and with what a perfect hatred I detest this war without an enemy, but I look upon it as *opus Domini*, which is enough to silence all passion in me. The God of peace in his good time send us peace and in the meantime fit us to receive it. We are both upon the stage and must act those parts that are assigned to us in this tragedy. Let us do it in a way of honour, and without personal animosities, whatever the issue be, I shall never willingly relinquish the dear title of

Your most affectionate friend and faithful servant,
William Waller'

Sir Ralph Hopton who received this letter from his old friend dated 16 June 1643 was a former 'non-violent Parliamentarian', who had voted for Strafford's attainder and had presented the Grand Remonstrance, but gradually moved to the King's side, and raised the Royal Standard in his home county of Somerset. It was in the south-west that he distinguished himself, and met William Waller in battle on a number of occasions. In the early 1620s

abroad and did not return to England until after the Restoration. Although the battle ended with the defeat of the King and the subsequent loss of territory in the north, it did not bring the war to an end. Two of the commanders, Leven and Fairfax, in the confusion of battle and thinking the day was lost, fled the battlefield taking with them contingents of their armies.

The problems of the Parliamentary armies were not confined to the military sphere. The victory over the King's forces at Marston Moor sharpened the political divisions within the Parliamentary side as well as increasing religious animosities. Pym, who had steered a precipitous middle course between the peace and war factions in Parliament, had died in 1643. In the same year, Charles arranged a 'Cessation', a ceasefire with the Irish rebels and in a similar way to Parliament's alliance with the Scots, he mobilized Irish troops for service in his campaign in England. Once again, suspicions were raised about Charles' leanings towards Catholicism and the hated spectre of popery raised its head. Only in this context can the treatment of Irish troops be understood, for when they were captured as prisoners of war they suffered cruelty not meted out to their English counterparts.

they had both been among the gentlemen volunteers who had gone to fight on the Continent in the cause of the Queen of Bohemia, where they became firm friends. Their friendship lasted in spite of the enmity of war, and their surviving correspondence is one of the most affecting memorials to the conflict.

Waller had moved gradually to a firmer Presbyterianism in 1642, which distressed Hopton, and led Waller to follow the Parliamentary cause. He became one of the great tacticians, known as the 'night owl' for his nocturnal manoeuvres. Hopton acknowledged Waller's skill after the Royalist defeat at Alton in December 1643. He wrote to Waller, whom he had previously beaten at Lansdown above Bath, 'God give a sudden stop to this issue of English blood', but the slaughter continued, with Waller's forces defeating Hopton's again at Alresford opening the way to take Winchester and Hampshire.

They met finally in the opposing forces at the second Battle of Newbury on 27 October 1644, after which Hopton was 'so perfectly tired with the drudgery of it'. Both men's stars were in eclipse thereafter: Hopton, failing to breach Waller's defence of Sussex and Surrey, went into exile in the Channel Isles, from where he led occasional forays, before retiring to Utrecht where he died in 1652; and Waller went to Holland, from which he returned only to be imprisoned and to live in seclusion after the Restoration. Both friends were drained by fighting their war without an enemy.

Sʳ Wᵐ Waller.

...the 'night owl', Sir William Waller (1597-1668).

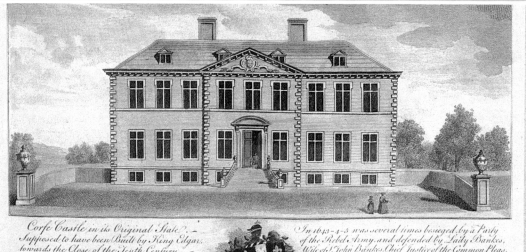

Women of Fortitude

Corfe Castle in its Original State.
Supposed to have been Built by King Edgar,
towards the Close of the Tenth Century.
Here Edward the Martyr, Son & Successor of Edgar,
was murdered by Elfrida his Mother in Law.
Was sometimes the Residence of the West Saxon Kings.
And the Place of Imprisonment of Edward 2.

In 1643-4-5 was several times besieged, by a Party
of the Rebel Army, and defended by Laidy Bankes,
Wife of S.r John Bankes, Chief Justice of the Common Pleas.
Feb.y 27 1645 was taken by Treachery, & Demolished.

Kingston hall, built by S.r Ralph Bankes in 1663.
The Seat of Henry Bankes Esq.r his Grandson,
to whom also belongs Corfe Castle.

Kingston Lacy, Dorset, the house the Bankes family built to replace the destroyed castle at Corfe.

There is a rollcall of defiant women in the Civil War, holding out for months and sometimes years on end in defending their family property while their husbands and sons were engaged elsewhere. At Corfe Castle in Dorset Lady Bankes withstood the Parliamentary forces for two long sieges while her husband Sir John was with the King in Oxford. The great fortification finally succumbed in 1646, after extensive undermining operations outside the castle, and treachery inside; and as she left the castle, Lady Bankes was presented with the keys, which still hang in the new house the Bankes built for themselves in 1663, Kingston Lacy. In the north of Dorset in September 1642 Lady Digby, wife of the reckless Earl of Bristol, found that her Royalist household was under siege by her brother, the Earl of Bedford. She walked into the Parliamentary lines to confront him: 'If you persist in your plans, you will find my body in the ruins.' The fortified Old Castle was taken and destroyed in 1645, but Lady Digby in the New Castle was assured of her safety.

Meanwhile, just over the border in Wiltshire, Lady Arundell defended Wardour Castle until it too was taken and her children imprisoned; in the siege of Sheffield Castle in Yorkshire, Lady Savile only gave up after fierce fighting in which she helped hurl missiles on the enemy, when her troops found her on the point of going into labour.

Perhaps most poignant of all was Lady Brilliana Harley at Brampton Bryan Castle in Herefordshire. While her husband Sir Robert, one of the leading lights in Parliament's cause, was away in London, Lady Brilliana held out against Royalist forces for six weeks from 25 July 1643. Her tender, loving letters to her children terminate with those she wrote from the besieged house. 'The Lord direct me what to do' she wrote, 'and, dear Ned, pray for me that the Lord in mercy may preserve me from my cruel and blood-thirsty enemies.' Lady Brilliana and the castle survived this siege, and the troops withdrew to Gloucester; but soon after she died, of sheer exhaustion, when the castle was threatened again. Brampton Bryan finally fell to the Royalists in April 1644; three of the Harleys' children, 67 men, and a year's provisions were taken, and the stronghold was destroyed.

*'Siege pieces',
which were struck
in beleaguered
strongholds: Carlisle,
Beeston, Colchester,
and Pontefract.*

The military victory over the King at Marston Moor opened up the possibility of more than just military success for it raised the dilemma of what a total victory over Charles would mean. Religious and political differences between the commanders in the Parliamentary armies made co-operation among them difficult and contributed to a number of defeats in the south and south-west in the autumn of 1644. Tensions increased and profound dissatisfaction arose over the Parliamentary military administration and its leaders, who it would seem were unwilling finally to defeat the King on the battlefield. In an attempt to end the military stalemate and potential political disaster, two measures were put to Parliament by Cromwell. The victories of his cavalry, the Ironsides, had strengthened Cromwell's position among the Parliamentary leadership, although Manchester and Essex were at odds with him. Conflicts had arisen between the two groups in Parliament with one calling for a settlement of church government along Presbyterian lines, for negotiation with the King and an end to war. On the other side were Cromwell and his supporters bent on religious reform and 'liberty of conscience' and for whom negotiation with the King at this stage was nothing less than betrayal of what they had been fighting for. In pursuit of the godly cause, Cromwell had asserted the right to leadership of the 'plain russet-coated captain that knows what he fights for and loves what he knows'. For the more conservative commanders, such sentiments were decidedly unwelcome. Curtailing the power of the monarch and his advisers was one thing, opening the floodgates to all manner of religious radicalism, social anarchy and the disruption of the social order quite another. The first of Cromwell's measures confirmed their fears; the Self-Denying Ordinance would require members of both Houses of Parliament to resign their military commands and their civil offices. The second called for the remodelling of the Parliamentary armies into a single army under a unified command. In early 1645, after much debate and disagreement, the measures were passed by both houses. Under the Self-Denying Ordinance most commanders gave up or lost their posts. Cromwell, himself an MP, managed to be exempt.

The wounded

Army regiments had surgeons attached who were supposed to treat wounded men, and captured enemies, who would respond to treatment. They often had quite horrific injuries, and although many of the wounded might be taken to makeshift town hospitals in the aftermath of battle, others were left on the battlefield along with the dead for the local populace to clear up and take care of. After Edgehill, for example, Hester Whyte petitioned Parliament that she wanted financial help for looking after seriously wounded men for three months. She claimed that 'She often sat up night and day with them, and in respect of her tenderness to the Parliament's friends, laid out her own money in supply of their wants.'

Where the surgeons did care for injured men, their charges were a serious drain on the purse of the army of King or Parliament. George Blagrave rendered an account to the Parliamentary army in September 1645. It cost £1 10s. [£1.50] to render assistance to John Bullock 'who had a very sore cut on the fore part of his head, which caused a piece of his skull, the breadth of a half crown piece, to be taken forth, also a very sore cut over his head.' Hugh Band was cheaper, although he had suffered with 'a thrust in the arm with a tuck and shot in the back', and Luke Severn, quarter-master, had received 'a thrust and cut in the arm, a very dangerous wound' that cost £1 to attend to. Blagrave had also cared for ten captured Cavaliers 'taken at the fight at Aske, whereof one was shot into the arm in the elbow joint and the bullet taken forth in the wrist near the hand. The rest were sore cut in their heads and thrust in the back' – probably pike wounds.

The surgeon's chest (above right) was to be taken on to the battlefield, for treating the many hideous wounds (right) the soldiers sustained.

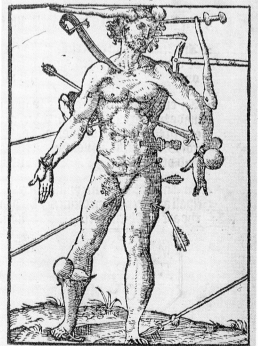

*Thomas Fairfax,
line engraving by
William Faithorne
after a painting by
Robert Walker.*

The New Model Army, formed from the existing armies of Waller, Essex and Manchester, was commanded by Sir Thomas Fairfax. Initially it suffered the same problems which beset all armies: shortage of money to pay the soldiers, disease and desertion. It also had to rely on conscription, especially for foot soldiers. In other respects, the New Model Army marked a break with the past. While the majority of its officers were gentlemen, they were appointed for their proficiency rather than their social status. Freed from local interests and a regional base, the New Model Army was much more mobile and flexible, with a greater social and geographical mix among its officers and men. Precisely because of its social composition, the Royalists were contemptuous of their opponents' army and underestimated its efficiency. Inevitably, it took some time for this new army to emerge as an effective fighting force and it was not until 1647 that it took on its political role and became a key factor in the nation's affairs. The experiences of the soldiers, mobile and free from local ties and traditional allegiances, contributed to the army becoming a hotbed of radical ideas and debates. Some of its officers and men would eventually demand sweeping social, religious and constitutional reforms which proved too radical for Cromwell to accept.

Weapons

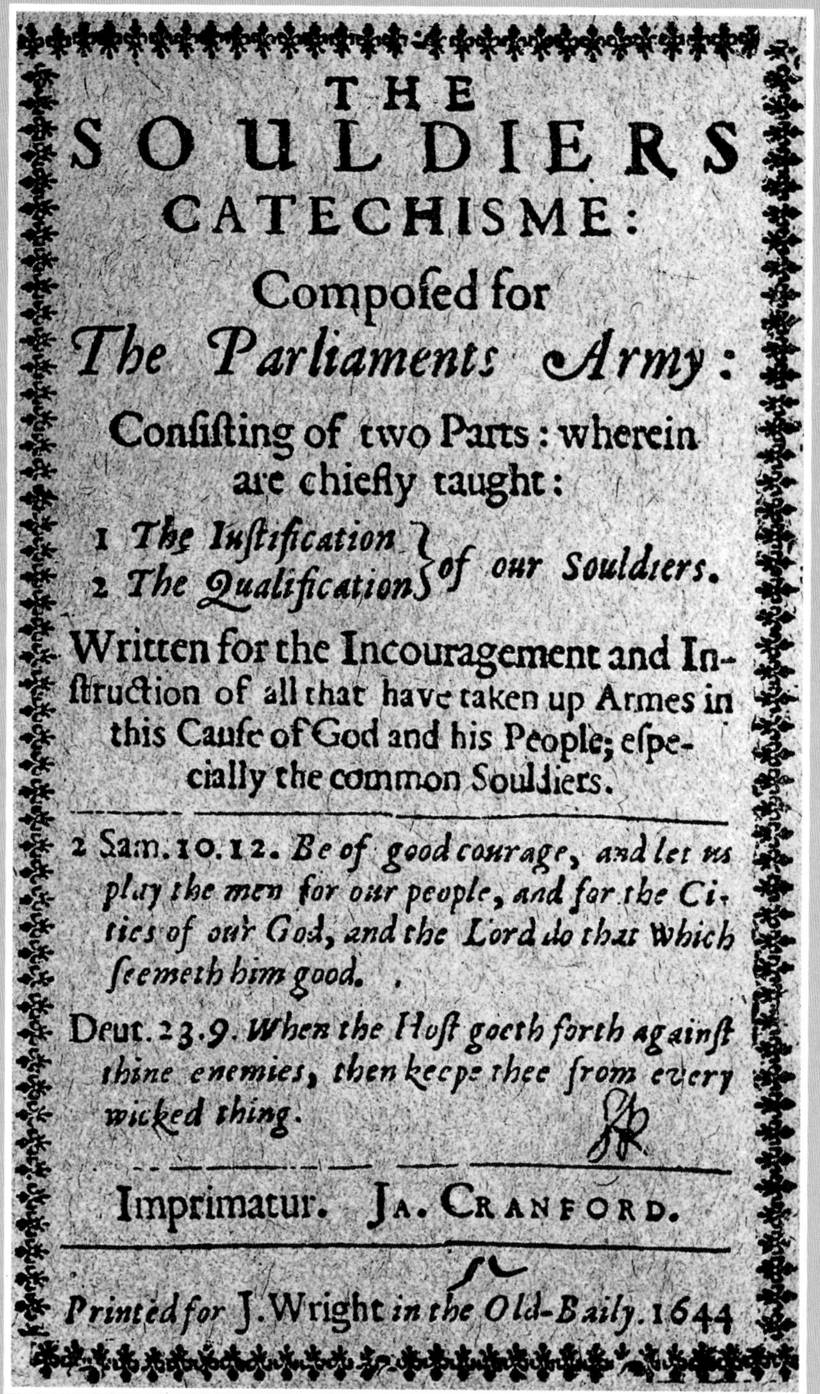

THE SOULDIERS CATECHISME:

Compoſed for

The Parliaments Army:

Conſiſting of two Parts : wherein
are chiefly taught :

1 *The Iuſtification*
2 *The Qualification* } *of our Souldiers.*

Written for the Incouragement and In-
ſtruction of all that have taken up Armes in
this Cauſe of God and his People; eſpe-
cially the common Souldiers.

2 Sam. 10. 12. *Be of good courage, and let us
play the men for our people, and for the Cities of our God, and the Lord do that which
ſeemeth him good.*

Deut. 23. 9. *When the Hoſt goeth forth againſt
thine enemies, then keepe thee from every
wicked thing.*

Imprimatur. JA. CRANFORD.

Printed for J. Wright in the Old-Baily. 1644

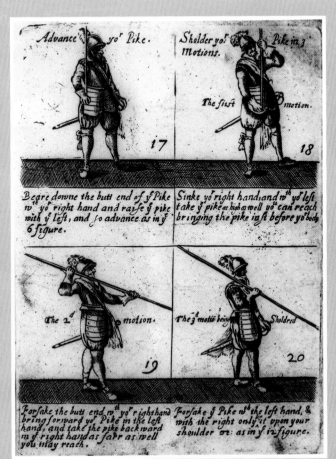

Advance yor Pike.

Sholder yor Pike in 3 Motions.

The first motion.

17

18

Beare downe the butt end of y^e Pike w.th yor right hand and raise y^e pike with y^e left, and so advance as in y^e 6 figure.

Sinke yor right hand, and w.th yor left take ye pike as high a well yo.^u can reach bringing the pike iust before yor body

The 2.^d motion.

The 3.^d motio being Sholdred

19

20

Forsake the butt end w.th yor right hand bring forward yor Pike in the left hand, and take the pike backward in ye right hand as fairr as well you may reach.

Forsake ye Pike w.th the left hand, & with the right only it vpon your shoulder oz: as in ye 12 figure.

The soldier was armed with prayer (opposite) and weaponry (right). The pike was capable of seriously wounding and killing.

The title piece to Nathaniel Burt's Military Instructions of 1644 (below).

Militarie Instructions, or the Souldier tried, for the Vse, of the Dragon, Being A part of Cavalrie, for fierings, on Horback, as the Harquebusier, & on foote, as Infantry, very necessary for such as desier to be studious, in the waye of the Art Militarie, neuer before published, by any, and now set forth by Captaine Nathaniell Burt

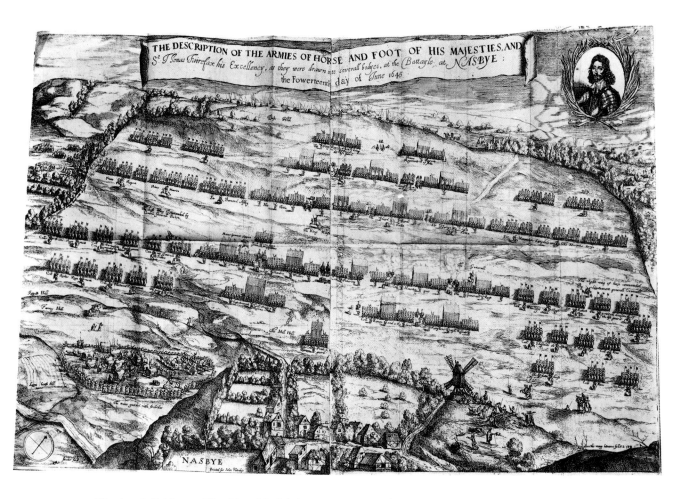

THE DESCRIPTION OF THE ARMIES OF HORSE AND FOOT OF HIS MAJESTIES, AND S.ʳ Tomas Fairefax his Excellency, as they were drawn into severall bodies, at the Battayle at NASBYE: the Fowerteenth day of June 1645.

NASBYE
Printed for John Wharfe

The battlefield at Naseby (above) in 1645, and relived in the present day (opposite)

The New Model Army was put to the test in June 1645. Parliament had ordered Fairfax to attack Oxford but he was forced to turn his attention to the main Royalist army on hearing that Rupert had launched a ruthless assault on Leicester when the town refused to surrender. Fired by the loss of Leicester, Fairfax moved his army to stop the enemy from further onslaught in the Midlands. The two armies finally faced each other on the fields at Naseby in Northamptonshire on 14 June 1645. In spite of his superior numbers, Fairfax was nearing defeat until the arrival of Cromwell's cavalry. Confident and disciplined, they routed the enemy, scattering the King's infantry, taking a vast quantity of arms and pillaging the Royalist baggage-train. Among the spoils was the King's correspondence which his enemies seized on with relish: here evidence was revealed of the King's intrigues in calling on Irish papists and the French to come to his aid. It was the final humiliation of a decisive military defeat. The New Model Army had proved its worth in its first battle, although one episode casts a shadow over the victors. Many Royalist prisoners were taken (estimates vary between 4,000 and 6,000), but atrocious revenge was taken on a group of women found with the baggage-train. Many were killed outright while others suffered the horror of having their noses slit and their faces slashed. The women

Naseby

On 14 June 1645, 23,000 men and 15,000 horses were assembled on the battlefield at Naseby, to the north of Northampton. In the fighting, where Fairfax and the Parliament's army won a decisive victory that was to give them the war, perhaps 1,700 men died. 'The slain', it was said, 'fell like ripe corn around the King.' The battlefield remained little-changed ever after. It was long possible to pick up musket balls and tunic buttons on the site.

That this is one of the decisive battle sites of English history has cut little ice with modern planners. Whereas on the Continent or in the USA major battlefields are given important status and are protected by statutory bodies, the sites on which the warring armies of King and Parliament fought in England have no such privileged status. Bodies like English Heritage or the National Trust do not have the protection of important battle sites within their remits, and so the history of the war has no voice. One of the few battle sites in Great Britain to be jealously protected is Culloden, where the flower of Scotland's youth was cut down behind Bonnie Prince Charlie in 1746.

The requirement for a major road linking the M1 and the A1 has over-ridden historical sensibilities, and the new road planned for construction in 1991 will cut through the heart of the battle site. The campaign for and against its routing has been long and hard: on one side the planners who see the road as a necessity, on the other historians and preservationists arguing that the site is of national importance and alternative routes are feasible. Battle has

been joined for over twenty years, amid allegations of foul play – from the Department of Transport that protestors underplayed the environmental impact of their counter-proposals, from the protestors that the Department has conveniently shrunk and relocated the battle site to fit its plans, gagging public inquiries. The story is an object lesson in conflicting pressures of 'heritage' and 'progress', and in the undervaluing of the significance of the Civil War.

were thought to be Irish, although it seems more likely that they were Welsh, and as such were not given the protection of the normal rules of war. The action against them foreshadowed the awful events that were to afflict Ireland in the future.

The major Royalist army was defeated and for Cromwell and the New Model Army a victory was secured, a sure sign that the providential hand of God was with them. With the surrender of Oxford in 1646, the first Civil War was finally over. Military victory had been achieved and the outcome of the conflict between Charles and his Parliament finally appeared to be decided. But if the King accepted military defeat would it necessarily follow that he would concede political defeat? The King had proved slippery often before. A settlement with Charles and a political solution still remained beyond the grasp of the Parliamentarians.

MAD FASHIONs,
OD FASHIONS,
All out of Fashions,
OR,
The Emblems of these Distracted times.

By *Iohn Taylor*.

LONDON,
Printed by *Iohn Hammond*, for *Thomas Banks*, 1642.

CHAPTER FOUR

Liberty

Any rapid and traumatic upheaval within a society brings about a change in perceptions, a chance to question the structures of that society, its values and its traditions. It is at such times that the voices and opinions of ordinary citizens can have the opportunity for expression. The Civil Wars provided just such a moment in English history. Although not strictly analagous to the French Revolution of the eighteenth century nor the Russian Revolution of the twentieth century, the period of the Civil Wars of the seventeenth century have been rightly designated the English Revolution.

The radical challenging of the old order, and the freedom of the people to voice their grievances and propose new models of society is the essence of any revolution. In 1989, events unfolded in Eastern Europe at an unthinkable speed; we witnessed thousands of ordinary people who took to the streets and came together in huge public demonstrations and meetings. Old structures and institutions were the subjects of mass protest, traditional powers and privileges were challenged and new freedoms called for. Comparisons can be made with the turbulent years of the Civil Wars in England three hundred years earlier; as the Digger, Gerrard Winstanley saw it 'the old world...is running up like parchment in the fire'.

The world seemed turned upside down.

The Civil Wars were not only fought on the battlefields; there was also a pamphlet war, a battle for hearts and minds waged in ideas, discussions and printed debates. By 1641 press censorship had collapsed and the powers of the Church courts were virtually non-existent. It was as if a new age had dawned with unprecedented freedom of expression for a variety of opinions and beliefs. The breakdown of consensus allowed both a greater involvement of ordinary people in the political process as well as the articulation of a range of challenging arguments and propositions. New authors rushed into print and reached a wider audience than ever before. Unlicensed printing allowed a flood of pamphlets to roll off the printing presses; it has been estimated that 9,000 per cent more pamphlets were published in 1642 than in 1640. Newspapers, which had first appeared in the 1620s, flourished during the 1640s.

As censorship ended so pamphlets flooded on to the market circulating new ideas and opinions. How long these had been simmering underground or were the direct product of the chaotic and disturbing events of 1640-42 is difficult to establish. Certainly, grievances had accumulated which now found open expression.

In the early 1640s, much of the debate was expressed in religious and theological terms. As we have seen in earlier chapters, religion was all-pervasive, defining the ways in which people understood their world. Religion and politics were inextricably linked. It is not surprising that challenges to the established order focused on religious belief and the institution of the Church and Church government. A strong tradition of anti-clericalism had existed in Britain throughout the Middle Ages. In the fourteenth century Chaucer had satirized the follies of churchmen and -women in figures like the Pardoner, the Nun's Priest and the Prioress. For centuries there had been popular protest against the widespread abuse of clerical privilege in such practices as absenteeism and the holding of more than one living, and with the existence of hundreds of untrained clergy capable sometimes of teaching no more than superstitious mumbo-jumbo and sometimes living in ways that were decidedly ungodly. Hostility was also directed at the enormous power and wealth concentrated in the hands of a small number of ecclesiastical leaders. All these grievances focused in opposition to the payment of tithes, the form of taxation in which parishoners were compelled to pay a tenth of their produce as salary to their clergymen and towards the upkeep of the Church.

In the fourteenth century this anti-clericalism had helped the spread of the ideas of John Wycliffe which became known as the Lollard movement. Wycliffe and his supporters believed that the Bible should be translated from Latin into English and placed in lay hands for individuals to interpret themselves. He was opposed to priestly power and called on temporal leaders to disendow a rich and lazy clergy. Lollardy was most prevalent amongst literate working people like weavers, wheelwrights, smiths, shoemakers and other tradesmen and in this helped to anticipate elements of congregational dissent in the seventeenth century some three hundred years later. Persecution of Lollardy as a heresy drove it underground although its influence persisted and acted as a strong influence on the English Reformation.

The protest embodied in Protestantism, against the abuses and the power of the Church of Rome inevitably unleashed forces which were hard to control.

Newsbooks circulated
the information and
propagation that
both sides wished to
make known.

Breaking and burning

One difficulty our century has with the Civil War years is understanding the phenomenon of iconoclasm. In orgies of destruction, coloured images and windows were smashed, choir stalls burned, painted interiors whitewashed, screens and railings broken, vestments torn. Churches today are the poorer for the loss of so much medieval work, the survivals the more precious. One key to the mid-seventeenth century must be to comprehend what iconoclasm was.

In the first instance, it was anti-Papist. The suvivals of the pre-Reformation church and the innovations enforced by Archbishop Laud seemed to represent naked Catholicism: graven images, corruption, pathways to heaven through good works, unseemly worship in music, chanting and in sacraments. A series of Parliamentary ordinances ordering the destruction of these items met increasing resistance in the parishes. Particular anger was directed against the bishops; episcopal authority was one of the most contentious elements in the early years of confrontation and conflict. The smashing of windows, monuments and images was also often a political act, destroying items which a landed family had installed or endowed, in the same spirit as football players who just happened to break down the hedges of enclosing landlords.

The greatest damage was wrought by the Army in the cathedrals. Lichfield Cathedral was partly dismantled and turned into an army barracks, and much of Carlisle Cathedral was razed to the ground, while in London St Paul's had the cavalry quartered in the nave and a market operating in the cloisters. Great Yarmouth appealed to Parliament for Norwich Cathedral to be pulled down and its stone re-used for building projects like the strengthening of their harbour wall. Other cathedrals were taken over as centres for preaching and, true to the Commonwealth form, were divided between different congregations. Exeter Cathedral, where the medieval choir and clergy stalls were destroyed and replaced by plain benches, had a stout central dividing wall erected that kept apart rival Independents and Presbyterians. The same thing happened in Holy Trinity Church, Hull, where Revd John Shaw, recorded, 'Mr Canne preached to the governor and the soldiers there...and their people in the chancel could not hear us (no, not when we sung a psalm); sure I am we could not hear them sing psalms, for they sung none.'

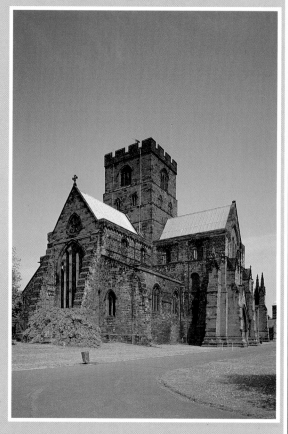

Carlisle Cathedral, devastated by the Scots in 1645.

The basis of all Protestant thinking was a belief in 'justification by faith alone', that spirituality was something that came from within, from direct communication with God and not through some form of intermediary. From the early days of the Reformation there was protest against the existence of any form of established church. Separatists such as the Familists and Anabaptists rejected the idea of a state church and ministries based on parishes with the clergy paid from compulsory tithes. Sometimes these radicals seemed to contemporaries like crazed anarchists who respected no form of authority and who justified any form of behaviour by saying that they were predestined for salvation and so could do no wrong. But in England by the late sixteenth century most of the radical Protestants had decided to work within the established Anglican church. There was constant tension during Elizabeth's reign between moderate Anglicans who believed in a hierarchical, established Church and Puritan extremists who wanted to reform the Church still further until it was organized around individual congregations or 'classes'. This tension almost resulted in the creation of a 'church within a church'.

The Puritan zealots put great emphasis on education and almost 'captured' the University of Cambridge as a centre from which they could disseminate their ideas. The other main feature of the Puritan attack was over control of the pulpit and the appointment of preachers. The thrust of much of the Puritan ministry was carried by these preachers or lecturers who were often elected by their congregations and their salaries paid by voluntary contributions. As many livings were too poor to support educated ministers, Puritan demands came to include the increasingly radical notion of abolishing the cathedral offices of bishops and the dean and chapters and using all the revenues thereby liberated to finance preaching.

By the mid-seventeenth century some sects had emerged which went even further in their aims. They wanted to establish their own congregations independent of the national church. More subversively, they positively welcomed and encouraged lay preachers. By this, and in other ways, they were disputing the central tenets of the doctrines of the established Church. The

Theatre

In 1642, as part of the programme of moral reform instigated by Parliament, the theatres were closed. What had been a vigorous part of life in London was taken away. Yet theatrical productions continued, in clandestine and private ways; like many aspects of life under the Commonwealth, wider tolerance was given than is commonly supposed. Soldiers would raid premises occasionally, clearing out the audience, arresting actors and confiscating costumes, but frequently they turned a blind eye until complaints were made or abuses became too flagrant.

Pre-eminent among the clandestine London theatres was the Red Bull, in the Clerkenwell district just north of the City. It had been a theatre before the wars, and came to specialize in the presentation of 'drolls', comic plays frequently with a lewd content, many written by its leading actors who always managed to stay one jump ahead of the soldiers. What the masses could enjoy the aristocrats also continued to patronize. In the private surroundings of nearby Rutland House, in the late 1650s, some of the earliest English operas like the 'Siege of Rhodes' were being performed, building upon the tradition of the Court masque which had flourished as part of the exclusive culture around Charles I. The Restoration theatre with its style quite distinct from that of pre-1642 did not appear after twenty years of total prohibition; rather it was the result of development.

Thomason's tracts

One of the many booksellers in St Paul's Churchyard in the early 1640s was George Thomason. With the calling of the Long Parliament he had begun systematically to collect every book, pamphlet and newspaper published in London, and as many as he could from the provinces. He continued collecting until Charles II's coronation in April 1661, and then he stopped.

Thomason had begun as a firm supporter of Parliament; in 1648 he wanted a treaty made with Charles; in 1651 he was arrested for his alleged complicity in a conspiracy with the Scots to secure the return of Charles II, and although named as a 'letter-box' for the King's correspondence he was released without trial. Thereafter he remained inconspicuous although continuing to collect the much smaller volume of publications permitted to appear with the re-introduction of censorship.

Like those who collected all the ephemera in Paris in 1789 or 1968, Thomason accumulated an unrivalled body of material: opinions, arguments, and counter-arguments in the political struggle, and the stuff of everyday life that accompanied it. Historians have been grateful to him ever since. Published between 19 and 22 January 1647, for example, were:

Strange Newes from Newgate; or a true Relation of the False Prophet that appeared in Butolphs Church Bishopsgate professing himself to be Christ.

A Catalogue of the severall Sects and Opinions in England and other Nations.

An Embleme of the Times or, a seasonable Exhortation drawn from the consideration of God's gracious dealing with England above all other her neighbour nations.

The Gunner's Glasse. Wherein the diligent Practicioner may see his Defects and amend all Errours that are incident to unskilled Gunners.

The King's Majesties Propositions to the States of Scotland, concerning his taking the Covenant.

The Kings Disguise.

The Kings Possessions; written by His Majesties own Hand.

A Bloody Plot discovered against the Independents.

A true and sad Relation of the Murder committed at Ratcliff in Stepney Parish upon the body of John Hunter, a seaman who was stabbed by one Mr. Smith and his wife.

All the news that was fit to print, all the tracts that people were eager to buy, in the 1640s.

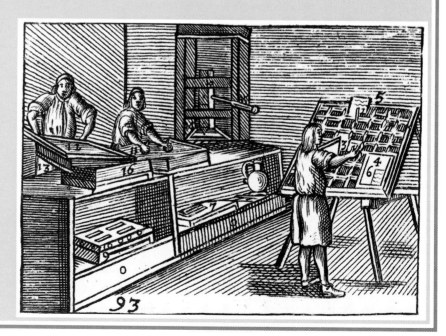

sects laid emphasis on the Spirit rather than the Word, that is on the workings of the Holy Spirit within the individual rather than on the ceremonials and institutions of the Church and the scriptures taught there. However, there was a great variety of beliefs within the sects and people tended to move easily between one congregation and another.

The independent sects represented the radical wing of Puritanism that prior to the outbreak of the Civil War had organized secretly and were the objects of persecution. Some of those who felt most beleaguered left England to find freedom of worship in America or the Netherlands, while others suffered imprisonment or the fate of the pamphleteers, Prynne, Burton and Bastwick, who endured the brutality of having their ears mutilated. Whatever the differences in doctrine between the sects and the moderate Puritans, they were united in their opposition to the innovations in the Church, implemented by Archbishop Laud. In the late 1630s and 40s popular iconoclasm was evident in many parts of the country; altar rails were pulled down, altars desecrated and statues destroyed. Furthermore, there was considerable opposition to the bishops expressed particularly in London with the 'root and branch' petitions which attempted to overthrow the authority of the episcopate. There was also a shared opposition to the Book of Common Prayer and to anything suggestive of popish forms of worship – crucifixes, pictures, images of the Virgin Mary, for example. It should be emphasized, too, that the sectaries (members of the sects) were not alone in challenging the powers and privileges of the clergy; in many areas petitions were drawn up against 'scandalous' ministers and in some instances, the clergy were forcibly ejected from their parishes by members of their own congregations.

With the collapse of censorship, various sects seized the opportunity to publish their views and practise their religion openly and defiantly. Controversy raged as all manner of religious argument and dispute went into print; the language reflected the disruption of war and conflict and the debates were often virulently expressed. One of the most visible attempts to democratize religion came with the insistence of the sects on the right of any man, and in some instances, any woman, to preach. Any individual who had received the Spirit and, in the process of personal illumination, had understood God's word was entitled, as much if not more so than priests and scholars, to preach publicly. This came from a belief that anyone with faith could be united with God personally and directly, rather than through the mediations of the parish priest. At a time when religious worship suddenly became free of restrictions, the sects operated outside parish boundaries and therefore outside the national Church. Challenging the traditional relationship between the clergy and their parish, itinerant lay preachers preached to congregations assembled in a variety of locations, from taverns to open air meetings.

This was disruptive not only theologically but also in terms of church administration, particularly the collection of tithes from which the clergy were paid. Some of the sense of new-found freedom and liberation in the 1640s and 50s comes to us in the words and actions of these lay preachers. Called 'mechanic' preachers, they were often uneducated men and women who claimed – and obviously experienced – divine inspiration and the desire to interpret the Bible in their own way and for themselves, rather than being taught the scriptures by their superiors. Such developments were at least unwelcome, if not feared. William Dell, a radical army chaplain, wrote with great irony of the established Church's opposition to new ideas:

'These are the men that would turn the world upside down, that make the nation full of tumults and uproars, that work all the disturbance in church and state. It is fit that such men and congregations should be suppressed...that we may have truth and peace and government again.'

It was not only men who were 'turning the world upside down', women too were claiming the right to speak, preach and participate in the debates of the period. Throughout the 1640s and 50s women challenged the teachings of the Bible as exemplified in the injunction of St Paul, 'Let your women keep silence in the churches: for it is not permitted unto them to speak.' Women argued for spiritual equality, often turning the scriptures to their own advantage and in support of their own claims. By arguing that they were the passive instruments of God's will, they challenged conventions and could take actions outside their prescribed roles. The presence of women preachers in the streets or in congregations horrified many Puritan clergy and gentry. The breakdown of the church hierarchy was cause enough for concern but an onslaught on sexual hierarchies and the patriarchal family was even more alarming. The outrage which greeted the publication in 1643 of Milton's *Doctrine and Discipline of Divorce* reflected the fear that the very foundations of society were being uprooted. Milton advocated, in the context of liberty of conscience, the right of divorce (for men) on grounds of what we would call today incompatibility and at the same time denounced the tyranny of arranged marriages.

In the turbulent years of the Civil War and the period of the Commonwealth, some women, like their male counterparts, shared the hopes and dreams of a new society. These visions of a different future were often expressed in prophecies, a form of pronouncement which many radical women adopted. However, prophecies were not confined to the radicals; millenarian beliefs were widespread. It was widely believed in the seventeenth century that these were the latter days of the world, that the dissolution of the world was approaching and would be followed by the thousand-year rule of the saints. In the freedom of the 1640s, biblical prophecies, especially those in the Books of Daniel and Revelations, were reinterpreted by scholars as well as ordinary people as referring to present-day England where the Civil War represented the struggle with the Anti-Christ. Parliament called upon the people to fight God's cause against the Anti-Christ, no longer perceived as the Pope in Rome but as the King and the Church in England. The second Coming, the establishment of Christ's Kingdom was at hand; some believed on the basis of scientific research that it was destined to be in the 1650s. Millenarianism provided the impetus for much of the radical religious debate of this period; combined with the utopian hopes of many of the religious sects, which were also shared by the more radical secular groups, it helped to fire the English Revolution.

However, when the Parliamentarians had rallied support for their 'godly' cause, they certainly had not bargained for such vociferous claims over what was meant by godly nor who were the true representatives of the godly. For many moderates

Preaching the word

The Orthodox true Minister,

the Seducer and false Prophet.

*'A glass for the times': a satire on lecturers
and unorthodox preaching.*

To bring England to God, to reform *England's Impenitency under Smiting*, Nicholas Proffet urged in 1645, 'instructions and corrections must be used; Magistrate and Minister, the Word and the Sword must be joined.' It was a familiar idea, that by hearing sermons the people would be made more godly, while careful control of their behaviour would bring moral reformation. Lectureships, set up in many towns in the 1620s and 30s, were one of the targets of Laudian counter-reform. Preachers accompanied the Parliamentarian army, urging them that God watched over their endeavours. The explosion of godliness in the Civil War and immediately after, was accompanied by a wave of sermons the like of which England had probably never seen or heard before, or since. Yet the population as a whole proved remarkably resistant. In his Essex parish of Earl's Colne, Ralph Josselin divided his flock into 'our society', the deeply religious; 'my sleepy hearers', most who attended his services; and 'the families that seldom hear'. One writer regarded congregations as 'those blocks that go to church as dogs do, only for company and can hear a powerful minister for

twenty or thirty years together, and mind no more what they hear than the seats they sit on', and a servant in Lancashire had summed up sermons as 'sharp shitting in a frosty morning'.

Sermons remained the backbone of most forms of worship in the 1650s, but Revd Richard Baxter 'found by experience, that an ignorant sot that has been an unprofitable hearer so long, has got more knowledge and remorse of conscience in half an hour's close discourse, than...from ten years' public discourse.' Catechizing, 'getting within', came to be regarded as the most effective means of advancing and reinforcing godliness. Henry Newcome, pastor of Gawsworth in Cheshire, recorded in 1659, 'We had now many private days, and I found that I was often unfit for them; yet they did us much good, for they either sent us away refreshed by enlargedness, or humbled for our straitness.'

Some were successful. On one happy occasion, Ralph Josselin was to enter in his diary, 'the church where I preached full, multitudes standing without at windows.' Unfortunately, he was recording one of his most vivid dreams.

during the 1640s and 50s, religious toleration was fast getting out of control as debates and practices seemed increasingly to smack of heresy and blasphemy. While the majority were looking towards reform within a national church, the radical sects seemed set on religious anarchy and experiment rather than reform. The sects represented only a tiny percentage of the population but their ideas and questionings of the structure of society had a significance beyond their numbers. Subversive religious ideas are inevitably threatening to the social order too, more so at a time of political and social upheaval. The Civil War was such a time and the Parliamentarians were faced with a vocal minority who threatened a more fundamental overthrow of society and its institutions. For the moderates rightly recognised that demands for democracy in the Church could all too easily slide into secular demands for a more democratic state. Ironically, those demands came from within the ranks of the Parliamentary army, the same army which had been largely responsible for defeating the King. The radicals in the army, more secular than religious, had a significance too beyond their actual numbers, partly in the response which their ideas invoked and also in the forms their radicalism took and the specific nature of that radicalism.

In June 1645, Charles was defeated at the Battle of Naseby but isolated strongholds held out into 1646. Peace proved elusive as the King refused to concede his defeat and negotiate a settlement with Parliament. He dragged out attempts at settlement throughout 1646 and most of 1647. In this context the victors of the Civil War divided into two camps, the conservatives in Parliament, now known as the Presbyterians, and the radicals, known as the Independents, who believed further reform was needed. The dispute between these two groups now focused on the issue of disbanding the army.

Soldiers' pay had been a problem for both sides during the war and the New Model Army, although better and more regularly paid, was now facing a situation where arrears of pay were mounting up. Furthermore, the army was also incensed by Parliament's failure to protect it from legal action being taken by some local authorities against soldiers for what could be seen as war crimes committed during the Civil War. Parliament refused to offer any sort of indemnity and there were reports of soldiers being hanged for having seized horses or supplies for war service. Against this background, some of the regiments mutinied. By the end of March 1647, the rank and file began to take action. The soldiers elected two delegates from each regiment to speak on their behalf, 'agitators' as they were called. The officers followed the rank and file by electing their own agitators to petition Parliament for redress of their grievances. The continuing intransigence of Parliament towards the army led to its increasing politicization with demands moving beyond military grievances to embrace political and religious freedoms and to constitute what was virtually a political programme.

Considering the nature and formation of the New Model Army, it is not altogether surprising to find it becoming a political force. Unlike local regiments under the command of a familiar local leader, the New Model Army was much more of a social mix. More mobile as it moved around the country, its soldiers were less deferential to their officers and more open to and aware of the influence of sectarian congregations and political radicals. Chaplains in the New Model Army preached both to civilian populations and to the soldiers, and they included many radicals. Where there were no chaplains, many soldiers organized their own services and took on the role of preacher, rather like the mechanic preachers of the radical sects. A strong religious ideology developed within the army as many in the ranks saw themselves as the instruments of divine providence. A sense of being the vanguard in the struggle against the King was matched by a sense of betrayal by Parliament when the hostilities ceased and the soldiers' services were no longer required. Moreover, the army felt that Parliament was failing to secure those things they felt they had been fighting for – religious freedom and reform of Parliament itself, among others. The King was 'captured' from his Parliamentary prison at Holdenby House and was kept under the army's control. A General Council of the Army was created and when the army marched into London and impeached eleven Members of Parliament in August 1647, it marked a turning point – the entry of the army into national politics. The army felt slighted by Parliament's refusal to concede their demands and so the General Council drew up its own proposals for a settlement with the King. Known as the 'Heads of Proposals', their authors were Cromwell's son-in-law, Henry Ireton and John Lambert, with the approval of Cromwell but without recourse to the rank and file within the army. The terms of the 'Heads' included new ideas and safeguards on the powers of Parliament and the monarch as well as a number of reforms – both legal and fiscal – and a proposal for religious settlement.

Charles inevitably refused to accept anything which gave more powers to Parliament. More significantly, the proposals were rejected by the rank and file of the army who viewed them with suspicion. For them, the 'grandees' in the army were conceding too much to the King while failing to press for a settlement of their grievances. The more radical elements of the rank and file had been forming alliances with a group of London political and religious radicals. Led by three brilliant pamphleteers, John Lilburne, Richard Overton and William Walwyn, this group was known as the Levellers. Originally used as a term of abuse by their opponents, it has proudly remained the name of a group who raised the possibility of fermenting a revolution within the revolution.

The Levellers were so called because they insisted that since all men were equal before God so should they be equal before the law. They were never a political party in the modern sense, but they did put forward a number of Leveller programmes. On the basis of these programmes, the Levellers gained support and allies, particularly in London where most of their activities were centred. They were able to raise thousands of signatures for their petitions and thousands turned out for their demonstrations; their support ranged from religious radicals to craftsmen, small masters and shopkeepers. In the same tradition as many religious radicals, they appealed for freedom of religious belief. In pamphlets and petitions they demanded liberty of conscience, the disestablishment of the Church and the abolition of compulsory tithes. As time went on, their outlook became more secular with demands for legal reforms and for equal application of the laws, the end of imprisonment for debt, the abolition of trade monopolies and the end of press censorship. They appealed to many people who had expected and hoped that the end of the war would herald a new order but instead were faced with high taxes, economic depression and a Parliament which abused its powers.

Churches of the Commonwealth years

Set up above the west door of the church at Staunton Harrold in Leicestershire is the inscription:

In the year 1653
when all things Sacred were throughout ye nation
Either demolished or profaned
Sir Robert Shirley, Barronet,
Founded this church;
Whose singular praise it is,
to haue done the best things in ye worst times,
and
hoped them in the most callamitous.
The righteous shall be had
in everlasting remembrance.

Shirley had built a Gothic, Perpendicular church – which still stands largely unaltered – expressing a past way of Anglican life. It is more 'Laudian' inside than any of the churches with surviving fittings from the 1630s: it has screens, altar rails; carved woodwork, an organ, and a painted ceiling depicting the Creation. Cromwell was so incensed that he ordered that if Shirley could pay to build a church he could also afford to raise a regiment – and when Shirley refused he was incarcerated in the Tower of London. He knew the place well, having been gaoled there on six occasions, and he died there, aged twenty-seven. Staunton Harrold is one of the few attempts at church-building in the 1650s, and is certainly the most flagrantly provocative. In the West Riding and Westmorland, Lady Anne Clifford built and repaired churches on her estates. She too had High Anglican and Royalist sympathies (her second husband was the Earl of Pembroke, one of Charles I's intimate friends) but her buildings were considerably more low-key, and well out of sight.

The parish church dedicated to Holy Trinity in Berwick-on-Tweed is one of the few parish churches of the Commonwealth period, built in a mixture of Gothic and Classical styles by Colonel George Fenwicke, the Governor of the fortified border town. The fact that the church has no tower is due, it is always alleged, to the intervention of Cromwell, who vetoed the building of one when he passed through on his way to Dunbar. Its pulpit, erected like the church in 1652, is now nowhere near as prominent as in a few other 'preaching-box' churches that survive, fitted out in the 1650s – the chapel at Littlecote House in Wiltshire, where the pulpit is placed centrally in the east wall with a reading desk below, or the tiny Norfolk marshland chapel of Guyhirn.

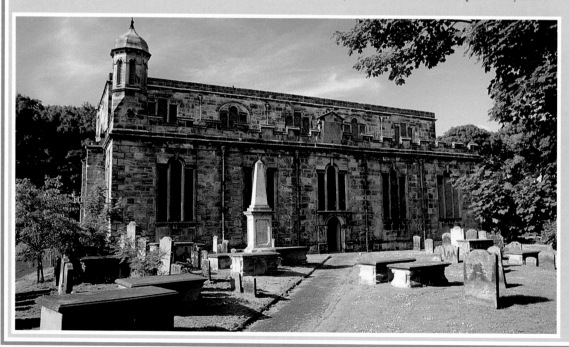

The interior of the new church at Staunton Harrold(left), and the 1652 parish church of Berwick on Tweed (opposite).

Lilburne

The central figure in the Leveller movement was a man whose career mirrored the many twists and changes of thought and action in the Civil War years. In 1638 John Lilburne's opposition to the episcopate was punished severely by Laud in Star Chamber, and he was regarded as a hero in the early years of Parliament's struggle. After entering the fighting, when in his late twenties, he resigned his commission in opposition to the Solemn League and Covenant, and began his lengthy campaigning against corruption in public life and for religious and political liberties. For his pains he was imprisoned seven times between 1645 and 1652, when he was banished for life. Lilburne continued to remain a thorn in authority's flesh: he returned to England the following year, was put on trial for treason for the third time, and although acquitted was put back in gaol. He died in 1657, a Quaker like many disillusioned radicals, and he left to posterity around eighty pamphlets which were in defence of the rights of citizens. In his *Just Defence* in 1653, he had written his testament:

'There being not one particular I have contended for, or for which I have suffered, but the right, freedom, safety and well-being of every particular man, woman and child in England has been so highly concerned therein, that their freedom or bondage has depended thereupon, insomuch that had they not been misled in their judgements, and corrupted in their understandings by such as sought their bondage, they would have seen themselves as much bound to have assisted me, as they judge themselves obliged to deliver their neighbour out of the hands of thieves and robbers. It being impossible for any man, woman or child in England to be free from the arbitrary and tyrannical will of men, except those ancient laws and ancient rights of England, for which I have contended even unto blood, be preserved and maintained.'

The truly revolutionary programme of the Levellers emerged from their attack on the unrepresentativeness of England's constitution. They looked back to the period when the Norman conquerors had imposed their tyrannical laws on the people of England and looked forward to a new order in which the sovereignty of the people was central and when representative institutions were democratically elected. The alliance with the army was not as strange as might first appear, for the army had entered the arena of national politics and their claim that they were 'not a mere mercenary army' but defenders of the people's liberties clearly had resonances with the Levellers. In the heady mixture of radical ideas, stirred by unrest among the soldiers for the delay in the settlement of their grievances, the Levellers drew up their challenge to the commanders of the army. In October 1647 in *The Case of the Army Truly Stated*, they strongly argued for actions to be taken speedily to redress the soldiers' grievances. From the specifics relating to the army the *Case* moved on a more general attack on Parliament and demands for long-term constitutional reforms.

Meester Lilburn achter een kar gegeeffelt.
Mr. Lilburne whipt after the Carts tayle.

John Lilburne (1615-57), celebrated (left) and reviled (above).

Fairfax, the Commander-in-Chief of the New Model Army, knew that if he was to retain unity he must respond quickly. A General Council was summoned to a meeting at Putney church in London on 28 October 1647. These discussions, now famous as the Putney Debates, have become historically significant because they attempted to provide a new constitution for England. At the centre of these debates on democracy was another Leveller manifesto, *The Agreement of the People*, jointly drafted by civilian and army Levellers. The civilian Levellers were represented by John Wildman, a lawyer, and a London tradesman called Maximilian Petty. Among the senior officers present were Cromwell and his son-in-law, Ireton, as well as Colonel Rainsborough. Rainsborough's famous statement, 'I think the poorest he in England has a life to lead as the greatest he', suggests that at least some of the senior officers were convinced by the Levellers' arguments.

The *Agreement* called for the same freedoms as the other Leveller manifestos but went further in its claims for the rights of the people within a new

The franchise is debated at Putney

Putney church, in London, scene of the Leveller debates in late 1647.

constitutional and democratic framework. The basic principle of the new constitution was that it was to be subscribed by the people who would elect a representative parliament, answerable only to the people and not to the King nor the House of Lords. 'Therefore these things in the Agreement, the people are to claim as their native right and price of their blood, which you are obliged absolutely to procure for them. And these being the foundation of freedom, it is necessary that they should be settled unalterably, which can be done by no means but this Agreement with the people.' Controls on parliamentary power would be effected by biennial Parliaments and the decentralization of power from central government to local authorities, also democratically elected. To achieve this, an extension of the franchise was imperative; although the Levellers were accused of speaking for 'hobnayles, clouted shooes and leather aprons', they did not argue for universal suffrage – servants, apprentices, beggars and women (the latter never even mentioned) were excluded. To twentieth-century eyes, this is a remarkable omission but the Levellers wanted the vote for those who were truly independent and the argument against giving it to servants, apprentices and women was that their vote could too easily be

General Ireton. The exception that lies in it is this: it is said, they are to be distributed according to the number of inhabitants, 'The people of England', etc. And this does make me think, that the meaning is that every man that is an inhabitant is to be equally considered, and to have an equal voice in the election of those representers, the persons that are for the general representative, and if that be the meaning then I have something to say against it, but if it be only that those people that by the civil constitution of this kingdom, which is original and fundamental, and beyond which I am sure no memory of record does go –

Interjection. Not before the Conquest –

But before the Conquest it was so. If it be intended that those that by that constitution that was before the Conquest, that has been beyond memory, such persons that have been under that constitution should be the electors, I have no more to say...

Captain Clarke. ...the grand question of all is, whether or no it be the property of every individual person in the kingdom to have a vote in election? and the ground is the law of nature, which, for my part, I think to be that law which is the ground of all constitutions...

Captain Audley. ...I would die in any place in England, in asserting that it is the right of every free-born man to elect according to the rule, that which concerns all ought to be debated by all...

Maximilian Petty. We judge that all inhabitants that have not lost their birthright should have an equal voice in elections...

Lieutenant-General Cromwell. If we should go about to alter these things, I do not think that we are bound to fight for every particular proposition. Servants, while servants, are not included. Then you agree that he that receives alms is to be excluded.

Lieutenant-Colonel Reade. I suppose it's concluded by all, that the choosing of representatives is a privilege; now I see no reason why any man that is a native ought to be excluded that privilege, unless from voluntary servitude.

Petty. I conceive the reason why we would exclude apprentices, or servants, or those that take alms, it is because they depend upon the will of other men and should be afraid to displease....

Mr Everard. ...We have declared in what we conceive these principles do lie...Now in the progress of these disputes, we find that the time spends, and no question but our adversaries are harder at work than we are...we have nakedly and freely unbosomed ourselves unto you. Though these things have startled many at the first view, yet we find there is good hopes; we have fixed our resolutions and we are determined, and we want nothing but that only God will direct us to what is just and right. But I understand that all these debates, if we should agree upon any one thing: this is our freedom; this is our liberty; this liberty and freedom we are debarred of, and we are bereaved of all these comforts...

influenced by their 'masters'. Even so, the Levellers' programme was too radical to be acceptable to Cromwell and the other army grandees and neither side was prepared to make concessions.

Before any resolutions could be found, the whole debate was overtaken by the course of events. On 11 November 1647, the King, fearing his life was in peril, escaped from army custody at Hampton Court and made his way to the Isle of Wight. In the circumstances the unity of the army was an urgent necessity. Further discussions of the *Agreement* were pre-empted although the issues raised did not go away. Two regiments of soldiers, with copies of the *Agreement* in their hats, mutinied at Ware. Three of the leaders were court-martialled and sentenced to death; military discipline had been enforced and the authority of the commanders re-established. The Levellers had failed to capture the army and as the possibility once again of any settlement with the King receded, war broke out again in the spring of 1648 and the country once more descended into political and military chaos.

After his escape, Charles had signed a secret agreement with commissioners from Scotland known as the Engagement. The opportunity of a Scots army entering England on the King's side was the excuse for the Royalists to plan an uprising which they hoped would reverse the outcome of the Civil War. In March 1648 a Presbyterian-Royalist revolt in Pembrokeshire began what is called the new war. The revolt in Wales was soon put down by Cromwell while Fairfax crushed a Royalist revolt in Kent. Fairfax pursued the Royalists into Colchester where a long, drawn-out and increasingly bloody siege followed. At this point a Scots army invaded England. Cromwell turned north and smashed the Scots at the battle of Preston and marched on to Edinburgh. A Royalist-led mutiny in the navy which could have helped the Royalists bring reinforcements from the continent, was put down. Meanwhile in Essex, Fairfax finally captured Colchester and in an act of uncharacteristic butchery summarily shot some of the Royalists after they had surrendered. Within a few months all resistance had been crushed but the fighting of the Second Civil War had been bloodier and more brutal than anything known in the earlier years of the fighting.

The political outcome of the Second Civil War is the subject of the next chapter. A return to fighting did not halt the progress of the radical impulse which during the 1640s and 50s opened up the possibility of a fundamental overturning of seventeenth-century society. During 1648 the *Agreement of the People* continued to be discussed and a compromise reached. Some reforms recommended by the Levellers were adopted by the government of the new republic, the Commonwealth, which abolished the House of Lords and the monarchy the following year. The failure to concede the more fundamental reforms was greeted by Lilburne, Walwyn and Overton with a series of pamphlets denouncing the new government as hypocritical and despotic. They were all arrested and imprisoned in the Tower. Cromwell, recognizing their threat to the stability of the new Parliament, warned 'if you do not break them, they will break you'.

The Rump Parliament which created the Commonwealth depended on the army for its survival. Yet sections of that army, inspired by the Levellers,

Hampton Court Palace, where negotiations about settlement with the King were conducted in the autumn of 1647.

*David Leslie,
Baron Newark, who
accompanied Charles
when he invaded
England from Scotland.*

continued to display a social and political radicalism which signified a revolutionary vision of a more democratic state with greater participation by the people, challenging the more cautious and conciliatory programme adopted by Parliament. Furthermore, there was continuing discontent among the soldiers over pay which erupted into mutiny by two regiments. Fairfax and Cromwell reacted swiftly to put this down; the mutineers who were on the run sought shelter in Burford church near Oxford but they were rounded up and their leaders executed. A further mutiny by soldiers refusing to take part in Cromwell's expeditionary force to Ireland met a similar fate and was effectively crushed. Meanwhile, in London, Walwyn and Overton were released and Lilburne tried and acquitted, but the Leveller challenge was over.

By the beginning of 1649 English society had been shaken to its very foundations. The ravages of the Civil Wars with all their bitterness, horrors and disruption had been followed by the execution of the King and the abolition of the House of Lords. The stability of familiar institutions, customs and assumptions about society had collapsed. In addition, the economic situation was disastrous; a ruinous harvest in 1648 had led to widespread hunger and unemployment. The increasing number of poor and hungry were threatening the social order and the discontent in the army and among demobilized soldiers

A great and bloudy

FIGHT

AT

COLCHESTER,

AND

The ſtorming of the Town by the Lord Generals Forces, with
the manner how they were repulſed and beaten off, and forced to retreat from the Walls, and a great and terrible
blow given at the ſaid ſtorm, by Granadoes and Gunpowder. Likewiſe their hanging out the Flag of Defiance, and
their ſallying out upon Tueſday laſt, all the chief Officers
ingaging in the ſaid Fight, and Sir *Charles Lucas* giving the
firſt onſet in the Van, with the number killed and taken, and
Sir *Charles Lucas* his Declaration.

London Printed for *G. Beal,* and are to be ſold in the Old
Bayley, and neer Temple Bar, 1648.

Burford

Incised into the lead lining of the font in Burford parish church, in Oxfordshire, is 'Antony Sedley prisner 1649', a melancholy memento of the eclipse of soldiers' hopes after the Civil Wars. An annual commemoration in Burford church of the Levellers keeps alive the memory of the radicals and of the unfortunates like Sedley.

Amidst general dissatisfaction at the failure of Leveller programmes of reform to be put into effect, and the mobilization of troops to fight in Ireland, army mutinies had broken out in April and May 1649. Men in Colonel Scrope's regiment laid down their arms in Salisbury at the beginning of May, and made their way rapidly towards Banbury where another mutiny had taken place. The authorities acted swiftly to quell mutiny and Fairfax's army moved, at great speed, cutting the mutineers off in Burford.

On the night of 13 May these troops, under Cromwell's command, swarmed into the town. In all, 340 men were rounded up (although others escaped) and herded into Burford church; for four days it became their prison. Scrope, their colonel, was sent in to tell the prisoners they were all to die. Then they learned that the two ringleaders, and two other men selected almost at random, were to be shot. On the Thursday morning the four men were led out and ranged against the church wall. To Cornet Thompson, 'death was a great terror', but Corporal Perkins 'died gallantly as he had lived religiously', and John Church '...pulled off his doublet, he stretched out his arms, and bade the soldiers do their duties, looking them in the face...'

Cornet Denne, as he stood before the firing squad, was given a last-minute reprieve, and his confession of guilt and remorse was published immediately as a pamphlet. The rest were marched away, and disbanded soon after. They left behind a general realization of how firmly the Army commanders resisted any dissension, all residual hope of Leveller hopes being put into action, and the mess that 349 frightened soldiers barricaded inside a church make. The Burford churchwardens' accounts record, 'paid Daniel Muncke and others for cleaning the church when the Levellers were taken.' They did not remove Sedley's name.

continued. The vexed issues of 'liberty of conscience' and religious freedoms were still explosive. The new Commonwealth wrestled with the problems of a religious settlement; the independent congregations continued to have a political impact with their challenge to religious orthodoxy.

For many of the small sects and independent congregations the primacy of personal revelation over Scripture remained central. A small group, known as the Diggers, combined their religious beliefs with radical attempts to find new political and economic solutions.

In April 1649 a group of poor men and women collected on the common on St George's Hill in Surrey and began to dig up the land and form a squatter community. Led by the charismatic Gerrard Winstanley their actions symbolized the assumption of ownership of common land. Winstanley believed in universal salvation and in what we would now call communist theories, that all property should be held in common. His visions of common ownership, rather than private property, also extended to equality between the sexes. Drawing on a theory of natural rights, Winstanley also quoted the Bible to support his arguments. Rejecting the traditional teachings of the Church, his was a visionary form of spirituality.

The Digger colony on St George's Hill was not unique; there were others in Buckinghamshire, Bedfordshire, Gloucestershire and Nottinghamshire, as well as in other parts of the country. The Diggers or 'True Levellers' produced specific demands that confiscated Church, Crown and Royalists' lands be turned over to the poor. Set out in *The Law of Freedom*, Winstanley challenged existing

The cruel aftermath (opposite) of the siege of Colchester.

Winstanley

In 1643 the economic uncertainties that accompanied the Civil War helped bring about the business failure of Gerrard Winstanley, who left the Lancashire cloth trade, and was forced to become a farm labourer. He published about twenty tracts between 1648 and 1652, charting his move from religious mysticism to communism with the Diggers, and finally the collapse of his community at St George's Hill, Surrey. A communist society would represent the triumph of the spirit over the flesh, he believed and he expressed his views particularly cogently in his pamphlet *A New Year's Gift* (of 1650). Subsequently, when the Digger experiment failed, it is likely that Winstanley became a Quaker and he disappeared from political life.

'What other lands do, England is not to take pattern; for England (as well as other lands) has lain under the power of that beast, kingly property. But now England is the first of nations that is upon the point of reforming; and if England must be the tenth part of the city, Babylon, that falls off from the beast first, and would have that honour, he must cheerfully (and dally no longer) cast out kingly covetous property, and set the crown upon Christ's head, who is the universal love or free community, and so be the leader of that happy restoration to all the nations of the world...for if ever the creation be restored, this is the way, which lies in this twofold power:

'First, community of mankind, which is comprised in the unity of spirit of love which is called Christ in you, or the law written in the heart, leading mankind into all truth, and to be of one heart and one mind.

'Second is community of the earth, for the quiet livelihood in food and raiment without using force, or restraining one another. These two communities, or rather one in two branches, is that true levelling which Christ will work at his more glorious appearance....

'For I tell you and your preachers, that Scripture which says "The poor shall inherit the earth" is really and materially to be fulfilled, for the earth is to be restored from the bondage of sword property, and it is to become a common treasury in reality to all mankind...'

property relations in the name of true Christian freedom and put forward his hopes for a communist Utopia. Earlier he had written: 'they that are resolved to work and eat together, making the earth a common treasury, doth join hands with Christ to lift up the creation from bondage, and restores all things from the curse.' Almost inevitably, the Digger colonies failed, some harassed by local residents, others by local justices. However, their importance lay in their ideas and their actions; in the twentieth century squatting has also been a way in which the poor and homeless have tried to find practical solutions for their needs, and 'trespass' protests by walkers and ramblers have claimed the rights of the people to the land above the interests of private and exclusive ownership.

During the 1650s, as we saw earlier, a plethora of groups, congregations and individuals questioned all forms of religious teachings and beliefs. Fundamental issues of authority, sin and the existence of hell, and practices of baptism were all thrown into the melting pot of ideas. Prophets predicted the Second Coming and numbers of ordinary men and women claimed direct illumination from God. Cromwell and the Commonwealth, believing in religious toleration, were being put to the test.

One group, now identified as Ranters, pushed toleration to the limit. In no way a sect nor an organized congregation, this loose group of individuals provoked fear and hostility quite out of proportion to their numbers. As individuals they were undeniably provocative; taking their belief in the individual's personal relationship to God to its extreme, they broke with all traditions and moral constraints. By the standards of their day they appeared sexually and socially immoral. For example, Abiezer Coppe's fondness for swearing and Laurence Clarkson's sexual licence contributed to the charge that their actions did not represent religious freedom so much as blasphemy. The Ranters are perhaps better understood in the context of a wholehearted rejection of the Puritan belief in sin and the guilt which Protestantism engenders in its adherents.

Mainstream Protestantism was, however, to face its biggest challenge from the Quakers. The Quakers of the seventeenth century had little in common with the Friends of today, known for their pacifism and quietism. The Quakers

Oliver Cromwell,
'our chief of men'.

originated in the north of England and found adherents among farmers and artisans as well as the poor. Like the Diggers, they believed in universal salvation and the notion of Christ within the individual. Their success in evangelizing is proved by the numbers of converts; in 1652 they numbered about 500, by 1657 there were perhaps 50,000. Their leaders were often flamboyant and aggressive in their beliefs; Quakers also demanded religious freedom alongside calls for social reforms. They were to be found disrupting services in the 'steeplehouses', their name for parish churches. They refused to pay tithes and challenged the authority of local magistrates. Their belief in equality of all men in the sight of God led them to eschew traditional forms of deference; they refused 'hat-honour', the removing of hats in front of figures of authority. Equality also meant that large numbers of women were attracted to the Quaker faith and shared in the preaching and dissemination of the Quaker faith. The trial of James Nayler was significant not just in the brutality of Nayler's

The Quakers

James Nailor Quaker set 2 howers on the Pillory at Westminster, whiped by the Hang man to the old Exchainge London, Som dayes after, Stood too howers more on the Pillory at the Exchainge, and there had his Tongue Bored throug with a hot Iron, & Stigmatized in the Forehead with the Letter:B: Decem: 17 anno Doi:1656:

The horrific punishment meted out to James Nayler (right) was one of the more extreme responses to the threat to social order that the Quakers (opposite) were supposed to represent.

·One of the most visible survivals of the period of Commonwealth is the Society of Friends, the Quakers. A religious group known for their pacifism and for their worship without liturgy, it seems difficult to imagine with what fear and loathing they were regarded when the sect emerged in the 1650s.

George Fox was a Leicestershire weaver who, like many in the early 1650s, began to seek new religious experiences. His came in Yorkshire, in a vision in 1652 on Pendle Hill in Ribblesdale, of 'a great people in white raiment by a river side coming to the Lord; and the place that I saw them in was about Wensleydale and Sedbergh'. He preached in Sedbergh at the hiring fair, and quickly attracted followers. The particular tenets of Quakerism – so-called because Friends were supposed to have religious ecstasies during which they shook, and were suspected of free love – involved a disregard for hierarchy, austerity, and opposition to tithes. They opposed the patriarchalism that was taken as the basis for social order, some of their activities were regarded as blasphemous, while their proselytizing zeal also made them suspect. In 1654, John Audland had travelled thirty miles a day, visiting twenty counties, in a few months preaching and converting. Two years later,

James Nayler, having entered Bristol half-naked and riding on a donkey, dressed as Christ with his followers laying down fronds, was sentenced to be branded and his tongue bored, then to be whipped, pilloried, and imprisoned for his blasphemy – a punishment that was the result of long debate about exactly how hideously he was to be treated.

Quakers were seen as perverting public order, as witches, as potential rebels. One scurrilous tract of 1659 accused them of bestiality with horses, 'why Quakers meet in meadows, woods, and pastures', and in the same year Somerset JPs were forced to advertise that 'there hath been a false report raised that Mr Beadon, Minister of Bawdrip, was killed by a Quaker... Mr Beadon is in perfect health, and was not affronted or wounded by any person', a rumour they believed had been started by Royalists in an abortive plot to restore the monarchy. When the monarchy was restored, the Quakers had some of the earliest anti-dissenter legislation directed against them. Gradually the Quakers' quietism made them a respected force and not to be feared, but only in the eighteenth century did they properly emerge from being a dangerous sect into wider acceptance and toleration.

THE QVAKERS DREAM: 14

OR,
The Devil's Pilgrimage in England:
BEING

An infallible Relation of their several Meetings,

Shreekings, Shakings, Quakings, Roarings, Yellings, Howlings, Tremblings in the Bodies, and Rhings in the Bellies: With a Narrative of their several Arguments, Tenets, Principles, and strange Doctrine: The strange and wonderful Satanical Apparitions, and the appearing of the Devil unto them in the likeness of a black Boar, a Dog with flaming eys, and a black man without a head, causing the Dogs to bark, the Swine to cry, and the Cattel to run, to the great admiration of all that shall read the same.

London, Printed for G. Horton, and are to be sold at the Royal Exchange in Cornhil, 1655. *Aprill. 26.*

A satire against Hugh Peters, the radical army chaplain, who had returned from Massachusetts, and was to be executed in 1660.

punishment but because it focused the confusion around the idea of liberty of 'godly conscience'. The Quaker menace brought a return to an established religious order with an attempt to impose compulsory religious worship on Sundays. But the national church was split irrevocably.

The Restoration of Charles II in 1660 signalled the end of twenty years of freedom of thought and the flourishing of new ideas. For many it had been a time of exhilaration, allowing for speculation, experiment and visions of a transformed society rising like a phœnix from the ashes of the old. The aspirations and dreams of the radicals existed side by side with practical demands for a major rebuilding of a new world founded on political and religious liberty with a democratic constitution. But the revolutionary demands ultimately failed. Part of the reason for the failure was the lack of unity between the disparate groups and lack of political unity was inevitably divisive. Demands for religious freedom led inexorably to political freedom and therefore a fundamental overturning of the State and the power of the State. But the power of the radicals of this period was never enough to dislodge the power of the men of property.

But there remains the power of ideas. While many of these disappeared underground again and some of the sects and radical groups disappeared forever, many would resurface and the tradition of democracy, liberty and equality would be fought for by succeeding generations. Tom Paine took up some of the ideas in the following century and transported them to the debate about freedom which helped bring the United States of America into existence. The Chartists revived some of the Leveller demands for suffrage reform in nineteenth-century industrial Britain. The Left in Britain today still looks back to the ideas of the Levellers, the Diggers and others, to the words of Lilburne and Winstanley, as a source of inspiration. The ideas of the English Revolution have had a strong lineage down through succeeding centuries and none stronger than those of the radicals who emerged to shine briefly in the ferment of revolutionary England.

CHAPTER FIVE

Execution

In the tangled and long-drawn-out events of what has become known as the Second
Civil War, the King proved himself to be entirely untrustworthy. He had led the Army
General Council to believe that they could negotiate with him. Then he had escaped
from the army's custody and negotiated adeal with the Scots. After Cromwell had defeated
the Scots army at the battle of Preston, the King thenentered into negotiations with the
Presbyterian wing in Parliament and signed the Treaty of Newport.Finally, the Army
General Council decided that they must act and this time against the King himself.

At St Albans in November 1648, General Ireton, Cromwell's son-in-law, representing
the junior officers, forced the Army General Council to adopt a radical policy. It was
decided that the Army must 'purge' Parliament of members unsympathetic to their
position and begin a trial against the King. A Remonstrance was presented to Parliament
declaring a complete loss of faith in Charles and outlining some of the Leveller demands
for constitutional reform. After several years of fighting, with all the chaos and instability
this had brought throughout the country, there was growing division amongst the
Parliamentary party itself. The basic issue was the question of Church reorganization. The
Independents were more sympathetic to the Levellers and the army radicals. They wanted
an all-out victory over the King now that the war had been decisively won. The
Presbyterians were more socially conservative and cautious. They were fearful that
religious toleration would bring social chaos. They had no wish to see the political
revolution go too far and the Parliamentary Presbyterians now sent commissioners to
negotiate with Charles.

Charles I, in a portrait painted while awaiting his trial.

It was in this context that the Treaty of Newport with the King was approved by the Presbyterian wing in Parliament. A major crisis now erupted between Army and Parliament. The Army commanders sent Colonel Thomas Pride with a military guard to Westminster and on 6 December 1648 he barred more than a hundred members from taking their seats in the Commons. Some of the excluded members were imprisoned. The purge removed from the scene those members who had favoured any form of negotiated settlement with Charles. The remaining members, later known perjoratively as the 'Rump', then set about putting the English Revolution into practice. Hopes were high of achieving great changes in religion, in the law and in Parliamentary and social reform. Some radicals returned from the New World excited by the revolutionary possibilities. Others believed that events ushered in the Second Coming of Christ and that the rule of the Saints was imminent. All revolutions have their moments of heady idealism and in England this moment was in December 1648.

The first problem facing the Rump was what to do with the King. The logic of the situation was simple. Charles had fought a Civil War and lost. By attempting an accommodation with nearly all his opponents separately he had lost the trust and the support of all of them. And whilst alive he acted as a focus for resistance to the new regime and a threat to the progress of the revolution itself. Now was the time for him to pay the price. But men held back from the pull of this logic. Not only was the King 'God's anointed' on earth, but standing at the peak of the social pyramid around which society was built, his removal would open up the way for the whole hierarchy to be turned upside down. If Parliament could remove the King, could not servants disobey their masters and wives their husbands? It was difficult to imagine what social anarchy would ensue.

It was these fears that held men back from the course of action that seems inevitable from the vantage point of three hundred and fifty years later. The dilemma that faced the Army and the remaining members of the purged Parliament at the end of 1648 has been faced by many other revolutionary councils since, such as the Girondins in France and the Bolsheviks in Russia. In France in 1793 and in Russia in 1918 the survival of the monarch came to be a thorn in the side of revolutionary progress. In Romania in December 1989, the survival of Ceausescu threatened to undermine all the work of the people's revolution and to act as a rallying point for counter-revolution. But in Romania, as in other situations, the problem was how to remove the leader whilst keeping some semblance of legality about the proceedings. In January 1649, Parliament, egged on by the Army, set the precedent that other revolutionaries were to follow in succeeding centuries.

On 1 January 1649, the remaining members of the House of Commons passed an ordinance for the trial of Charles I. When the House of Lords refused to go along with this, the purged House of Commons responded with a resolution declaring 'that the Commons of England in Parliament assembled do declare that the people are, under God, the original of all just power; and do also declare that the Commons of England in Parliament assembled, being chosen by and representing the people, have the supreme power in this nation'. A High Court of Justice of 135 members was established to try and to judge Charles. The original intention was that the Lord Chief Justice of England would preside over

Lord President Bradshaw of ye High Court of Justice yt condemned Charles I.st to death. Hugh Peters By Dobson

the tribunal but he refused and it proved difficult to find anyone willing to take on the job. Eventually, a relatively obscure provincial judge known for his republican sympathies, John Bradshaw, was appointed as President. After much discussion about procedure, the trial of the King began on 20 January in the awesome setting of Westminster Hall. Throughout the period of the trial security was intense as it was feared that there would be an attempt to rescue the King. Guards were posted on roofs, cellars were searched for bombs. Bradshaw wore a steel-lined hat in case an attempt was made to assassinate him.

It is often claimed that the King's trial was an empty charade carried out by a tiny minority. There is some truth in this. But in other ways the trial is fascinating and the arguments heard there have echoed down through history ever since. The first problem faced by the prosecutors was, what could the King be accused of? Since the fourteenth century, treason had been defined as hostility to, or making war, upon the King. How could Charles be accused of making war against himself? Here Parliament came up with a new definition of treason, reversing the traditional meaning by declaring that 'it is treason in the King of England...to levy war against the Parliament and Kingdom of England.' This was one of the central points at dispute throughout the trial: could the Head of State be tried by law or was he above the law?

For Charles the issues were clear. The King was God's representative on earth and the Bible called upon all subjects to obey their King. It was the King who gave expression to the law through his judgements and therefore the House of Commons, who were in any case not a court, could not create a court of justice

Peter Lely's portrait of the regicides John Bradshaw and Hugh Peters.

The Trial of the King

Lord President. Sir...How great a friend you have been to the laws and liberties of the people, let all England and the world judge.

The King. Sir, under favour, it was the liberty, freedom, and laws of the subject that ever I took – defended myself with arms. I never took up arms against the people, but for the laws.

Lord President. The command of the court must be obeyed. No answer will be given to the charge.

The King. Well, sir.

The King was not permitted to speak in his own defence, although he had prepared this text:

Having already made my protestations, not only against the illegality of this court, but also that no earthly power can justly call me (who am your King) in question as a delinquent, I would not any more open my mouth upon this occasion more than to refer myself to what I have spoken were I in this case alone concerned. But the duty I owe to God in the preservation of the true liberty of my people will not suffer me at this time to be silent. For how can any freeborn subject of England call life or anything he possesses his own, if power without right daily make new and abrogate the old fundamental law of the land, which I now take to be the present case...I will show you the reason why I am confident you cannot judge me, nor indeed the meanest man in England. For I will not (like you) without showing a reason seek to impose a belief upon my subjects.

There is no proceeding [that is] just against any man but what is warranted either by God's laws or the municipal laws of the country where he lives...

Besides all this, the peace of the kingdom is not the least in my thoughts. And what hope of settlement is there, so long as power reigns without rule or law, changing the whole frame of that government under which this kingdom has flourished for many hundred years? Nor will I say what will fall out in case this lawless, unjust proceeding against me do go on. And believe it, the Commons of England will not thank you for this change, for they will remember how

happy they have been of late years under the reigns of Queen Elizabeth, the King my father, and myself, until the beginning of these unhappy troubles, and will have cause to doubt that they shall ever be so happy under any new. And by this time it will be too sensibly evident that the arms I took up were only to defend the fundamental laws of this kingdom against those who have supposed my power has totally changed the ancient government...

The next day, the Lord President, John Bradshaw, summed up:

Lord President. Sir, you spake very well of a precious thing that you call peace, and it had been much to be wished that God had put it into your heart that you had as effectually and really endeavoured and studied the peace of the kingdom as now in words you seem to pretend. But, as you were told

*The execution (previous page)
and death warrant (right) of Charles I.*

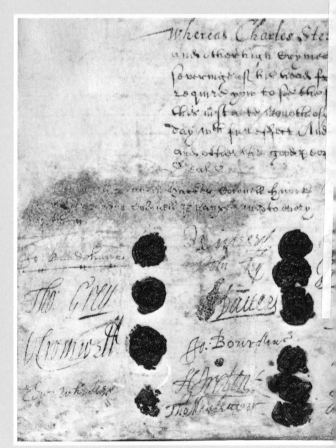

the other day, actions must expound intentions; your actions have been clean contrary...For, sir, you have held yourself and let fall such language as if you had been no ways subject to the law, or that the law had not been your superior. Sir, the court is very well sensible of it – and I hope so are all the understanding people of England – that the law is your superior, that you ought to have ruled according to the law – you ought to have done so. Sir, I know very well your pretence hath been that you have done so. But, sir, the difference hath been: who shall be the expositors of this law, sir? Whether you and your party, out of courts of justice, shall take upon them to expound the law, or the courts of law who are the expounders – nay the sovereign and highest court of justice, the Parliament of England, that is not only the sole expounder but the sole maker of the law...

But then sir, the weight that lies upon you in all those respects that have been spoke, by reason of your tyranny, treason, breach of trust, and the murders that have been committed, surely, sir, it must drive you into a sad consideration concerning your eternal condition...Sir, you said well to us the other day, you wished us to have God before our eyes. Truly, sir, I hope all of us have so. That God that we know is a King of Kings and Lord of Lords, that God with whom there is no respect of persons, that God that is the avenger of innocent blood – we have that God before us that does bestow a curse upon them that withhold their hands from shedding of blood, which is in the case of guilty malefactors and those that do deserve death...

Sir, I say for yourself we do heartily wish and desire that God would be pleased to give you a sense of your sins, that you would see wherein you have done amiss, that you may cry unto him that God would deliver you from bloodguiltiness...

The death sentence was passed.

The Eikon Basilike, *filled with symbolism and with the words of a martyr king.*

in which to try him. After the Charge of High Treason was read, Charles refused to plead one way or the other. He answered by saying: 'Remember, I am your King – your lawful King – and what sins you bring upon your heads and the judgement of God upon this land, think well upon it.'

Charles insisted that he was the only true guardian of the liberties of the people. Two days later, the King was again called upon to answer the charges. He refused, saying:

'A King cannot be tried by any superior jurisdiction on earth. But it is not my case alone – it is the freedom and the liberty of the people of England. And do you pretend what you will, I stand more for their liberties – for if power without law may make laws, may alter the fundamental laws of the kingdom, I do not know what that subject he is in England that can be sure of his life or anything that he calls his own. Therefore, when that I came here I did expect particular reasons to know by what law, what authority, you did proceed against me here…My reasons why – in conscience and the duty I owe to God first and my people next, for the preservation of their lives, liberties and estates – I conceive I cannot answer this till I be satisfied of the legality of it.'

When President Bradshaw interrupted the King and told him that prisoners should not require anything of the court, Charles snapped in response 'Prisoner? Sir, I am not an ordinary prisoner!'

Bradshaw refused to allow Charles to make the speech he had prepared in his defence but the speech was published a few days later. Still the King refused to recognise the jurisdiction of the court and challenged the basis on which the Commons could claim to represent the people of England. He rightly pointed out that not only was the House of Lords not present but also that many members of the Commons had been excluded by Pride's Purge. Charles claimed that anything the court did would threaten the welfare and the liberty of the people of England with a new form of tyranny.

The essence of the prosecution's case was presented by Bradshaw in his speech on 27 January. He claimed that the law was superior to anyone, including the King. As no more than someone holding an office in trust, the King was answerable to Parliament as 'the sovereign and highest court of justice…the sole maker of the law'. The influence of Leveller thinking was clear in Bradshaw's exposition of the case against Charles when he claimed that ultimate sovereignty rested with the people of England and that Parliament, the law and, of course, the Sovereign also, were finally answerable to the people. The outcome of the trial was a foregone conclusion. Sentence was pronounced:

'For all which treasons and crimes, this court doth adjudge that he, the said Charles Stuart, as a tyrant, traitor, murderer and public enemy to the good people of this nation, shall be put to death by the severing of his head from his body.'

With all the pressures involved and bearing in mind the speed of mounting the trial, the clarity with which both sides expressed their case was remarkable. The Parliamentary cause rested on the fact that there was a higher authority than the King and that Charles had fallen foul of this. The King's defence was not expressed in personal terms and his real success lay in defending the cause of the monarchy itself, thus ensuring its survival in the long run. The arguments Charles used in his defence haunted Englishmen for the next decade and, as many historians have observed, Charles's martyrdom was his finest moment. Although he had lived miserably he died magnificently.

Only fifty-nine members of the Court, less than half, actually signed the death warrant against Charles, but nonetheless the execution was carried out on 30 January 1649 on a scaffold erected outside the Banqueting Hall in Whitehall. It was here, in 1635, on the lavish ceiling of the Banqueting Hall that Charles had portrayed the grandeur of the Stuart dynasty and his glorious perception of kingship. It was here, fourteen years later, that he made his final speech. Wearing only his nightcap and a cloak, Charles protested his innocence to the last, claiming that he had not started the war, that Parliament had made war on

Cromwell

Oliver Cromwell had the most extraordinary of all English political careers. A minor Huntingdonshire farmer and gentleman, he spent the first forty years of his life in relative seclusion, away from the worlds of fighting and politics. Then in the late 1630s, with links to leading oppositionists, he began to find himself within the growing action against Charles I. Elected to the Long Parliament, he fought long and hard in the war, being one of the new brooms sweeping the Army back into shape. Historians still debate his motives and the drive behind his rise to fame and power. To what extent was Cromwell's impetuousness and temper the mainspring of his actions? Did he have a greed for power that was often divided against itself by a disdain for authority, or was he fortuitously on each occasion the right man in the right place at the right time? Evident to all, then and since, was Cromwell's firm conviction that God's Providence was working exclusively through him.

Cromwell has always brought out the strongest views and emotions. His steward John Maidstone described him most straightforwardly.

'His body was well compact and strong, his stature under six feet I believe about two inches, his head so shaped as you might see it a storehouse and shop, both of a vast treasury of natural parts...His temper was exceedingly fiery, as I have known; but...soon allayed...A larger soul hath seldom dwelt in a house of clay.'

Whereas Gerrard Winstanley in *The Law of Freedom* (1651) addressed Cromwell as one whom 'God hath honoured with the brightest honour of any man since Moses', and John Milton addressed his sonnet to 'Cromwell, our chief of men', others were less sure. A biography published soon after the Lord Protector's death by 'L.S.' found a disturbing ambiguity.

'We find in the beginning of England's distractions a most active instrument to carry on the cause for King and Parliament; this pretence holding water, and proving prosperous, he then became the main stickler for liberty of conscience without any limitation. This toleration became his masterpiece in politics; for it procured him a party that stuck close in all cases of necessity.'

L.S. thought that Cromwell's life showed 'policy and piety may both lie in a bed and not touch one another', the Essex clergyman Ralph Josselin recorded in his diary at the Lord Protector's death, 'Cromwell dead, the people not much minding it.' The disillusioned divine, Richard Baxter, looked back later with a more jaundiced eye. 'Cromwell meant honestly in the main, and was pious and conscionable in the main part of his life till prosperity and success corrupted him. Then his generous religious zeal gave way to ambition which increased as successes increased. When his successes had broken down all considerable opposition, then he was in the face of his strongest temptations, which conquered him when he had conquered others.'

John Dryden apostrophized Cromwell in his *Heroique Stanzas:*

His ashes in a peaceful urn shall rest
His name a great example stands to show
How strangely high endeavours may be blest,
Where piety and valour jointly go.

The strictures against Cromwell got ever-greater, support for him ever-smaller, until Thomas Carlyle in *On Heroes, Hero-Worship and the Heroic in History* (1841) began to think again.

'His dead body was hung in chains; his "place in History" – place in History, forsooth! – has been a place of ignominy, accusation, blackness and disgrace; and here, this day, who knows if it is not rash in me to be among the first that ever ventured to pronounce him not a knave and liar, but a genuinely honest man! Peace to him. Did he not, in spite of all, accomplish much for us?...Let the Hero rest. It was to men's judgement that he appealed: nor have men judged him very well.'

Oliver Cromwell, attended by Fame, tramples on Error and Faction in a print of 1658.

*Oliver Cromwell,
portrayed 'warts and all'
in terracotta.*

him. He maintained his belief in the Crown's superiority over the law to the end. 'A subject and a sovereign are clean different things,' he claimed. Minutes later the axe came down and in a single blow severed his head from his body. The executioner held up the head and showed it to the crowd that had gathered in Whitehall.

In March, the Rump of Parliament backed by the army abolished the House of Lords calling it 'useless and dangerous'. The monarchy was formally abolished at the same time as being 'unnecessary, burdensome and dangerous to the liberty, safety and public interest of the people'. The nation was now to be called 'the Commonwealth and free state' of England. The next decade was the only period in the last 1,500 years of history during which Britain was a republic. This epoch is indelibly associated with one man, Oliver Cromwell, and his figure straddles the decade like a colossus leaving his influence on the whole course of British history.

Cromwell had arrived late to the events of December 1648 and January 1649. He missed the beginning of the debate on the Army's Remonstrance, having dallied at the siege of Pontefract, and it is probable that he delayed his return to London in December in order to avoid being directly implicated in the purge of Parliament. But during the private meetings of the High Court, he became a dominant voice, rallying doubters and encouraging supporters. This ambivalent behaviour of Cromwell has led to many accusations against him. He has been charged with overwhelming ambition but also with indecisiveness and a desire to avoid the awkward moment. Furthermore, his political career is littered with what has been called the betrayal of his one-time colleagues. However, his

Accommodation to the new regime

Although the antiquary John Selden said 'the wisest way for men in these times is to say nothing', and withdrew from public life, the pamphlet war continued after the fighting had ceased and the King had been executed in 1649. One of the greatest questions was the legitimacy of the government which had replaced the King, and how far Parliament's rule would be heeded. The Engagement Oath of 2 January 1650 was designed to secure loyalty to the Rump Parliament – which was the vestige of the body that had waged war against the King, had been keenly divided within itself on the question of trying and then executing Charles, and had subsequently abolished the 'kingly office' which was undoubtedly an unpopular move within the nation at large.

Anthony Ascham, who helped lead the moves to try the King, and was assassinated in Madrid in 1650 where he went as the Commonwealth's ambassador, wrote in defence of the legitimacy of the new regime – and of self-interest.

'There is a war for dominion, and a war for possession. If it be for dominion, we may contribute our money, arms and oaths to the expelling perhaps of an innocent family. If it be for possession (which is the worst), then it is for the slavery of thousands of innocent families. And before either can be com-passed, we may assure ourselves that thousands may be as innocently killed by the means of them who contribute to the strengthening of an unjust party. But because I state this question in a war already formed, and actually introduced upon the people, therefore in answer to this positive demand, I as positively say, *that for a justifiable obedience, it is best, and enough, for us to consider whether the invading party have us and the means of our subsistence in his possession, or no*'.

Many more pamphlet voices were raised against the legitimacy of the new regime. An anonymous 'godly minister in Lancashire' spoke for many in 1650 against the Engagement Oath.

'I consider if men at their inition and settlement will walk so arbitrarily, and domineer with so high a hand, what will they do (may we expect) when they come to a full settlement, by the consent of all the people of the nation?

'The grieving and troubling the hearts and consciences, not of loose, perverse and seditious, but of grave, sober, pious and peaceable men is made nothing of; but they are trampled upon, and wholly neglected, whilst many atheists, Cavaliers, and base wretches that will take the Engagement, are embraced, privileged and respected.'

The oak became one of the enduring symbols of England and the restored Crown. Here, Cromwell is shown destroying the native tree.

political life shows one underlying consistency. He would never act until he could discern what he took to be the will of God in a particular situation. Sometimes it would take time for him to make up his mind, sometimes he would need some external event to signify to him God's intention. He would deliberate until certain of his view but then act forcefully and without hesitation. He was a man of action but not before he was convinced of the rightness of his action.

The spirituality that motivated Cromwell from the early 1630s was the guiding force in his life. He was constantly quoting the Bible and he called himself a 'seeker'. He did not know exactly what God intended for him or for England but he knew that God intended something. And as one who believed passionately in the need for a moral reformation he grew convinced that England had been chosen to shine God's light as a beacon for others. For him, military victories were a sign of God's pleasure. His fury against Charles for fighting the Second Civil War was because he believed Charles had failed to understand God's message in bringing victory to Parliament, and that a return to war was contrary to divine judgement. Although he was a Parliamentarian, when it seemed to him that Parliament was being led astray he could soon shift his allegiance and support to the Army when he believed it was more likely to advance the cause of the godly. This pragmatism did not make him popular and it certainly did not make it easy to predict his actions. But it lay at the source of his energy and at the root of his motivation. The next ten years of history belong to Cromwell.

Drogheda

All that can be done here is to sketch out the complex story of the years following the execution of Charles. The events of the decade of the 1650s are described only as a working out of the story of the conflict of the 1640s and one thing soon became clear: the execution of Charles had solved nothing. It was the great dramatic climax in the theatre of constitutional change that was going on in England but contemporaries at home and abroad were shocked by the act. It never commanded more than minority support and the major weakness of the Commonwealth was that it started life with the backing of only a small minority of Englishmen. Many centuries later, Mao Tse-Tung wrote that 'political power lies in the barrel of a gun'. With the Army as the ultimate source of authority in the 1650s, never was this slogan more true to English history than in this decade.

Weak and insecure, the first task facing the leaders of the infant Commonwealth was to defeat the foes surrounding its borders. Accordingly, Cromwell turned first to Ireland where the rebellion against English rule had continued in a desultory fashion throughout the Civil Wars. With the accounts of the massacre of Protestant settlers by the natives in 1641 still ringing in his ears, Cromwell arrived in Dublin in August 1649 with an army of 15,000 men, all well trained and experienced veterans. His first action was against the town of Drogheda which straddled the road north and where many English Royalists held out. Cromwell laid siege to Drogheda which continued to resist but his superior firepower soon won the day. What followed was one of the worst atrocities in the entire period of the Civil War. The garrison and many civilians, almost 3,000 people in all, were put to the sword and the few

'Cromwell came over, and like a lightning passed through the land', Bishop Nicholas French wrote from exile after leaving Ireland in the wake of the Cromwellian conquest. The first shaft of lightning was to be directed against the town of Drogheda, twenty-five miles to the north of Dublin. There were 2,600 men garrisoned there, with few provisions and little ammunition. On 3 September 1649 Cromwell's forces arrived, an army of 10,000 men. After a week-long siege, and a call to surrender had been sent out and was refused, the bombardment began. By late afternoon the next day entry was forced into the town, and the army moved in. Cromwell had ordered that no quarter was to be given – an order he later said he gave 'in the heat of the action' since he had lost many men in the storming of the town, and the governor Sir Arthur Aston, his officers and over 2,000 others were put to the sword. Many were non-combatants, like the friars who all died. The next day two forts were brought to submit, and the few who survived this carnage were transported to Barbados.

Drogheda, scene of the bloodiest massacre.

Cromwell himself claimed that the agony of blood-letting Drogheda had suffered 'will tend to prevent the effusion of blood for the future, which are the satisfactory grounds to such actions, which otherwise cannot but work remorse and regret.' By the strict rules of war, Cromwell had been entitled to show no mercy, since he had offered terms of surrender which had been refused. Elsewhere, he had tempered those rules with humanity, but at Drogheda and almost immediately after at Wexford the carnage had been almost total. In the context of what had been happening on the Continent in the previous thirty years, Drogheda and Wexford did not weigh very heavily in the scale of atrocities; but in the context of the Civil Wars in the British Isles they were vicious indeed. Although there was some lessening of resistance, other towns continued to hold out against the Cromwellian forces; but Irish resistance had almost entirely disintegrated by the time Cromwell was recalled in May 1650, and the conquest was complete in 1653. The damage had been done. Many had died, towns and countryside had been laid waste, and Oliver Cromwell had become one of the most hated figures in Ireland's history.

A Cromwellian edict for Ireland, with the Lord Protector's portrait and the Commonwealth arms in place of the King's.

survivors were transported to the West Indies. Strictly according to the rules of war, Cromwell's behaviour was acceptable. He had warned the defenders of the consequences of prolonged resistance. But the massacre at Drogheda was quite unlike anything that had occurred before in the Civil War. It can only be explained by attempting to understand Cromwell's contempt for the Irish and his sense of Protestant vengeance for 1641. Cromwell wrote of the massacre to Parliament saying:

> 'I wish that all honest hearts may give the glory of this to God alone, to whom indeed the praise of this mercy belongs...I am persuaded that this is a righteous judgement of God upon those barbarous wretches who have imbrued their hands with so much innocent blood.'

The massacre at Drogheda was followed by another, a month later, at Wexford which had long been a rebel town. Here 2,000 Irish were put to the sword against twenty of Cromwell's men killed. If the intention had been to terrorize the Irish into submission, Cromwell was certainly successful. In a whirlwind campaign the towns of Ulster and Munster surrendered before his advancing army. Only Connaught in the west remained outside English control when in May 1650 Cromwell left Ireland. Following his departure came massive land

A King in exile

After a year and a half away, Charles II was smuggled back to the Continent after his failure to regain his throne and the humiliation of Worcester. With him went much hope of active royalist conspiracy in England; although plots continued and occasionally flared up, or were intercepted by the Cromwellian espionage system, no great rising was to occur. Instead, Charles was consigned to nine long years of penury, dragging himself and his apology for a court around France, Germany and the Low Countries, trying to make ends meet with little or no means, and keeping his mother at arm's length.

The most important man at Charles' side throughout the exile was Edward Hyde, to be rewarded as Earl of Clarendon after the Restoration, who in late 1652 found himself unable to pay for a fire or buy warm clothes, and only ate one meal a day. The King was kept warm by a succession of mistresses. A pension for Charles from the French crown proved meagre in sum and usually tardy in payment, while occasional collections from royalists at home pro-

vided some funds. In July 1654 Charles removed himself to the German states, to take the waters at Aachen, and to settle in Cologne. Apart from the occasional treat, the court's straitened financial circumstances continued there. So did the plotting with royalists and disaffected elements in England and Scotland – often, Charles (following in his father's footsteps) adopted parallel policies hoping one would work, but alienating many in the process. The arrest of many of his supporters in the secret Sealed Knot society after plots had failed in 1654, and the failure of the 1655 rising, put paid to most hopes of regaining the throne through some counter-coup.

In 1656 Charles gained the support of Spain, in return for various promises including the return of parts of their empire which Cromwell was attacking. He became the client of another foreign power; but as the 1650s ground on, the prospect of a restoration brightened, and by 1659 Charles was waiting for the call in the Low Countries.

Charles II hiding in the oak tree at Boscobel, after defeat at Worcester.

confiscations and the beginning of the vast transfer of land that left much of Ireland in English Protestant hands for centuries to come. Essentially, Cromwell had been motivated by strategic considerations, to prevent Ireland from threatening the 'back door' of England. But his behaviour towards the Irish was governed by his sense of Protestant mission. He wrote: 'If ever men were engaged in a righteous cause in the world, this will scarce be a second to it...We come by the assistance of God, to hold forth and maintain the lustre and glory of English liberty in a nation where we have an undoubted right to it.' Although he spent only nine months in Ireland, Cromwell remained for centuries a villain in the Irish folk-memory. Generations of Irish boys and girls were brought up knowing Cromwell as a bogey-man. 'Cromwell will catch you' they were warned if they misbehaved. Cromwell's brief reign of terror was long to be remembered in Ireland.

Cromwell returned to England because of a new threat from Scotland. The Scots were particularly incensed by the execution by the English of Charles, whom they regarded as *their* King, without their even being consulted by Parliament. They had recognized Charles's eldest son as King and in June 1650 Charles II landed north of Aberdeen. He received a warm welcome as he marched south. In London, the Council of State debated sending an expedition against Scotland. Fairfax refused to lead it and instead chose to retire. His contribution to Parliament's military victory in the 1640s had been supreme. But now he leaves the story and Cromwell was appointed Commander-in-Chief. In July he marched north with an army of 5,000 horse and 10,000 foot.

Cromwell's army made contact with the larger Scots army led by David Leslie. After several weeks of manoeuvring Cromwell finally found himself caught with his back to the sea at Dunbar. Before dawn on 3 September 1650, Cromwell launched a daring attack uphill against the superior numbers of the Scots army. It was the only way of getting out of his impossible situation. His desparate plan worked and Cromwell routed the Scots and marched on to Edinburgh. After the battle of Dunbar Cromwell is said to have laughed hysterically for hours. His victory against all odds and expectations was another sign to him of divine

Western designs

Providence and partisanship, it has been said, pushed Cromwell westwards in his colonial plans of conquest, of which the most significant fruit by far was the capture of Jamaica from Spain. Spain was the old, Catholic enemy, and it had been made the more inimical by its protection of Charles II after 1656. The West Indies offered hopes of gold and empire, and Jamaica's sugar, indigo and tobacco plantations and slaves were wrested from the Spanish in an action in 1655. Despite two Spanish attempts to regain the island, the English held fast. Edward Doyley, the English commander, recounted a whole series of episodes showing how, in the taking of Jamaica, a bountiful God was on the side of Protestantism. The Governor of Puerto Rico, for example, who had been preparing a counter-attack and unsuccessfully attempting to capture Englishmen on the Dutch island of Tortula, 'was on his return cast away by the hurricane, only one mulatto escaped'. Moreover, some [Spaniards] are come in to us almost starved, the Negroes formerly their slaves using them roughly, and denying them provisions...I shall not fail in my endeavours to prepare for their coming [again], and doubt not, but that the King of Spain's lessening his garrisons, may in time produce good effect to our nation.'

providence. But one military victory was not enough to defeat the Scots and as more recruits flooded in, Charles II was crowned at Scone on 1 January 1651. Another Scots army led by the new King finally advanced across the border in August 1651 and cautiously moved south, harried by the English militias as it went. Finally Cromwell with an army of some 30,000 men confronted Charles with his depleted force of 12,000 outside Worcester. On the afternoon of 3 September, a year after his victory at Dunbar, Cromwell's army engaged the Scots and after 'as stiff a contest, for four or five hours, as I have ever seen', the Scots were defeated. The Duke of Hamilton died of his wounds, Leslie and the other generals were captured and taken to the Tower. The Earl of Derby was convicted of high treason and was executed. Charles escaped and spent six weeks on the run trying to evade capture before finally slipping away from Brighton on 14 October to France. The battle of Worcester was the last battle of the Civil War.

It now seemed as if the security of the Commonwealth was assured and Cromwell returned to the Rump Parliament. One striking success of the Rump, as of all the republican governments of the 1650s, was in the area of foreign policy. The new republic followed a commercially aggressive policy that brought it to war initially with the Protestant Netherlands and finally with Catholic Spain. All the deliberations of the decade must be seen in the context of an adventurous but also costly foreign policy that brought immense gains overseas, in Europe, in the Baltic, in Africa and in the West Indies. These new connections generated commercial interests that were to be long-lasting.

However, on the domestic front the Rump was beset with problems it seemed unable to solve. The countryside was still racked with disorder and a series of bad harvests drove prices up. Everywhere there was scarcity. Few of the local gentry families across England, the families from which the magistracy were drawn, gave the Rump much support. Hence there was a drive to impose centralized control throughout the country. In 1650 all office holders and ministers had to take the Engagement to the Commonwealth. Local magistrates who refused were replaced, frequently by army officers whose loyalty to the new regime was more certain. In 1652 the Rump revoked all the town charters and tried to remove the last vestiges of Royalist control over the municipalities. Some towns like Bristol, Taunton and Hull passed to radical Puritan control. But in many others one oligarchy was replaced by another with very little in the way of real change.

As a reforming body, the Rump failed to live up to its revolutionary expectations. In religion a form of toleration was established. Adultery was made punishable by death. Strict observance of the Sabbath was made compulsory and there was an attempt to stamp out blasphemy and swearing. But nothing was done to change the economics of the church and no attempt was made to tackle the old bugbear of tithes. The lawyers in the Rump managed to frustrate any attempts at legal reform and, despite harsh economic difficulties in the countryside, little was done to reform the Poor Laws.

In April 1653 members of the Rump began to discuss plans to retain their own seats in perpetuity. The radicals felt that it was not living up to its promise and that a more godly body was called for. In a fit of rage, Cromwell dissolved the Rump, declaring 'You have sat too long here for any good you have been doing.

The Rump

The Rump Parliament was greeted with glee by those left inside, with outrage by those excluded – 'the highest and most detestable force and breach of privilege and freedom ever offered to any Parliament of England' one former member called it, who felt that events had come a very long way since Charles had attempted to arrest the Five Members. It was, as one pamphleteer called it, *The Parliament under the power of the sword*, 'the converting of our well-regulated Monarchy into a military Anarchy, with a popular Parliament only at the beck of the Army.'

Professor David Underdown, whose research into the purge of the members of the Long Parliament showed clearly how the Presbyterian and accommodating elements were excluded, described the Rump that governed the new republic until Oliver Cromwell threw it out in 1653 as 'a curious blend of religious and republican zealots, self-interested time-servers, and erstwhile Presbyterians, many of them as ferociously repressive of radical former friends as of monarchist enemies.' Yet what the Rump clearly believed it stood for was liberty, and liberty which had overcome the divine right absolutism of the previous Stuart reigns. Speaker Lenthall, survivor of the King's intrusion in January 1642, hailed the Commonwealth as 'the perfect recovery of the liberties lost in that long succession of tyranny'. The new great seal of England showed the map of the nation on one side and Parliament in session on the other, with the inscription 'In the first year of freedom by God's blessing restored'. Few believed then that freedom had been restored, and their numbers were to shrink rapidly.

The Rump and dreggs of the house of Com remaining after the good members were purged out.

The Rump, satirized.

Depart, I say, and let us have done with you in the name of God, go!' Thus ended the story of the first twelve years of the Long Parliament that had been reluctantly called by the King in November 1640. Cromwell noted that few mourned its passsing, observing 'There was not so much as the barking of a dog, or any general or visible repining at it.'

Cromwell knew that open elections would probably return Presbyterians and crypto-royalists and so he drew up a list of 140 men nominated by the army leaders and by the Independent congregational churches. Cromwell summoned them in July and they voted to form a new Parliament. This body became known as the Barebones Parliament, which was intended as a derisory sneer against its social composition as exemplified by one of its members, Praise-God Barbon, a London Baptist leatherseller. The possibility of radical religious reform, including the abolition of tithes, a proposal to abolish excise duty,

Praisegod Barebones, whose assembly was satirically dignified with the title of a parliament.

The Picture of the Good Old Cauſe drawn to the Life

In the *Effigies* of Maſter *PRAISE-GOD BAREBONE.*

WITH

Several Examples of Gods Judgements on ſome Eminent Engagers againſt Kingly Government.

1. Doriſlaus, *one that had a great hand in the Kings murther, was ſtab'd at the* Hague *in* March 1649. *when he was ſent to treat with the* Dutch *in the name of the Free-State or Common-wealth of* England.
2. Anthony Aſcham *ſerved in the like manner at* Madrid *in* Spain, *near the ſame time, being ſent from the* Rump *on the like errand.*
3. Milton *that writ two Books againſt the Kings, and* Salmaſius *his Defence of Kings, ſtruck totally blind, he being not much above* 40. *years old.*
4. *Alderman* Hoyle *of* York, *one of the Juncto, and high Court of Juſtice, and (though he ſigned not the Kings Sentence) the ſame day twelve moneth, the King was murthered, hanged himſelf in his Chamber at* Weſtminſter.
5. *Sir* Gregory Norton *died raving mad, which by his Phyſicians was not imputed to the diſtemper of his body, but a troubled, diſquieted mind; He was one of the Kings Judges.*

The Portraiture of Mr Praiſe God Barebone

6. Lockier, *once an Agitator in the Army, at his late Majeſties pretended Triall, ſpit* Jew-like *in the Kings Face, and likewiſe blew Tobacco-Aſhes upon him; Afterwards turned* Leveller, *and was ſhot to death by his* Fellow-Rogues *in Saint* Pauls *Church-yard.*
7. Collonel Ven, *a Citizen of* London, *formerly a great Profeſſour of Religion, but turned with the Times, was a Member of the* Rump, *a great Engager againſt Kingly Government, on* July the 7. 1650. *He going to bed as perfectly well and in health, as ever in his life, his Wife lying by him, he fell aſleep by her immediately, and ſlept ſoundly without complaint of the leaſt diſtemper, but the next morning about 6 a Clock, his Wife found him ſtark dead by her, never having made the leaſt groan, or ſpoken one word to her ſince the day before; and thus God baniſhed him firſt out of the Land of the Living.*

Many more inſtances may be given, but I am loth to be too tedious.

OUr late modern Saints (as if *Guy Fawkes* ſtood for a Lobber in our *Engliſh Calender*) have canonized themſelves in ſuch a Rubrick of blood, that the very Enemies of Chriſtian Religion would have relented at, and meer humanity regretted: ſuch an univerſal quarrel againſt Government, Order, all Divine Inſtitution, ſuch impudent affront and bold contempt of Authority, and the Sacred Majeſty of Kings was never before heard of. Nor did the moſt deſperate Heretiques, (no not that accurſed *Munſter* crue,) or the moſt ſavage Heathen ever deſign or attempt the quarter of the Villanies committed by our *godly party* within this 20. years: Inſomuch, that they have brought not only the Proteſtant Catholique Religion, but the very Chriſtian Faith, Divine Truth it ſelf, to contempt and deriſion.

Neither have they palliated only theſe audacious facinorous Practices under the diſguiſe of religion, but avowedly maintained their deſtructive Principles to be conſiſtent and agreeable with it, and entitled God and his Providence to all their moſt Horrid and execrable actions, daring the Face of the Sun with their Egyptian darkneſs, and crying liberty and reformation, when there was nothing but ſlavery and confuſion.

The *præludium* of theſe miſcheifs, was begun by the zealous Puritans, they quarrel at the Biſhops Surplices, and Lawn-ſleeves, and their ſacrilegious brood ſtrip them of their very ſhirts, and rob God and the Church of its revenue, and his Miniſters of all manner of ſubſiſtence. From hence came the Title of gifted Brethren; when a prevailing corrupt party of the late long parliament divided the ſpoils of the Church among their *Corahs* and *Abirams*: it was the *corban* of Religion that furniſhed our *Holders forth* with canting and jugling Doctrines and Uſes.

We had alſo ſome of a higher form, the Brethren that were above Ordinances, people inſpired as full of deviliſh Revelations as any blown bladder; this was the ſeventh Son, the laſt and worſt Devil, the very expreſs image and picture of a Non-Conformiſt, that could do miracles, all but blowing wind in the *Rump* to have preſerved it from periſhing.

The Perſon preſented here to your view, is one, or rather all of theſe ſorts, that have ſo much infeſted and infamed our Age and Countrey, was a diſpenſer during the perſecution of the Biſhops, (as they call'd it) when Truth ran into their corners, *and could never be ſeen again among them*, and Satan learnt them *Profeſſion* was as convenient. Yea verily beloved, this is he, although he look like a ſimple skin, he is a Wolf in ſheeps cloathing, a hide bound covetous Leatherſeller, but has a Conſcience as wide as his windows, when it raind ſtones into them at the funeral Pile of the *Rump*. You would take his cloudy face for a vizard if you knew not his black ſoul within him, and that Nature did her beſt in it to expreſs him to the life. I cannot better pourtrait his mind then by the enſuing Petition, where you will find the ſubſtance and abridgement of *Puritaniſme* in its natural and compleat dreſs, and this was the *Embrio* and baſe iſſue of his Trayterous deſign.

Mr. PRAISE-GOD BAREBONE his Petition, as it was preſented to the *Rump-Parliament*, Thurſday the ninth of *February*, 1659. In behalf of himſelf and many Thouſands. With their Anſwer thereunto.

To the *Parliament* of the Common-wealth of *England, &c.*

The Repreſentation and addreſs of the Well-affected Perſons, Inhabitants of the Cities of London *and* Weſtminſter, *and places adjacent, being faithful and conſtant Adherers to this* Parliament, *who are reſolved (by the aſſiſtance of Almighty God) to ſtand by, aſſert and maintain their Authority, againſt all Oppoſers, notwithſtanding the preſent confidence and bold attempts of the Promoters of Regal Intereſt, by the declared Enemies of their Cauſe and Authority.*

WHereas the good Old Cauſe was for Civil and Chriſtian Liberty againſt Oppreſſion and Perſecution; the Oppreſſors and Perſecutors were chiefly the King, his Lords, and Clergy, and their Adherents; who to effect their Deſigns, raiſed War againſt the Parliament: whereupon the Parliament in defence of Civil and Chriſtian Liberty, call the oppreſſed and perſecuted to their aid, by whoſe aſſiſtance the oppreſſors & perſecutors have been ſubdued, Kingſhip and Peerage aboliſhed, and Perſecution checkt; by which, the number of conſcientious friends to the Parliament have been ſo exceedingly encreaſed, that they are now (by Gods aſſiſtance) in a far more able capacity of keeping down their Enemies, then they were in thoſe times when they ſubdued them.

Neverthelеſs, ſo watchful hath the reſtleſs Enemy been to make advantage, that what (time after time) he hath loſt in the Field, he hath endeavoured to regain, even in the Parliaments Councel. Where, becauſe they had not the Face openly to bring in the King with the former Oppreſſions and perſecutions, they Shrouded and Vailed themſelves, one while under a Perſonal Treaty; Another while, under a Cloak of Zeal againſt Blaſphemy and Hereſie; their endeavour being to bring in the King upon any tearms; to cheriſh the perſecuting Party, and to Brow-beat their moſt conſcientious Oppoſers.

Upon which pretences, nevertheleſs they have through tract of Time, and the unſettledneſs of Government, prevailed ſo far, as under the Notion of a Moderate party, to get the ſubtilleſt of their Friends into many places of Truſt and Command both Civil and Military; through whoſe countenance and encouragement, albeit the Parliament upon good grounds Voted the Government by Kings and Lords, uſeleſs, burthenſome and dangerous, and declare very largely for Liberty of Conſcience; yet of late, a general boldneſſe hath bin taken to plead a neceſſity of returning to the Government of King and Lords, a taking in of the Kings Son, or which is all one, for a return of the juſtly ſecluded Members, or a Free Parliament, without due Qualifications, whereby the good Old Cauſe of Liberty and Freedom (ſo long contended for, againſt Regal Intereſt, with the expence of much blood and Treaſure) and the Aſſertors thereof will be proſtituted to ſatisfie the Luſts of the Enemies of the Common-wealth; wherein they have prevailed ſo far, that unleſs all conſcientious perſons in Parliament, Army, Navy, and Common-wealth, do ſpeedily unite, and watchfully look about them; as the Sword will certainly (though ſecretly and ſilently) be ſtollen out of their hands, ſo alſo will they find all Civil Authority fall ſuddenly into the hands of their enraged Enemies, and a return of all thoſe Violences, Oppreſſions and Perſecutions, which have coſt ſo much Blood and Treaſure to extirpate.

The ſerious apprehenſions whereof hath ſtirred up your cordial Friends to deſire you to uſe all poſſible endeavours to prevent the Common-wealths Adverſaries in this their moſt dangerous Stratagem; And as the moſt effectual means thereunto, We pray,

1. That you will admit no perſon or perſons to ſit or Vote in this, or any future Parliament or Council of State, or to be in any Office or Judicatory, or any publick Truſt in the Common-wealth, or Command in the Army, Navy, or Garriſons, or to be a publick Preacher to the people at Sea or Land or any Inſtructer of Youth, except ſuch only as ſhall abjure, or by Solemn Engagement renounce the pretended Title or Titles of *Charles Stuart* and the whole Line of the late King *James* and of every other perſon as a ſingle perſon pretending, or which ſhall pretend to the Crown or Government of theſe Nations of *England, Scotland* and *Ireland*, or any of them, and the Dominions and Territories belonging to them, or any of them, or any other ſingle perſon, Kingſhip Peerage, or any power co-ordinate with the peoples Repreſentatives in Parliament; And all coercive power in matter of Religion, according to a Vote of a Grand Committee of the 11. of *September*, 1659.

2. We further pray, that it may be Enacted, That whoſoever ſhal move, offer, or propound in Parliament, Councel or in any other Court or Publick Meeting, any matter or thing in order to the introducing of *Charles Stuart*, or any of that Family, as aforeſaid; or any other ſingle Perſon, Houſe of Lords coercive power in matter of Religion, or any power co-ordinate with the peoples Repreſentatives in Parliament, may be deemed and adjudged guilty of high Treaſon, and may ſuffer the pains and penalty thereof. And that whoſoever ſhall in Parliament, Councel, or any other publique Court, or Meeting, move for, or propoſe the Revocation of this Law (when by you enacted) may be deemed and judged guilty of high Treaſon, and ſuffer the pains and penalties thereof.

In proſecution whereof, we ſhall ſtand by you with our Eſtates and Lives, to aſſert and maintain your Authority againſt all Oppoſitions whatſoever, notwithſtanding the preſent Confidence and bold Attempts of yours and our Enemies.

Signed *Praiſe-God Barebone*, with the promiſe of the Subſcriptions of many Thouſands.

Reſolved by the Parliament, that the Petitioners have the Thanks of the Houſe for their Expreſſions of their good Affections to the Parliament.

The Petitioners being again called in, M. Speaker gave them this Anſwer.

Gentlemen, The Houſe have read your Petition, and they do find that you have been ſuch as have conſtantly born them good Affections, and that your Affections are the ſame ſtill: and for the Expreſſions of your good Affections, the Houſe hath commanded me to give you Thanks, in their Names I do give you Thanks, accordingly.

It is deſired, That all ſuch as are Lovers of the *Good Old Cauſe*, do ſend in their Subſcriptions to this Petition unto the place appointed in thoſe Papers that come to their Hands: Yea, and with all the ſpeed that may be, to teſtifie their Zeal to the *Good Old Cauſe*, by their being in readineſs to aſſert it.

See here the Quinteſſence of Treaſon not to be parallell'd in any times or perſons, but this did King *James* prophetically intimate in that uſual *Saying* of his no Biſhop, no King, as alſo is to be ſeen in his Βασιλικὸν Δῶρον directed to his Son *Hen.* Prince of *Wales*.

'In King *James's baſilicon Doron*, in theſe words he adviſes his Son, 'p. 41, 42. Take heed therefore my Son of theſe *Puritans*, the very 'Peſts in the Church and Common-wealth, whom no deſerts can 'oblige, neither Oaths nor promiſes bind, breathing nothing but 'Sedition and Calumnies, aſpiring without meaſure, railing without reaſon, and making their own imaginations (without any warrant of the word) the Square of their Conſcience.

'I proteſt before the great God (and ſince I am here, as upon my 'Teſtament, it is no place for me to lye in) that you ſhall 'never finde with any High-land or Border-Theeves greater ingratitude, and more lyes and viler perjuries, then among 'theſe PHANATICK Spirits, and ſuffer not the Principals of 'them to brook your Land, if you liſt to ſit at reſt, except you 'would keep them for trying your patience as *Socrates* did an evil 'wife, and in p. 40. *He ſaith*, I was often calumniated in their popular 'Sermons; Not for any vice or evil that was in me, *But becauſe I 'was a King, which to them is the higheſt evil.*

'Tis not to be doubted, that any the moſt ſpecious Pretences of Religion, any ſeeming extraordinary piety ſhall ever be able to ſhake our Allegiance; or that late poſterity will not with Horrour and Amazement *read the Hiſtory of our Age*, and yet it is queſtionable whether they will wonder more at theſe mens Treaſons, and deteſtable Impieties, or his moſt Sacred Majeſties Mercy and Clemency afforded in his General Pardon, to which this wretch hath already betaken himſelf.

London, Printed, And are to be ſold at divers Book-ſellers Shops, 1660. July 14 4

sweeping reforms in the law along with the acceleration of the appointment of radicals in the localities, all began to alarm the less zealous members. In December the conservative majority persuaded the assembly to surrender its powers to Cromwell as Lord-General, on the grounds that it was he who had called them into being.

A new constitution called the Instrument of Government, probably drafted by Major-General Lambert, was presented to Cromwell and he accepted it. In it Cromwell was given the position of Lord Protector. Protectors had been known before in England acting on behalf of kings who were under age and there was a temporary, *ad hoc* flavour to the title. It probably represented a compromise between those who wanted Cromwell to be made King and Cromwell's own refusal of the title which he had abolished only five years earlier, along with a widely held realization that the nation needed an individual to lead it in some form. The Lord Protector and his Council were given extensive powers, for instance to legislate without Parliament, far beyond anything that Charles I had ever demanded. A Parliament was to be summoned but not until September 1654 and in the meantime Cromwell and his Council busily set about passing laws and raising taxes under the authority of the Instrument.

The Protectorate Parliament consisted of 400 members for England and Wales and thirty each from Scotland and Ireland representing the creation of a single state within the British Isles. Fearful of parliamentary rights and privileges, the members refused to validate the Instrument and instead debated their own constitutional bill calling for government by a single person with regular parliaments. Without approving the funding to maintain the army and before a single act was passed, Cromwell dissolved the Parliament but continued to collect taxes, customs and excise. When the legality of these taxes was challenged by a merchant, George Cony, Cromwell was only able to obtain a favourable verdict against him by sacking a judge and prosecuting Cony's counsel. All this smacked far too much of Charles I's personal rule in the 1630s and the opposition to the collection of tunnage and poundage without parliamentary approval.

A small local uprising in Salisbury provoked fears of a Royalist plot to overthrow the Protectorate. As is often the case, those in charge of security exaggerated the danger and Cromwell's Secretary of State, John Thurloe, prepared countermeasures. The rising was the excuse used to usher in the next political experiment of the Protectorate. In 1655 the country was divided into eleven districts and a Major-General was appointed to govern each area. The Major-Generals had extensive powers and they set about training a new militia to be financed out of a tax popularly known as the 'decimation tax' on all royalists (because it was levied at the rate of 10 per cent). In addition the Major-Generals were given various duties with regard to the 'reformation of manners' and they attempted to suppress sports and control alehouses. This naked use of martial law was as deeply unpopular in England in 1655 as such regimes have been in Third World countries in the late twentieth century and the rule of the Major-Generals helped to damage further the reputation of Cromwell.

Another Parliament was called in 1656 but at its first meeting a hundred members were excluded on the grounds of being 'unfit persons'. Money was voted for a war with Spain, England's traditional enemy, but the House refused

Espionage

On 8 March 1655 Mr Bryan wrote to Mr Jackson a merchant in France:

'Sir. After I had received your orders to compound for your debts, I made all the haste conveniently I could hither, where I found all your accounts in such disorder by the absence of your friends, and the restraint of others who are bound for you, and the despair of those you addressed me to...I had almost forgot to tell you that your most faithful servant Knoply is not able to serve you for the present... because most of Mr Axford's family lives with him.'

This letter was intercepted, and the code easily broken. Jackson was the exiled King, Bryan one Daniel O'Neill, Knoply the county of Kent, Axford was the army. The letter concerned an attempted Royalist rising – the last to be attempted – and it was frustrated by incompetence, lack of will, and by the effective espionage network under John Thurloe, Cromwell's Secretary of State.

Civil War battles re-enacted by present-day enthusiasts often take place as the Sealed Knot – the name of the pro-Royalist conspirators for Charles II's restoration. Messages passed between England and the court, advising action or caution as circumstances dictated. This last attempt at insurrection was made by the exiles around the King, against the Sealed Knot's advice. The Protectorate's agents and spies were in every foreign capital and every port, and correspondence was regularly intercepted. The Earl of Rochester (the Restoration libertine's father), was the messenger for the plot from Paris. He landed secretly at Margate in late February 1655 and made his way to Yorkshire, despite the order of restraint sent out to ports and being questioned twice en route. But of 4,000 men expected to rally, symbolically at Marston Moor, only a hundred appeared. The plans were cancelled. Disguised as a Frenchman, in a fetching yellow wig, Rochester made his way back to London, where his talkativeness under the influence of drink in taverns compromised a number of his associates, who were arrested. Rochester gave authority the slip and reappeared at The Hague.

His success at evading capture suggests that the Cromwellian espionage system was perhaps not always quite so thorough. Nevertheless, one key to the continued survival of the regime was the network of spying, interception and correspondence which usually kept Cromwell and Thurloe one step ahead.

Andrew Marvell (above), Cromwell's political secretary, and Secretary of State Thurloe (below).

*Tumbledown Dick,
still commemorated in
the pub at Wortham,
Suffolk (opposite),
in the 1840s.*

to pass a bill continuing the militia under the Major-Generals. Stalemate was avoided by the moderate members who framed a Humble Petition and Advice to the Lord Protector, proposing yet another constitution. This new formula was a reversion to the old pattern of two Houses in Parliament, but now with members of the Upper House being nominated by the Protector. Its main initiative was to offer Cromwell the crown. The vast majority in Parliament called on Cromwell to accept. The Army fiercely opposed the offer. After much deliberation, Cromwell refused the crown but accepted most of the rest of the new constitution. But when the excluded members were readmitted to the next Parliament which met in January 1658 they immediately set about criticizing the very nature of the new arrangements and Cromwell angrily dissolved them in much the same way as he had dissolved the Rump and the earlier Protectorate Parliaments some years before.

In the summer of 1658 after a series of victories in foreign wars, the standing of the Republic in Europe had never been higher. The loyalty of the army to Cromwell also seemed certain. But still a way had not been found to balance the wishes of the radicals with the constitutionalism of the moderates. The cost of the foreign wars made the calling of another Parliament inevitable and yet stalemate between Parliament and Protector seemed unavoidable. It was in this context that Cromwell's health slowly worsened, and after the death of his favourite daughter from cancer he went into a fatal decline. Before he died on 3 September 1658 he nominated his eldest son, Richard, as his successor as he was entitled to do under the Humble Petition.

There has been much debate about whether the course of British history would have been different if Cromwell had lived several years longer or if he had nominated his younger son, Henry, a strong and determined governor of Ireland, or his son-in-law Fleetwood, who was second in command in the army as his successor. Certainly Richard was no match for the tasks facing him. But in fact events were already following an inexorable logic. When in the spring of 1659 Parliament set itself on a collision course with the army, the generals pressured Richard into dismissing his first Parliament. On 5 May the army restored the Rump and Richard retired into oblivion uttering his famous remark that he did not want to see 'a drop of blood' spilt over him. The Protectorate was replaced by a restored Commonwealth but after an initial few months of harmony, Parliament again fell out with the army who in October 1659 dissolved the Rump once more.

In the autumn of 1659 there was no legal civil government in Britain. On previous occasions, as when the Rump had first been dissolved, it was the stature of Cromwell that had enabled the basic tenets of government to continue, taxes to be collected and laws enforced. But this time there was no such universally respected figure. There was another frantic burst of pamphleteering with widespread debate about the nature of government. The City of London, which since 1640 had exerted a powerful Puritan and Parliamentarian influence on events, now refused to co-operate with the military government. With the threat of anarchy hanging over the nation the leader of the army in Scotland, General Monck, acted. Prompted partly by a request from some of the Council members, his army marched south to the border. General Lambert led an army north to oppose Monck. But no one now had the stomach for another civil war.

Tumbledown Dick

From the early 1650s Oliver Cromwell did as much as he could to make his government civilian rather than military, whatever the route he and his aides had taken to power. Many of his fellow-soldiers who had been victorious in war were increasingly disillusioned with the direction the Commonwealth was taking – when the Instrument of Government founded the Protectorate in 1654, and when after the Humble Petition and Advice Cromwell was given the right to name his successor in 1657. He chose his eldest son Richard. It signalled that he was establishing a dynasty; but it also indicated that he was choosing a civilian style, which shy and retiring Richard exemplified, rather than a militaristic. Cromwell's second son Henry, an accomplished soldier, would not have done.

Richard would not do either. Succeeding as Lord Protector after his father's death on 3 September 1658, he found himself caught between two extremes of policy. Trying to continue with greater vigour his father's policy of loosening the military's grip, he was confronted by his brother-in-law General Charles Fleetwood, the Commander-in-Chief. In a move reminiscent of many modern coups, army officers eased him from office in April 1659. To their consternation, the officers found their army still committed to the republican 'Good Old Cause', and in May they were forced to recall the Rump and re-establish a Commonwealth.

Richard has gone down in history as 'Tumbledown Dick', a nonentity after a strong father, and was still a joke in popular memory 200 years later. At the Restoration, Richard Cromwell took himself overseas, and from 1680 lived in retirement under an assumed name in Buckinghamshire until his death in 1712 on the eve of the end of the Stuart dynasty.

Richard Cromwell, 'Tumbledown Dick'.

In December 1659 the generals recalled the Rump again but Monck continued to march south and when he entered London in February 1660 there was no real doubt that he was in control and could impose a settlement. Monck's precise political motives are not clear although some historians have argued that he was driven by a belief that the army was subordinate to the legal civil power and should stay out of politics. His actions over the next few weeks were decisive. He recalled the members excluded from the Rump in 1648 and formed an allegiance with the City of London. The surviving members of the Long Parliament, first called by the King in November 1640, voted to dissolve themselves after calling for free elections to a new Parliament. Whilst these were taking place, Charles II issued a Declaration from the Dutch town of Breda where he was waiting, having deliberately left Catholic France. In this he offered Parliament the opportunity of settling all the outstanding problems whilst guaranteeing a general pardon to his father's enemies, a settlement of disputes about land sales, payment of arrears to the army and liberty of conscience for all. When the new 'Convention' Parliament met (so called because of the lack of royal writs of summons) it declared that the government of the country properly resided in the King, Lords and Commons and it invited Charles to come and take up his rightful position. Charles set sail and landed in England on 25 May 1660.

The speed of collapse of the British Republic has continued to surprise historians. But perhaps it really reflects no more than the fragility of its creation. It could never resolve the many contradictions underlying its existence. There was a widespread desire for a civilian form of government that could never be reconciled with the fact that from December 1648 authority ultimately came from the Army. There was a constant tension between the democratic pressures that had come down from the Levellers, through the charges that were made against Charles at his trial, to the belief that the will of the people was supreme, on the one hand, and the demands that government should be saintly and its principal duty was to reform the manners and morals of the nation, on the other. The Republic in one sense had been no more than a military dictatorship but it had always been a reluctant one, trying to cloak its actions in legality. But as with many revolutionary regimes that fail to gain recognition, it had to become more repressive in order to survive. And it was this that finally alienated the people altogether, provoking a longing for peace and stability. In the euphoria of compromise that conquered all in 1660, it seemed as though the Civil Wars had finally come full circle.

CHAPTER SIX

Legacy

Throughout the kingdom, the Restoration of Charles II was met with jubilant celebrations. For many people the festivities marked a return to the 'good old days' before the Civil Wars had torn the nation apart. Across the country bonfires were lit, parties were held, hogsheads of beer and baskets of bread were handed out to the poor. At Sherborne which had been one of the most Royalist of the west country towns, the cross of St George flew from the tower of the Abbey, the streets were decked with flowers and George Digby, the son of the Earl of Bristol, led a procession of Dorset gentlemen through the town. A hundred maids in white followed behind a drummer. There were 'consorts of music', trumpet fanfares and volleys of shot. That evening some 'witty wags' held a mock trial at which effigies of Bradshaw and Cromwell were tried and dragged through the town, hacked to pieces and then thrown on a bonfire along with the emblems of the Commonwealth.

Even in towns and villages that had a less staunchly Royalist past than Sherborne the celebrations were loud and long. In the eleven years since the execution of Charles I, the Commonwealth had become increasingly unpopular and associated with the interests of a small minority. The Royalist cause, on the other hand, had become linked in the popular mind with freedom from the strictures of the fundamentalist religious reformers. So less than twenty miles from Sherborne, in the county town of Dorchester which had been a Puritan stronghold throughout the years of the Civil War, the bells were also rung, young people paraded with banners and salutes were fired. Even here the Town Clerk spoke of the King's return rescuing them from 'a world of confusions' and 'unheard-of governments'. And yet there was no excessive drinking or revelry. The Dorchester Company of Freeman distributed £2 among the poor of the town but there was no free beer and the merry-making was more restrained. Everywhere Royalists and Parliamentarians celebrated with what no doubt was a genuine sense of relief at seeing a return to harmony and peace over the chaos of recent years. But the Restoration of the King symbolized not only the return to social order and cohesion after twenty years of conflict and instability but for many it also marked a return to the 'Golden Age of Maypoles' and merriment that had disappeared during the Puritan regimes of recent years.

Celebrating the Restoration of Charles II.

More than just the King was restored in 1660. The desire to turn away from the activities of the last twenty years was matched by a feeling that the rule of law must be preserved. This was to cause some major problems. The wholesale confiscation and sale of lands had created a complex and tangled situation. All Church, Crown and confiscated Royalists' lands were returned but lands that had been sold privately to pay political fines were not. Though there were complaints, large amounts of land did not change hands during the period of the Civil War and the Commonwealth. Few new landed families emerged in Charles II's reign having acquired lands in the 1640s and 50s.

An Act of Indemnity and Oblivion pardoned all offences arising from the conflicts of the last twenty years 'out of a hearty and pious desire to put an end to all suits and controversies that by occasion of the late distractions have arisen'. Only fifty-seven people were excepted – mostly those who had signed

Christmas was abolished in 1652, to be celebrated with renewed vigour after 1660.

The King returns

Samuel Pepys was among those who travelled across the Channel to bring Charles II back in May 1660.

'23 May...We weighed anchor, and with a fresh gale and most happy weather we set sail for England – all the afternoon the King walking here and there, up and down (quite contrary to what I thought him to have been), very active and stirring.

'Upon the quarterdeck he fell in discourse of his escape from Worcester. Where it made me ready to weep to hear the stories that he told of his difficulties that he had passed through. As his travelling four days and three nights on foot, every step up to the knees in dirt, with nothing but a green coat and a pair of country breeches on and a pair of country shoes, that made him so sore all over his feet that he could scarce stir. Yet he was forced to run away from a miller and other company that took them for rogues...

'24 May. Up, and made myself as fine as I could with the linen stockings and wide canons that I bought the other day at [The] Hague. Extraordinary press of noble company and great mirth all the day...

'25 May. By the morning we were come close to the land and everybody made ready.

'...so got on shore when the King did, who was received by General Monck with all imaginable love and respect at his entrance upon land at Dover. Infinite the crowd of people and the gallantry of the horsemen, citizens, and noblemen of all sorts.

'The mayor of the town came and gave him his white staff, the badge of his place, which the King did give him again. The mayor also presented him

Samuel Pepys, by Hayls.

from the town a very rich Bible, which he took and said it was the thing that he loved above all things in the world.

'A canopy was provided for him to stand under, which he did; and talked awhile with General Monck and others; and so into a stately coach there set for him; and so away straight through the town towards Canterbury...The shouting and joy expressed by all is past imagination.'

Friday *the Four and twentieth day of* December, 1652.

Refolved by the Parliament,

THat the Markets be kept to Morrow, being the Five and twentieth day of *December*; And that the Lord Major, and Sheriffs of *London* and *Middlefex*, and the Iuftices of Peace for the City of *Weftminfter* and Liberties thereof, do take care, That all fuch perfons as fhall open their Shops on that day, be protected from VVrong or Violence, and the Offenders punifhed.

Refolved by the Parliament,

That no Obfervation fhall be had of the Five and twentieth day of *December,* commonly called *Chriftmas-Day*; nor any Solemnity ufed or exercifed in Churches upon that Day in refpect thereof.

Ordered by the Parliament,

That the Lord Major of the City of *London*, and Sheriffs of *London* and *Middlefex*, and the Iuftices of Peace of *Middlefex* refpectively, be Authorized and Required to fee this Order duly obferved within the late Lines of Communication, and weekly Bills of Mortality.

Hen: Scobell, Cleric. Parliaments.

London, Printed by *John Field,* Printer to the Parliament of *England.* 1652.

A complete angler

One of the most lasting testaments of the years of the Commonwealth is also perhaps one of the most surprising. In May 1653 *The Compleat Angler, or, The Contemplative Man's Recreation* was published. Izaak Walton's book has passed into the realms of fame, the classic fishing book of all time, the most-reprinted book in English after the Bible and Book of Common Prayer. What has drawn readers to *The Compleat Angler* is not only the practical information, but also its evocation of a lost age, when angling really was a sport conducted from lush river banks beneath honeysuckle hedges.

The irony is that Walton was himself evoking a golden age. His book begins on May Day, a suppressed festival. There is a sub-text to *The Compleat Angler*: the monarchy has been abolished, it will probably not come again, and contemplation and withdrawal are the most seemly ways to behave. Izaak Walton was by 1653 a wealthy City draper who had retired to Staffordshire. He had many literary connections; John Donne, for example, was his vicar in St Dunstan's-in-the-West, and Walton was

Donne's first biographer. Throughout the Civil War, Walton remained a firm Royalist; in 1651, after the Battle of Worcester, he was entrusted with smuggling part of the Garter regalia to a prisoner in the Tower of London, from whom it was conveyed to Charles II in exile. Walton's own reaction to the nation's new masters was to stay out of public life, avoiding public protest, following however unwillingly the edicts of the Commonwealth. His was probably a common reaction. Fishing provided an excuse to escape, and it was a pastime in which many sequestered clergy indulged, allowing them opportunity to talk and complain and dream together.

With the Restoration, Walton became steward to George Morley, Bishop of Worcester and then of Winchester, where he continued his literary output of poems and biographies, and tinkered with *The Compleat Angler*. In the four subsequent editions its original purpose was overwhelmed by classical allusion and more information. It remains the book for which he is remembered, the book of a golden age which Walton also believed had already past.

Izaak Walton (left),
whose fishing manual
was a lament for a
lost, royal age.

Charles II's
coronation procession
(above) entering the
City of London.

Charles I's execution warrant in January 1649. Of these, thirty were condemned to death but only eleven were finally executed. The others escaped or were allowed to disappear, most of them abroad including some to America. After such a long and bloody period of fighting this seems an extraordinarily forgiving and lenient policy, especially when compared, for instance, to the bitterness and the recriminations against collaborators that followed the Second World War in countries like France or Holland which had gone through the experience of Nazi occupation for some years.

The legal settlement of the Restoration was based on the Declaration of Breda. It took several years for all the elements to be worked out but there was a strong feeling that the constitutional niceties must be preserved. All the legislation of 1641 and 1642 to which Charles I had given his assent remained on the statute book except for two items – the Act which excluded bishops from the House of Lords and the Triennial Act which forced the King to meet Parliament once every three years. Both these Acts were repealed. The Long Parliament was formally dissolved and the Convention that had recalled the King was turned into a legal Parliament. It continued the work that had been started in 1641 by abolishing purveyance and feudal tenures and it confirmed the abolition of the Court of Wards. Charles II was compensated for loss of revenue by a grant in perpetuity of a portion of the excise revenue from beer, cider and tea. In one sense this marked a triumph of the Parliamentary cause. But on the other hand, the dispute which had actually sparked off the Civil War was finally settled in the Militia Act of 1661 which vested the command of the armed forces in the King. On this central issue Parliament gave way. The principle is still seen today in the annual ceremony by which officer cadets when graduating from Sandhurst swear an oath of allegiance not to Parliament or to 'the people' but to the Crown.

With the restoration of the King came the restoration of the Church of England. Although the Declaration of Breda promised religious toleration for all, this did not in fact come about. Instead, the pendulum swung against the Puritans and the 'Cavalier' Parliament elected in 1661 enthusiastically passed legislation that has become known as the 'Clarendon Code', named rather misleadingly after Charles II's senior minister, the Earl of Clarendon. The Corporation Act of 1661 excluded from the government of borough corporations anyone who would not take the Anglican sacrament and the oaths of allegiance and supremacy. Furthermore, all office holders had to swear not to take up arms against the King in the famous 'Non-Resistance Oath'. In the following year the Uniformity Act made all clergy swear the same oaths and take a further declaration of their 'unfeigned acceptance' of the Book of Common Prayer. The Conventicle Act of 1664 forbade meetings held 'under colour or pretence of any exercise of religion' of five or more people. And the Five Mile Act of 1665 prohibited any ministers or preachers who had been ejected by the earlier legislation from coming within five miles of the parish where they had been incumbent.

In all this, Parliament's supremacy over the church was clearly established. Never again were churchmen to hold senior political office in the way that Laud had done in the 1630s. Although the church courts were restored, the House of Commons firmly resisted an attempt by the bishops to revive the High

Indemnity and Oblivion

When Charles II returned, one of the most pressing pieces of business was to reward those who had supported him, punish those who had opposed him, and mollify as many people as he could. One result was the Act of Indemnity and Oblivion of 1660 – which many glossed as an Act of Indemnity for the King's enemies, and Oblivion for his friends.

The Act was the great gesture intended to reunite Charles' kingdom. Its principal targets were those who had tried Charles I and signed his death warrant. Some of them were obscure men, some famous. In the 1659 Declaration of Breda, Charles had already offered pardons to all but seven of the regicides. In the event, the Bill named thirty-three regicides; nineteen of whom had surrendered themselves and were spared execution. The King seems to have been mild in his treatment of those who had

taken his kingdom away and taken his father's life, while the two Houses of Parliament argued between themselves so sparing the lives of men who might have expected to die. For Royalists, the difficulty was that there were families enjoying lands and privileges which they felt rightfully to be theirs – and yet it seemed the King dare not go too far in restoring what had been taken from them. His priorities were to reward those who had been in exile with him, Royalist conspirators of the 1650s, and those in control of the country, like Monck, when Charles was invited to return. This he did; Royalists who had kept quiet but failed to work for Charles' return got shorter shrift, although many received preferment and aid.

The provisions of the Restoration were achieved with little blood-letting, few recriminations, and many advancements.

The Declaration of Breda, at which Charles II offered pardons and terms for his return.

The Crown Jewels

The execution of Charles I in 1649 had been followed by the systematic destruction of the royal symbols of sovereignty – the crowns, sceptres, orbs, and other ornaments which were integral parts of the coronation ceremonies. Many of them were early medieval in origin, and St Edward's crown may even have dated from the time of the Confessor himself, a Saxon diadem 'of gold wirework set with slight stones and little bells'. The hammers wielded by the Parliamentary Commissioners broke up the regalia, and their metal content was consigned to the Mint, the jewels dispersed. The only object to survive was the gold Ampulla, the eagle-shaped vessel for oils used in anointing which probably dated from 1399.

When Charles II came to be crowned, therefore, considerable efforts were made to replace the regalia, and most of the items used in coronations since date from 1661. St Edward's crown was the most important: the new sovereign assumed the responsibility for good kingly rule which Edward the Confessor had exemplified. There was no charge made for the 80 ounces of gold used in its making in 1661, and there is more than a suspicion that the 79 ounces of gold delivered to the Mint after the regalia had been broken up were never used (according to the records, coins issued by the Commonwealth were made from bullion ingots). What was changed was the shape: the new St Edward's crown has a characteristically depressed centre and a wide spread, which was designed to top the new King's luxuriant black curls.

Charles II at his Coronation (left), wearing the newly-created regalia.

Edward Hyde, Earl of Clarendon(above), the chronicler of the years of the Great Rebellion.

Commission which still smacked of the abuses of royal power under Charles I. In 1664 the clergy surrendered the right to separate taxation in Convocation. The foundations of the relationship between church and state were established that have survived largely unchanged into the twentieth century.

The intention of this legislation was clearly to exclude the extreme forms of Puritanism that had flourished for nearly twenty years from the government of the country. In this it was undoubtedly successful at one level. 1,700 ministers resigned their livings rather than comply with the new Uniformity Act. The key to the social and political hierarchy came to be membership of the established Anglican church. Education and the universities were barred to non-members of the church as was access to municipal or government offices. The upper classes wanted to close the door for good on the religious radicalism and experimentation of the Commonwealth and return to an older, more stable form of worship. But Puritanism did not disappear – it was simply driven outside the establishment. For some years the radical Puritans were harried mercilessly. They were subjected to heavy fines and harsh imprisonments for their beliefs. But by the royal Declaration of Indulgence in 1672 things were changing. Many dissenters emerged from underground to accept royal licences and as long as they accepted a new political quietism the energy to pursue them faded away. Doubtless many Puritans were prepared to swear their allegiance in public whilst carrying on in private much as before. The Puritan radicals of the 1650s therefore slowly evolved into the Dissenting sects of the post-Restoration era.

So although the Church was restored along with the Crown, the nobility and the 'old ways' in 1660, the unified world of the Elizabethan era had gone forever. The Independents, the Congregationalists and the Baptists became the Non-conformists of the late seventeenth century. George Fox transformed the radical edge of the Quakers into a belief in pacifism and a withdrawal from politics. The overall legacy was that rich tradition in English life and culture that produced Bunyan (many of whose great works were written in prison as an unlicensed preacher in the 1660s), Defoe and ultimately Wesley. In religion, as in many other areas, the Restoration marked the end of the English Revolution but the beginning of a new chapter. A clear line can be discerned linking the Puritan radicals of the mid-seventeenth century with the Nonconformists of industrial Britain a century and a half later. In 1660 the parson was restored along with the squire in every parish but the monopoly of the church over the cultural and intellectual life of the nation had been shattered forever.

It was on the governmental level that the Civil War most clearly marked a critical transition in the emergence of modern Britain. The power of the monarch was not the same in the 1660s as it had been in the 1630s. Parliament clearly established the principle in the early Restoration legislation that the people of England could not be taxed without their consent expressed through the men of property in the House of Commons. The abolition of military tenures and the sale of the crown lands altered the nature of kingship. The feudal notion of the king as the principal landowner and the source of ultimate justice was definitely now a thing of the past. The crown was still at the centre of the political scene, as it still is in a formal and ceremonial sense today, but with a different kind of authority. Fewer people believed in the 'divinity that doth hedge a king' and it is significant that Charles II was hardly ever called

Cromwell and his henchmen, seen as supping with the Devil.

Sufferings and sufferers

The process of ejecting clergy from their livings, first in the 1640s and then at the Restoration, produced many stories of woe and poverty, as well as fuelling the growing divisions among dissenting congregations in the years after the Restoration. Many who had refused to take the oaths were forced to wander or to keep away from towns, and formed dissenting congregations of their own. The propaganda war continued after the Restoration, and the tales of the sufferings of clergy of both types were collected and disseminated. Each is a miniature version of the story of mid-seventeenth century religious ferment.

William Sheldrake, for one, had been presented to the lectureship in Wisbech, the Cambridgeshire town where Secretary of State John Thurloe built his grand house, Wisbech Castle. Lee informed Thurloe about opinion in Norfolk, in December 1657 describing with disgust the observance of Christmas in Wisbech. Sheldrake was substitute for Thomas Lee, the lecturer who had been ejected in 1645 for his antipathy to Parliament's cause, and praying 'now Charles fight for thy kingdom, trust in thy God, and he shall give thee the victory.' He returned briefly to his rectory after Sheldrake was ejected in 1660. For a while Sheldrake then followed his father's trade 'to deal in wool and yarn, to get a maintenance for his family...He was a person of uncommon sagacity, and capable of managing the greatest business, or of being a considerable statesman.' Yet Sheldrake continued to preach the word, but outside Anglican communions as he had been excommunicated. He became the pastor of the Congregational church in Great Yarmouth, and he was fined and prosecuted on a number of occasions before his death in 1685.

The Congregationalists sheltered many clergy ousted at the Restoration. Humphrey Philips, who had been assistant at Sherborne Abbey in Dorset, was fined for continuing to preach in the town and subsequently imprisoned for eleven months. On his release he went to Holland, and later came back to find his patrons had turned Sabbatarian Baptist. He then became an itinerant preacher on the Somerset-Wiltshire border, and 'fines were often imposed and levied upon him, and he had much trouble from the bishop's court, which drove him from his home', before spending his declining years in and around the clothing town of Frome.

William Adams had been the minister at Totnes in Devon, deputizing for the vicar who had become meanwhile rector of St Bartholomew the Great in London's Smithfield. His godliness was insufficient in the turbulent early 1650s, and he was ejected in 1652, dying in London leaving his wife and children 'with no more than a single threepence, to the mercy of the wide world.' Francis Whiddon became the lecturer in 1658, and celebrated communion in the parish for the first time in thirteen years. He was ejected in 1662, and continued to preach in and around Totnes, where he fell foul of the restrictions placed upon Nonconformist ministers on many more occasions before he died in 1679.

In his sermons in the early 1640s, Cuthbert Dale was accused of preaching to his congregation in the Suffolk parish of Kettleburgh 'That the angels did mediate for the children of God, and that men might drink one pot for necessity, a second for recreation, and a third for good fellowship'. He was ejected, and lived in poverty until reinstituted in 1660 for the last eight years of his life. Such stories abound.

upon to perform miracles like the treatment of scrofula that had been part of the mystical and magical powers of earlier kings. As historians have observed, the execution of Charles I was the central political event of the century.

This new attitude towards the monarch is best illustrated by events a generation later in 1688. James II, who succeeded Charles II in 1685, was a Catholic. Having tried to pack Parliament with his own supporters he then granted full religious liberty to Catholics. When he appointed the Catholic Earl Tyrconnel as Lord Lieutenant in Ireland and began to bring Irish soldiers to England, his actions revived too many memories and fears of 1641-42. There followed a military coup in which the Dutch Prince William of Orange, who was married to James's eldest daughter Mary, was invited to come to England

William of Orange arrives at the Glorious Revolution.

Anti-clerical satires (opposite) continued into the eighteenth century.

and to take the crown. James's supporters deserted him en masse and he fled to France. The bulk of the landed classes rallied to Prince William and in order to preserve the constitutional niceties a form of words was found in which sovereignty was offered jointly to William and Mary. The gap in the Restoration settlement of the 1660s was sealed when in 1689 Parliament enacted a Bill of Rights barring Catholics from the throne in future. Two further acts completed the constitutional settlement when in 1694 the Triennial Act established that Parliament must meet every three years and the Mutiny Act made the maintenance of an army legal for one year at a time only. These limitations on the crown were the price William paid for the continued financial support by Parliament for a long and expensive war against Louis XIV of France who continued to uphold James II's claim to the English throne.

A MASTER PARSON with a GOOD LIVING.

Although the events of 1688 were called a 'Glorious Revolution' they still left a measure of compromise in the constitutional arrangements between Crown and Parliament. The government was that of a constitutional monarchy and the broad parameters by which the system operated were now clearly defined. The King could not be a Catholic. He could not suspend the law. He was dependent upon Parliament to vote money for government. Although the King appointed his own ministers they were in the end answerable to Parliament and no royal pardon could overrule the will of Parliament. But, on the other hand, the Crown still had many important prerogative powers which William was anxious to use and as a reaction against the political turbulence of the century there was a widespread readiness to exalt the King in Parliament.

Two loosely structured political parties began to emerge expressing these different views. The Tories were closer to the King and the established church and emphasised a sense of hierarchy and social deference. The Whigs emphasised the privileges of Parliament and sometimes found it useful to invoke the rights of free born Englishmen. The development of these two parties reflected the fact that there was no real consensus on what relation existed or should exist between those in authority and those they nominally represented. Indeed, a system which allowed for these different interpretations of the nature of power and for the development of political parties, all of which operated *within* the system rather than outside it, is perhaps the most long lasting political legacy of the seventeenth century constitutional struggle. There were no clear winners and losers in the conflict between Crown and Parliament and the question of where ultimate sovereignty finally lies was left open.

Nowhere are the consequences of the mid-seventeenth century crisis more apparent in the eighteenth century, and indeed today, than across the Irish Channel. The seventeenth century was a crucial century in the history of modern Ireland. It had begun with the confiscations of land and the establishment of Protestant settlers from Scotland and from London in the Ulster Plantation. As part of a broad colonial adventure, these Plantations left the native Catholic Irish aggrieved and resentful while the Protestant settlers felt beleaguered and isolated. The growing resentment of the native Gaels, dispossessed of their lands, led to the Irish Rising in the autumn of 1641 which was the critical event in provoking war in England. The presence of Irish soldiers in the King's army from 1643 had led to the worst atrocities in the Civil War. Cromwell's savagery in Ireland in 1649-50 left lasting scars and completed the process of English colonization and conquest of Ireland that had begun in the twelfth century. Most of the land that had been given to officers as a form of payment was left in their hands. About two-thirds of the cultivatable land of Ireland was owned by Protestants, many of whom did not live in Ireland but simply extracted their rents from the country.

Cromwell's land settlement in Ireland left a Protestant English landowning class dominating a country of Catholic Irish. When James II appointed Tyrconnel as the first Catholic Lord Lieutenant in over a hundred years it looked as though the whole of Protestant rule in Ireland might be rolled back. Not surprisingly, when James fled England he soon turned to Ireland for support in the campaign to regain his crown. Once again, the scene was set for English wars to be fought out on Irish soil.

James's army, well supplied with arms and money from Louis XIV of France, laid siege to the Protestant city of Londonderry. Here the Apprentice Boys prevented the commander of the garrison, Lundy, from surrendering the city in the summer of 1689. Despite terrible privations the city held out for fifteen weeks until it was relieved. The determination of the citizens to resist James is now a part of the Ulster folk memory, celebrated annually in the Apprentice Boys Parade in the city.

The final battle in the Civil Wars of the seventeenth century took place in July 1690 on the banks of the river Boyne in Ireland. Parliament had voted William a huge sum to raise an army against Ireland and although William was half-hearted about the campaign it befitted his general strategic aim of trying to destroy French arms and influence wherever he could. When William finally met James in battle at the Boyne he defeated him decisively. James fled from Ireland and William occupied Dublin. The battle marked the final victory of Protestantism over Catholicism in the British Isles. It was also a triumph for William and Parliament over James who no longer had a secure base in Britain. William's succession as the Protestant ruler of Britain was never to be seriously challenged again.

Although William of Orange only spent a few weeks in Ireland he was to become a folk-hero to the Protestant Irish. Every year he is commemorated as tens of thousands of Orangemen swagger and strut through the towns and villages of Northern Ireland to honour the 'glorious and immortal memory' of King Billy. Parading behind bands and banners, the Irish Protestants are really celebrating the final victory of the Protestant ascendancy in Ireland. The battle of the Boyne was the third defeat of the native Irish in a century and William's victory was to set the seal on the English control of Ireland for two hundred years to come. When the drums beat to proclaim the Protestant victory of King Billy at the Boyne, the Protestants of Northern Ireland are ironically recalling the last of the great setpiece battles of the seventeenth-century Civil Wars.

In Scotland and Wales too, the legacy of the Civil Wars was to be the submission of their power to the centralised authority of London. Following his defeat of the Irish, Cromwell in 1650 had turned to Scotland where Charles II had been recognized as King. The Scots were defeated at Dunbar and finally crushed at the battle of Worcester in 1651. Cromwell's conquest of Scotland had taken two years. In April 1652 the union of Scotland and England was officially proclaimed in Edinburgh and Scotland was governed by a military garrison. Unlike the situation in Ireland where there were massive land confiscations, Scotland suffered the indignity of direct rule from the English but no lasting transfer of land ownership. The authority of the Kirk was drastically reduced but there was no religious persecution against the Scottish Presbyterians, and free trade between Scotland and England was to lead to a period of relative prosperity under the Commonwealth.

Although at the time of the Restoration the union was repealed, the City of London still controlled many business monopolies in Scotland and slowly English culture spread throughout the Lowlands of Scotland. Inevitably, the union with Scotland would be revived and in 1707 out of a fear of division between two different heirs to Queen Anne, Parliament passed the Act of Union which has cemented Scotland to England ever since. The Union brought

King Billy on a wall in Derry. Only in Northern Ireland have the events of the seventeenth century remained so clearly in the popular imagination.

An anti-Jacobite satire: a plaque showing James II trampling on Justice and Law, with Louis XIV beside him trampling on a cornucopia.

prosperity to the landowners of the south and east of Scotland and to the merchants of Glasgow but for the Highland crofters it brought increasing poverty. It was in these remote areas that the Stuart cause found its residual support in the next century. James II's grandson, Charles Edward, saw his moment in 1745. The Highlands rallied to the Jacobite cause and Charles proved to be a romantic figure suited to the heroic role he was destined to play. Despite initial success, the Jacobites could not roll back the tide of history and England certainly did not want to see a return of the Stuarts. Defeat was followed by flight. The Highlands were conquered and in time became an impoverished wasteland. 'Bonnie Prince Charlie' acquired legendary status but the Highland Clearances completed the process of the conquest of Scotland by the English that Cromwell had begun in 1650.

A similar story can be told with regard to Wales and to the Royalist areas of counties like Cornwall. Everywhere the writ of English government and the influence of the London merchants was supreme. Indeed, London, already the unchallenged capital of England emerged as the dominant city of the British Isles. During the Civil Wars, when the court had left London, Parliament became the focus of government and had to develop new administrative systems. Financial departments were formed, often located in the halls of the City companies. In the 1650s Committees were established for all aspects of government, to supervise trade, to oversee the confiscation of lands, to administer customs and excise. A new breed of administrator began to flourish who, whilst still enmeshed in a network of private patronage, shared a belief that his duty was to serve the public need. Although to date the appearance of the modern civil service in the era of the Commonwealth is premature, the seeds for future development were sown and in the work of an ex-Cromwellian like Samuel Pepys one can see a committment to the public service under the Restoration monarch. London was not only supreme in business and in trade but was rapidly becoming the administrative focus of the British Isles.

Another important legacy of the Wars and of the Protectorate was a hatred of standing armies. Few areas of Britain had escaped the tramp of passing armies with all the disruption that this brought to the delicate balance of subsistence farming that prevailed in much of the country. Crops were trampled or devoured by cavalry horses. Labourers who could barely be spared from the land were conscripted or at best volunteered. From 1643 to 1645, agriculture from the Midland counties down to Wiltshire and Somerset in the south-west was devastated by visiting armies. The Wiltshire town of Chippenham, for instance, had to pay three 'contributions' to visiting Parliamentary armies and another two to the Royalists.

The memory of the rule of the Major Generals and of Cromwell, who from 1660 became indelibly associated with military tyranny, cast a dark shadow over future generations. As events of these years receded into memory, the lesson remained plain to many Englishmen: that the march of armies and the beat of the recruiting sergeant's drum were to be avoided at all costs. Over succeeding centuries as continental nations developed vast powerful armies Britain kept only a small standing army reliant upon volunteers and not conscription. Of course, much of this relates to the fact that Britain is an island with clearly defined boundaries unlike the great shifting land frontiers of Europe which have

King and Martyr

One of the most abiding images is of Charles I as martyr. Dying as nobly as he did was probably the King's finest action, and the speed with which the hagiographical *Eikon Basilike* circulated, drawing explicit parallels with Christ's sufferings, guaranteed the royal martyrdom would not be forgotten. It is still commemorated in High Anglican circles on the feast day of Charles King and Martyr, 30 January, the anniversary of his death, and in churches named or renamed soon after the Restoration. Probably the best-known is in Tunbridge Wells, the spa town which rapidly rose to prominence in the seventeenth century. The chapel was begun in 1676, and its dedication was a riposte to local puritanical zeal which had earlier named the local hills Mount Sion and Mount Ephraim. Earlier than this is the Church of King Charles the Martyr in Falmouth, Cornwall, endowed by Sir Peter Killigrew in 1662, whose family home in the village had been devastated in the Civil War. The Charles Church in Plymouth, a town which had held out so long for Parliament before the Royalists took it after prolonged siege, was renamed after the Restoration; the Gothic Revival church was actually begun in 1648, and most of the work was completed in the 1650s. (The building is now a shell, the result of German bombing in the Second World War.)

De staert van nyt en giericheyt bezeten
verspuwt de Vree' der Nederlandtsche staat
geen koonings moort en knaag noch syn geweté
soo houdt de boosheyt Regel, streeck noch maat

ZEE SLACH VANDEN COMMANDEVR
Ian van Gale. tegens. 8. Engelse schepen waer van
een in brant is en een met 40 stucke by ons verouert.

Engelsen Admierael in brandt

The Dutch offer peace to England in 1653, during the debilitating conflict over trade that was to resurface in the next decade.

been at the centre of conflicts down to the twentieth century. But a reaction to the rule of the military in the 1640s and 50s played its part in turning the nation away from the army and towards the navy which had played a minor role in the Civil Wars.

From the 1650s onwards Britain's foreign policy was increasingly influenced by commercial interests. This was signalled by three wars with the Dutch Republic which were only resolved when the Dutch finally accepted their subordination to England. London, again at the centre of the story, became a major entrepôt and trading capital in Europe, re-exporting much of the produce that was imported from the colonies. To achieve this it was necessary to seize the trading initiative from the Dutch and the Navigation Acts of 1650 and 1651 laid down a marker that the Dutch could hardly fail to respond to. The Dutch War of 1652-54 saw a great strengthening of the mercantile marine and the 1654 Anglo-Portuguese Treaty transferred the monopoly of trade with the Portuguese empire from Dutch to English merchants thus opening up vast new trading rights with Brazil and with West Africa.

A new attitude to the colonial empire was seen in the 1650s. The policy of the Commonwealth was to increase colonial production in order to supply England with some of the raw materials she needed and to prohibit trade between the colonies and foreigners (which basically meant the Dutch) ensuring that all trade was carried in English ships. In the Western Design of 1655, Cromwell put into effect a colonial policy that had been the dream of English seafarers since Elizabeth's time by focusing attention on the West Indies. The capture of Jamaica was symbolic of the shift from Spain to Britain as the senior trading partner in the region. The cruel, inhuman trade in slaves to meet the needs of the sugar plantations in the West Indies and as labour for the expanding colonies of America started to generate the huge Atlantic trading nexus of interests that made the ports of Liverpool and Bristol prosperous for over a hundred and fifty years to come.

From 1649, in an effort to subdue pirates and privateers, the navy began to police the seas. English sea power appeared in the Mediterranean. English traders negotiated access to Swedish ports in the Baltic where previously the Dutch had held the monopoly. Trade with China began. The old anti-Spanish policy that had lasted since the Elizabethan era was replaced by a policy directed against new rivals, initially Holland but ultimately the French. From the 1650s British foreign policy was entering a new era, in which the basis of British power was to be its overseas and colonial trade and the means of protecting this was to be provided by the navy.

A great revolution in thinking also dates from this time. Many people now felt that the solution to problems could be found by reason and argument, not by reference to theology or the Scriptures. In the early part of the century Sir Francis Bacon had encouraged men to observe and to study the world around them. But this new philosophy of scientific enquiry was largely stillborn until the 1640s and 50s. It was then that new ideas from before the Civil Wars found widespread acceptance like Harvey's discovery of the circulation of the blood and Copernicus's views on astronomy. Boyle rejected the medieval workings of alchemy and laid the foundation for the modern science of chemistry. Doubtless the Puritan striving for personal religious experience gave an intellectual boost

A new spirit of enquiry

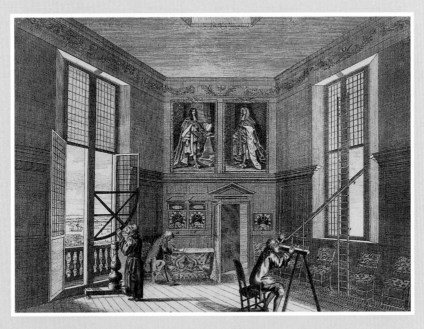

*The formation of the
Royal Society (opposite).*

*The octagon room at Wren's
new Royal Observatory, Greenwich.*

The pursuit of natural philosophy became one of the great fashions of the late Stuart age. It received its most public manifestation in the formation of the Royal Society, which received royal incorporation in 1662 having been founded within months of the Restoration of Charles II. The spirit of enquiry did not spring from nowhere; although some have claimed that the formation of the Royal Society brought new men and new thought onto the stage, the continuities before and after 1662 are quite apparent. The Commonwealth years had spawned many different scientific and philosophical endeavours, especially in a circle around Samuel Hartlib; and in 1657 Christopher Wren had been made Professor of Astronomy at Gresham College in the City of London, where the Royal Society was to have its first headquarters. What distinguished the new body was the broadness of its membership. It embraced those who had been in favour of the previous regime and those who had been opposed; it was not concentrated in a private circle around a patron; and the emphasis was placed upon experimentation and rational enquiry.

A passion for collecting and classifying – plants, shells, fossils, minerals, curiosities of all sorts – which had become a great gentlemanly pursuit in Stuart England, was channelled into the gathering of scientific information. Many of the new forms of study the Royal Society fostered had practical intentions. Henry Oldenburg, the Society's first Secretary, thought it was 'no slight point of philosophy to know... what animals may be tamed for human use and what commixtures with other animals may be advanced.' The Commissioners of the Navy consulted the Royal Society on the timber shortage, and one of the results was the founding-member John Evelyn's *Silva* (1664), one of the most famous of all books on trees. This scientific enquiry was not without its political points: Evelyn showed in various skilful ways how excessive tree-felling had been one of the ways in which confiscated estates had been run down during the Commonwealth, and tree-planting became almost a Restoration duty. Charles II planted many with his own hands – they were mainly oaks, of course.

to the spirit of scientific enquiry but unlike with many things Puritan these new attitudes were not rejected at the time of the Restoration.

Science became fashionable at the court of Charles II and in 1662 the King himself issued the Charter that established the Royal Society. In its early years the Society did much to encourage the practical application of scientific ideas in agriculture and in navigation which had lasting benefits. Progress was made in botany, chemistry, medicine, mathematics and astronomy. At the beginning of the seventeenth century, men and women had lived in a world where they felt constantly vulnerable to the forces of nature around them. Disease, death, fire, plague all seemed to be cruel and arbitrary in the way they could strike. By the end of the century many people felt they had more control over their world. Technical improvements in industry and agriculture, the advance in fire-fighting devices, progress in medicine and a greater understanding of the rules of nature all made for a changing outlook and attitude to the natural world. This new mechanical philosophy extended from the heavens above to the New Worlds beyond where the frontiers were constantly being pushed back.

Although science was fashionable at court, a rigid censorship was re-imposed in the Licensing Acts from 1662 onwards. This prevented the free exchange of ideas that had so enlivened the 1640s and 50s. Although there was considerable technological advance in the 1660s this soon faltered and the Royal Society became something of a gentleman's club. Oxford and Cambridge had been at the forefront of scientific advance but were now taken over by an intellectual conservatism. It was two hundred years before the universities caught up with the scientific lead they had established in the 1650s. The next great phase of technological innovation did not come until the late eighteenth century when a new industrial spirit prompted further advance.

In this climate, the great decline in educational opportunity after the return of Charles II is easy to understand. The Puritans had put enormous emphasis on the value of education as a weapon against the three evils of 'Ignorance, Prophaneness and Idleness'. They believed that everyone should have direct access to the Bible by being able to read it for themselves. As a consequence there was a great expansion in education from the Tudor era onwards. By the mid-seventeenth century there was perhaps one grammar school per 4,400 people. The numbers of young men entering higher education had increased by about 60 per cent between the 1560s and the 1630s. Although literacy levels in terms of those who can read and write are notoriously difficult to estimate, it seems that about a third of all adult males were literate and in the towns and cities the figure might have been nearly double this. The Long Parliament was probably the best educated in English history before the twentieth century. Plans were drawn up for a vast, comprehensive educational system on a national scale from elementary schools to universities. The Puritan zeal for education generated a substantial readership which devoured the pamphlets of these years. The great political debates of the time were not conducted between a tiny elite but were shared between a huge number of people participating for once in the political life of the nation.

After the Restoration it was widely believed by the new establishment that popular education had been the root cause of the Civil War enabling too many people to think beyond their station. Education was thought to lead to

Republicanism

The LOVER'S DREAM,
'A Thousand Virtues seem to lackey her, Driving far off each thing of Sin & Guilt.' Milton.

Gillray's cartoon of George IV when Prince of Wales at the time of his proposed marriage to settle his debts, in a satire against the royal family that would now be outrageous.

The Republican experiment of the Commonwealth years has had little use as a model in Britain. The Revolution of 1688 cemented new relationships between Crown and Parliament. The most active bouts of republican fervour undoubtedly occurred in the ferment at the turn of the eighteenth century, with the Revolutions in America and France. Tom Paine in *Common Sense* (1776) had raged:

'A French bastard landing with an armed banditti and establishing himself King of England, against the consent of the natives, is in plain terms a very paltry rascally original. It certainly hath no divinity in it,' harking back to the Norman yoke which had so exercised the political revolutionaries 130 years before. They would have recognized the disloyal toasts at radical dinners in the reign of George IV, 'May the last of Kings be strangled with the guts of the last priest'. However, the thrust of agitation in the nineteenth century was for representation and suffrage, and the form of government, monarchical or republican, was of less political moment. Whig historians like Macaulay were to congratulate the nation that it had had its revolutions in the seventeenth century.

Antipathy to monarchy reached its height with George IV, William IV, and Victoria. Prinny's excesses might have been forgiven were it not for his disgraceful treatment of Queen Caroline. *The Times* described his funeral, 'We never saw so motley, so rude, so ill-managed a body of persons', while William IV's was 'a wretched mockery'. The satirical cartoonists, like Gillray, Cruickshank, Rowlandson lampooned the monarchy mercilessly, and Queen Victoria was the butt of public and newspaper criticism until the 1870s: 'Queen of the Whigs' after her political partisanship early in the reign, the 'Widow of Windsor' after Albert's death, 'Mrs Brown' as comment on her closeness to her ghillie grew. In 1864 a notice was pinned to Buckingham Palace gates: 'These commanding premises to be let or sold, in consequence of the late occupant's declining business.'

If anyone saved the monarchy, it was Disraeli, who prised the Queen out of retirement and persuaded her to take part in the lavish imperial ceremonial of the Golden Jubilee, which was subsequently surpassed by the imperial glitter of the Diamond Jubilee. The monarchy was until then wasting away; yet the vacuum was not filled by active republicanism. Since then, republican initiatives in Britain have been few, and popular regard for the monarchy has probably never been higher.

disobedience and there was felt to be an urgent need to bring schooling under control. In 1662 the Act of Uniformity made all schoolmasters subject to an ecclesiastical licence. Grammar schools closed or went into decline. A classical education became the prerogative of the rich. Literacy levels plummeted and regained the levels of the 1650s in the early 1900s. The numbers going through higher education did not reach the same level until the Second World War.

There is no question that the radical Puritan revolution of the 1640s and 50s was defeated in the Restoration of 1660. This applies just as much to science, education and ideas as to the economic and political transformations of the Commonwealth. Many of the radical ideas of these years went underground which is not to say that they vanished altogether but that they disappeared from free circulation and historians can only occasionally divine their existence over following generations.

The years 1640 to 1660 came to be seen as an aberration, as a sort of political and cultural cul-de-sac the nation had been led up in error. The squire and the parson were firmly back in control and the use of violence to achieve political ends came to be seen as something that was distinctly un-English. A veil was drawn over these years and men preferred not to recall them, other than as an example of how religion and bigotry could mislead a nation.

By the end of the century many of the central constitutional debates of the era were still unresolved in theory but an arrangement had been developed that seemed to work out in practice. Parliament was powerful but the Crown was still left with important prerogatives. The supremacy of Parliament was matched by

And when did you last see your father?

The Victorians were obsessed with the Civil War, and their words and paintings give us the majority of our images of it. *The Children of the New Forest* still colours the popular imagination. The romantic genius of Sir Walter Scott, in *Woodstock* (1826), probably began it all with the exciting tale of intrigue in Charles II's escape in the wake of the Battle of Worcester. History paintings of the Civil War era became such a quintessential part of Victorian art, in which Charles I often symbolized rectitude in the face of folly. He was portrayed as an ideal husband and father: Henrietta Maria and Charles prefigured Victoria and Albert. Cromwell and the success of Parliament then came to epitomize the inexorable rise of Parliamentary democracy, which is seen to best advantage in the great sequence of Civil War canvases commissioned from Charles West Cope in 1857-67 for the rebuilt House of Lords. The figure of Oliver Cromwell was used to convey the sense of religious rightness and self-made position that the nineteenth century usually regarded as very particularly its own, most powerfully realized in Egg's painting of Cromwell in prayer on the eve of the Battle of Naseby.

In France, the English Civil War was widely portrayed as well, for the political interest of a revolution and counter-revolution that preceded the French Revolution by 150 years. As early as 1831, Paul Delaroche painted the first of a great series of Charles and Oliver pictures, showing Cromwell gazing at the dead King in his coffin – a powerful image of an entirely imaginary event.

Most famous of all the nineteenth-century images, perhaps, is W.F. Yeames' *And when did you last see your father?* (*opposite*). Exhibited in 1878, it was destined to become one of the most frequently-reproduced of all Victorian pictures and to be immortalized in the waxworks of Madame Tussauds. The image of the sober Puritan at a desk interrogating the proud little boy standing on a footstool, the silks and colours of whose clothes contrast with the sombre attire of the questioners and soldiers, has fixed for ever the confrontation of 'romantic, doomed Cavaliers and stern, relentless Puritans'.

the privileges of a constitutional monarch. And on the question of who commanded the army which in one specific sense had been the cause of the Civil Wars, no clear answer had been found. Generations of officers have sworn their loyalty to the crown. But the army was only kept in existence by Parliament renewing the Mutiny Act each year. Today the Army Act is passed every five years and the question still occasionally arises as to whether the army is ultimately responsible to Parliament or to the executive, which in the late twentieth century means the Prime Minister and the Cabinet. But by this typically British compromise over the issue of sovereignty, the nation has at least avoided the sort of political revolution that has shaken several of the continental powers over the last three hundred years and the army by and large has stayed outside the world of politics.

Arguments will continue to rage about the exact meaning of the events of these momentous years although there can be no doubt that they played a crucial role in the shaping of modern Britain. Perhaps no legacy of this era is more important than the desire for peace and prosperity as a reaction to the violence and hardship of the Civil War and the Commonwealth. The men of property, the 'natural' leaders were back in charge, the radical alternatives had been rejected. Britain was able to develop and to prosper having established a working political system that has endured without serious rupture down to the present day. And this was an important reason why Britain was able to act as the cradle of the next great phase in the history of the western world some hundred years later with the Industrial Revolution.

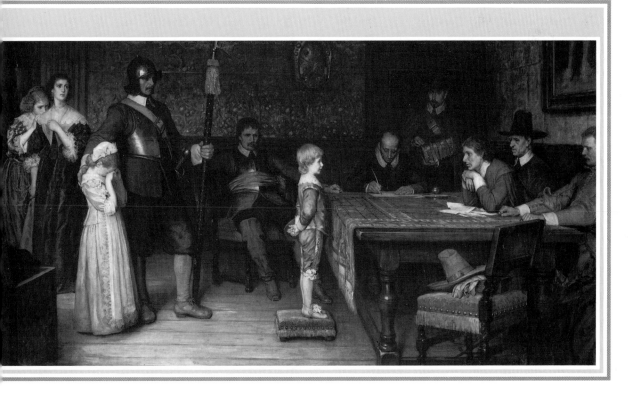

There is a very wide range of literature on all aspects of the Civil Wars and the period of the Commonwealth and the Protectorate. We have listed below a highly selective guide to further reading, primarily of books which are readily available, many in paperback:

There are a number of excellent single-volume histories of the period:
Maurice Ashley, *The English Civil War* (London, 1974; revised Gloucester, 1990)
G.E.Aylmer, *Rebellion or Revolution?* (Oxford, 1987)
Christopher Hill, *The Century of Revolution 1603-1714* (Edinburgh, 1961; revised Oxford, 1980)
John Kenyon, *The Civil Wars of England* (London, 1988)
Richard Ollard, *This War Without An Enemy* (London, 1976)
Ivan Roots, *The Great Rebellion* (London, 1966)
Austin Woolrych, *Battles of the English Civil War* (London, 1961)
Blair Worden (ed.), *Stuart England* (Oxford, 1986)

We also found the following books useful:
Susan Dwyer Amussen, *An Ordered Society* (Oxford, 1988)
Charles Carlton, *Charles 1* (London, 1983)
Taylor Downing (ed.), *The Troubles. The background to the question of Northern Ireland* (London, 1980)
Anthony Fletcher, *The Outbreak of the English Civil War* (London, 1981)
Peter Gaunt, *The Cromwellian Gazetteer* (Gloucester, 1987)
Christopher Hill, *Society and Puritanism in Pre-Revolutionary England* (London, 1964)
Christopher Hill, *God's Englishman* (London, 1970)
Christopher Hill, *The World Turned Upside Down* (London, 1972)
Christopher Hill, *Some Intellectual Consequences of the English Revolution* (London, 1980)
Derek Hirst, *Authority and Conflict* (London, 1986)
Elaine Hobby, *Virtue of Necessity* (London, 1988)
Ronald Hutton, *The Restoration* (London, 1985)
Ronald Hutton, *Charles II* (London, 1989)
Ronald Hutton, *The British Republic* (London, 1990)
David Lagomarsino and Charles T. Wood, *The Trial of Charles I* (London, 1989)
Brian Manning, *The English People and the English Revolution* (London, 1976)
John Morrill (ed.), *Reactions to the English Civil War 1642-1649* (London, 1982)
John Morrill (ed.), *Oliver Cromwell and the English Revolution* (London, 1990)
Conrad Russell, *The Causes of the English Civil War* (Oxford, 1990)
David Stevenson, *The Scottish Revolution* (Newton Abbot, 1973)
Lawrence Stone, *The Causes of the English Revolution* (London, 1972)
Keith Thomas, *Religion and the Decline of Magic* (London, 1971)
David Underdown, *Pride's Purge* (Oxford, 1971)
David Underdown, *Revel, Riot and Rebellion* (Oxford, 1985)
C.V. Wedgwood, *Oliver Cromwell* (London, 1964)
C.V. Wedgwood, *The Trial of Charles I* (London, 1964)
Blair Worden, *The Rump Parliament* (Cambridge, 1974)
Peter Young & Richard Holmes, *The English Civil War: A Military History 1642-1651* (London,1974)

We would also like to mention the work of the Partizan Press, who publish re-prints and specialist pamphlets of the period. Contact: David Ryan, 26, Cliffsea Grove, Leigh-on-Sea, Essex SS9 1NQ

A list of sites relating to the Civil War; buildings and churches of the period.

* usually open to the public; ** admission charge
[EH] English Heritage; [NT] National Trust;
[NTS] National Trust for Scotland; [HS] Historic Scotland;
[CADW] Welsh Historic Monuments

Abbey Dore, Hereford and Worcester; *church, furnishings and glass 1630s

Abingdon, Oxfordshire; **Town Museum, Civil War displays and excavations

Albury, Surrey; remains of John Evelyn's 1650s gardens

Alton, Hampshire; *church, musket shot marks from battle

Amersham, Buckinghamshire; *church, tombs 1636, 1654

Ampthill, Bedfordshire; *Houghton House [EH], ruins of 1640s house, classical loggias

**Appleby Castle, Cumbria; Lady Anne Clifford family portaits and relics

**Arundel Castle, West Sussex; considerably damaged in Civil War siege, later rebuilt

**Ashby-de-la-Zouch Castle, Leicestershire [EH]; mainly destroyed in Civil War siege, *Town Museum, Civil War displays

**Ashdown House, Oxfordshire [NT]; 1660s house, shrine to Elizabeth of Bohemia

**Auckland Castle, Bishop Auckland, Durham; restoration of partly-destroyed Bishop's Palace after 1660

Banbury, Oxfordshire; *Town Museum, Civil War displays

Barthomley, Cheshire; *church, scene of Royalist atrocity 1643

**Basing House, Hampshire; destroyed after longest Civil War siege; excavated

Bassingbourn, Cambridgeshire; *church, Buller monument, 1647

**Beeston Castle, Cheshire [EH]; besieged 1643; history displays

**Belvoir Castle, Leicestershire; slighted 1646, twice rebuilt; village demolished 1645

Berwick-on-Tweed, Northumberland; *parish church, built 1650s

**Bickleigh Castle, Devon; besieged in Civil War

**Bishop's Waltham Palace, Hampshire [EH]; ruined in Civil War siege

**Bolsover Castle, Derbyshire [EH]; part-abandoned Jacobean and mid-Stuart fantasy house

Boscobel, Shropshire; **Boscobel House, with descendant of oak tree in which Charles II hid after defeat at Worcester

Brading, Isle of Wight; *church, Oglander monument 1655

Bramber, Sussex; **St Mary's House, one of Charles II's hiding places after Worcester

Bramhope, West Yorkshire; *1649 chapel with furnishings

Brampton Bryan Castle, Herefordshire; *ruins of besieged castle; *church part rebuilt 1650s

Bridgnorth, Shropshire; *Town Museum, Civil War and siege displays; *castle ruins

Bridgwater, Somerset; *Admiral Blake museum (Commonwealth admiral's birthplace)

Briggflats, West Yorkshire; *Quaker meeting house and settlement, built 1675

Bristol, Avon; Brandon Hill; *monument to battle

Broad Hinton, Wiltshire; *church, Col. Glanville's monument of 1645

**Brodie Castle, Grampian [NTS]; Z-plan castle rebuilt after Civil War

**Brough Castle, Cumbria [EH]; repaired by Lady Anne Clifford 1650s

**Brougham Castle, Cumbria [EH]; repaired by Lady Anne Clifford 1650s

**Broughton Castle, Oxfordshire; home of Viscount Saye & Sele, leading Parliamentarian

Burford, Oxfordshire; *church with plaque commemorating death of three Levellers.

Cambridge, Cambridgeshire; Christ's College, Fellows' Building c. 1640; *Clare College, begun 1638; Peterhouse, *1630s chapel; Pembroke College, Hitcham Building, 1659, *chapel by Wren 1660s

Campton, Bedfordshire; *church part-rebuilt 1649

**Canons Ashby, Northamptonshire [NT]; site of skirmish outside house and church

**Carisbrooke Castle, Isle of Wight [EH]; King Charles I's final place of imprisonment

Carlisle, Cumbria; *Cathedral, part-demolished by troops in Civil War; **Castle, Civil War siege displays

Carsington, Derbyshire

** Castle Fraser; Grampian [NTS]; Z-plan castle completed 1636

Chalfont St Giles, Buckinghamshire; **Milton Cottage, poet's house, preserved from 1665

**Chavenage, Tetbury, Gloucestershire; Cromwell's and Ireton's bedrooms, Charles I's death mask

**Chepstow Castle, Gwent [CADW]; besieged 1648; republican Henry Marten's cell

**Chenies Manor, Buckinghamshire; Earls of Bedford's ancestral home and burial place

Chester, Cheshire; **King Charles Tower, Civil War displays; *City Walls

**Chingle Hall, Goosnargh, Lancashire; Battle of Preston fought partly in grounds

Cholmondeley Castle, Cheshire; **Cromwellian family chapel in park

**Claydon House, Middle Claydon, Buckinghamshire [NT]; Verney family home, van Dyck etc portraits; *Middle Claydon church, Civil War family tombs

Clonmel, Ireland; *Tipperary Museum, displays of 1650 siege

Colchester, Essex; **Colchester and Essex Museum, siege displays; Siege House, St John's Abbey Gateway, and *St Mary's Church Arts Centre all with external marks of fighting

Colwick, Staffordshire; *church tower and monuments 1640s

Conway, Gwynedd, Wales; **Conway Castle [CADW], besieged 1646; **Aberconway House [NT], ancient surviving house, local history displays

****Corfe Castle**, Dorset [NT]; ruins of besieged castle, held out by Lady Bankes

****Coughton Court**, Warwickshire [NT]; part-rebuilt after Civil War siege and bombardment

Coxwold, North Yorkshire; *church, Bellasis monuments

Cricklade, Wiltshire; school, c.1651

****Dartmouth Castle**, Devon [EH]; part-extended and besieged in Civil War

***Denbigh Castle**, Gwynedd, Wales [CADW]; besieged 1646

Denton, Lincolnshire; Welby Almshouses c. 1650

Devizes, Wiltshire; **Devizes Museum, Civil War displays; Battle of Roundway Down nearby; damage to town churches

Dinton, Wiltshire; 17th-century houses [NT] including Hyde's birthplace and Lawes' Cottage

Donnington Castle, Berkshire [EH]; **ruins of long-besieged castle

Dunbar, East Lothian, Scotland; *Local History Centre, Battle of Dunbar displays

****Dunnottar Castle**, Grampian, Scotland; besieged by Cromwell 1650; hiding-place of Scottish regalia

****Durham Cathedral**, Durham; 1665 choir stalls etc, replacing those destroyed by Scots

East Knoyle, Wiltshire; *church, late-1630s decoration by Christopher Wren

****East Riddlesden Hall**, near Keighley, West Yorkshire [NT]; stone-built manor, part 1648

****Eccleshall Castle**, Staffordshire; destroyed after siege, Bishop of Lichfield's residence

Edgehill, Warwickshire; *Castle Inn, commemorative tower above battle site (see also Farnborough Hall)

****Edinburgh Castle**, Scotland [HS]; Scottish Crown Jewels

Ely, Cambridgeshire; *Cromwell's house, 1635-45, recently restored as Tourist Information Office

Exeter, Devon; *Royal Albert Museum, siege displays; *City Walls

****Falkland Palace**, Fife, Scotland [NTS]; Stuart royal palace

Falmouth, Cornwall; *1662 Church of Charles the Martyr

****Farnborough Hall**, Warwickshire [NT]; Edgehill Battle Museum

Farndon, Cheshire; *church stained glass showing Civil War soldiers

****Farnham Castle**, Surrey; Charles I lodged there en route to his trial

Flitton, Bedfordshire; *church, 1650s monuments

****Forde Abbey**, near Chard, Dorset; acquired by Attorney-General Edmund Prideaux, original furnishings

****Gainsborough Old Hall**, Lincolnshire [NT]; used as school in Commonwealth

Gawsworth, Cheshire; **Fitton monuments in parish church 1630s-50s

Gloucester, Gloucestershire; **Folk Museum, 1643 siege displays; *East Gate, displays

****Godolphin House**, near Helston, Cornwall; 1630s front, house of Earls of Godolphin

Great Houghton, West Yorkshire; *chapel, 1650s furnishings and arrangement

Greystoke, Cumbria; *church 1645

Groombridge, Kent; *church 1625; Groombridge Place built 1654 , **gardens occasionally open

Guyhirn, near Wisbech, Norfolk; *1650s chapel

***Hall Place**, Bexley, Kent; exterior rebuilt 1649-53

****Ham House**, near Richmond, Surrey [NT, V&A]; grand Stuart house, royal decoration, portraits

***Hambledon Hill**, near Blandford Forum, Dorset [NT]; site of battle with Clubmen, 1645

Hanbury, Staffordshire; *church, 1650s monuments

****Harlech Castle**, Gwynedd, Wales [CADW]; fell 1646

****Hartlebury Castle**, near Kidderminster, Hereford and Worcester; rebuilt after Civil War siege

****Helmsley Castle**, North Yorkshire [EH]; destroyed 1644

Hereford, Hereford & Worcester; **Old House, Civil War displays; siege mortar 'Roaring Meg' outside **Churchill Gardens Museum

****Holdenby House**, Northamptonshire; gardens remain of house where Charles I captured and first imprisoned

****Holyroodhouse**, Edinburgh, Scotland [HS]; Stuart royal palace

Hull, North Humberside; *City Museum, Civil War displays

Huntingdon, Cambridgeshire; *Cromwell Museum

****Hurst Castle**, Hampshire [EH]; Charles I held there 1648

Iwerne Courtney, Dorset ; *church, 1650s monuments

****Kellie Castle**, Grampian [NTS]; rebuilt after Civil War

****Kingston Lacy**, Dorset [NT]; Bankes family house post-1660, memorials of Corfe Castle siege

Knotting, Bedfordshire; *church, 1637 gates to chancel to prevent cock-fights

Langley, Shropshire; *chapel, well-preserved furnishings

****Lanhydrock**, Cornwall [NT]; house completed 1650s (although much rebuilt after Victorian fire)

Lansdown, Bath, Avon; *Bevil Grenville monument [EH] to Battle of Lansdown Hill

Leeds, West Yorkshire; *St John's church, 1630s

Leicester, Leicestershire; **Newarke Houses and Royal Leicestershire Regiment Museum, Civil War displays

Leighton Bromswold, Cambridgeshire; *church re-fitted by George Herbert, 1630s tower

****Leith Hall**, Scotland [NTS]; building originally erected in Civil War

Lichfield, Staffordshire; *Cathedral, badly-damaged in Civil War sieges; **St Mary's Centre, museum Civil War displays

****Littlecote**, near Hungerford, Berkshire; Cromwellian militia armour; 1650s chapel

****Little Dean Hall**, Gloucestershire; Civil War associations, nearby battle 1643

Little Gidding, Cambridgeshire; *church and community founded by Nicholas Ferrar

London, **Banqueting House; Charles I's place of execution

London, *Putney parish church; scene of the Putney Debates 1649

London, *Queen's Chapel, St James' Palace; built by Inigo Jones for Henrietta Maria

London, **Queen's House, Greenwich [National Maritime Museum]; built by Inigo Jones for Anne of Denmark and Henrietta Maria, recently restored to Stuart splendour

London, *St Katherine Cree church; Laudian City church

London, **Tower of London; Crown Jewels; Royal Armouries

Lyddington, Leicestershire; *church, unusual 1630s communion rails

Lydiard Tregoze, near Swindon, Wiltshire; *church, St John family memorials

Marlborough, Wiltshire; *church part-rebuilt after 1653 fire

Maulden, Bedfordshire; *church, 1650s memorials

Medbourne, Leicestershire; *church transept rebuilt 1650s as school

Menstrie Castle, Central, Scotland; **Nova Scotia Room [NTS], Scottish baronetcy displays

Messing, Essex; *church woodwork and stained glass c. 1640

Montgomery Castle, Powys, Wales; scene of siege and battle 1644

Moreton Corbet Castle, Shropshire [EH]; ruined after Civil War attack

Morpeth Castle, Northumberland; ruined after siege

Moseley Old Hall, Staffordshire [NT]; Charles II's hiding place after defeat at Worcester

Mount Grace Priory, North Yorkshire [EH]; 1654 house built in monastic ruins

Nantwich, Cheshire; *Nantwich Museum, Civil War and siege displays

Naseby, Northamptonshire; **Naseby Battle and Farm Museum

Newark-on-Trent, Nottinghamshire; *Newark Museum, siege and Civil War displays; *Newark Castle ruins, earthworks

Newburgh Priory, near Coxwold [q.v.], North Yorkshire; Cromwell's reputed burial place in daughter's house

Newbury, Berkshire; *Newbury District Museum, battle and siege displays

Newcastle-upon-Tyne, Tyneside; *Guildhall, built 1655-8

North Walsham, Norfolk; *church, Commonwealth arms on reverse of Stuart royal arms painting

Norton Conyers, near Ripon, North Yorkshire; house of Graham family; post-Marston Moor hiding place

Nottingham, Nottinghamshire; **Castle, rebuilt after 1670 as grand house, now museum

Nunwell House, Isle of Wight; associated with Charles I

Over Peover, near Knutsford, Cheshire; **Peover Hall, 1650s stables, classical designs; *1640s chapel in parish church

Oxford, Oxfordshire; *Museum of Oxford, Court and siege displays; *Castle mound; Brasenose College, 1650s-60s;

*porch of St Mary's church, 1630s; *St John's, Canterbury Quad built by Laud 1630s with royal statues

Packwood House, Warwickshire [NT]; 1650s extensions to house and gardens, including celebrated Yew Garden

Parnham House, near Beaminster, Dorset; family divided between Parliament and King

Pembroke Castle, Pembroke, Dyfed [CADW]; survivor of long siege

Pendennis Castle, Cornwall [EH]; besieged 1646

Plaxtol, Kent; *church, part 1649

Plymouth, Devon; *Citadel, fortifications rebuilt 1660s; Charles Church, 1648-53, ruined in World War II

*Pontefract Castle, North Yorkshire; long siege, fell 1649

Portland Castle, Dorset [EH]; besieged twice, fell 1646

Portsmouth, Hampshire; *Gates [EH], survivors of Civil War sieges

Powderham Castle, Devon; besieged in Civil War

Preston, Lancashire; *Harris Museum & Art Gallery, Civil War displays

Ripley Castle, North Yorkshire; scene of killing of prisoners after Marston Moor

Ross-on-Wye, Hereford and Worcester; *church, Col. Redhall monument of 1651

Rousham House, near Steeple Aston, Oxfordshire; attacked in 1645, battle-scarred

Rycote Chapel, near Thame, Oxfordshire [EH]; grand 1630s fittings

St Mawes Castle, Cornwall [EH]; unlike Pendennis opposite, surrendered quickly in siege

Saffron Walden, Essex; *Town Museum; Castle ruins; house where officers of New Model Army met 1647

Salisbury, Wiltshire; *Cathedral, Gorges tomb 1635, modelled on Temple of Solomon; *St Edmund's church, tower c. 1650

Scarborough Castle, North Yorkshire [EH]; besieged 1644-5

Scone Palace, Perth, Tayside, Scotland; place of coronation of Charles II 1650

Sherborne Old Castle, Sherborne, Dorset [EH]; slighted after siege

Sherborne New Castle, Sherborne, Dorset; Digby family seat; family museum in cellar, Civil War relics

Shrewsbury, Shropshire; Castle, headquarters of Charles I and Prince Rupert; **Rowley's House Museum, 17th-century displays

Skipton Castle, North Yorkshire; fell 1645

*South Wingfield Manor, South Yorkshire [EH]; ruined in Civil War

Sproxton, North Yorkshire; *church c. 1660

*Staunton Harrold, Leicestershire; church [NT] built defiantly 1653

Stokesay Castle, Shropshire [EH]; withstood attack; *church, 1650s repair and decoration

Sutton, Hereford and Worcester; *church, rare Commonwealth font

INDEX

Photographs and illustrations reproduced by kind permission of the following:
14; National Portrait Gallery, London: 15; Mary Evans Picture Library: 18; Tate Gallery, London: 20 and 21; Weidenfeld & Nicolson Ltd: 23; by gracious permission of Her Majesty the Queen: 24; Mary Evans Picture Library: 26a; Bridgeman Art Library: 16b; Mary Evans Picture Library: 27; The National Trust Photographic Library: 28 and 30; Weidenfeld & Nicolson Ltd: 31; Department of the Environment (Crown Copyright): 32; Weidenfeld & Nicolson Ltd: 34a; Fotomas Index: 34b; by kind permission of Lord Saye: 35a; David Souden: 35; Weidenfeld & Nicolson Ltd: 37; Royal Commission on the Historical Monuments of England: 38; Weidenfeld & Nicolson Ltd: 39a; Fotomas Index: 39b; A.F Kersting: 40; Weidenfeld & Nicolson Ltd: 41; Fotomas Index: 42; Pencarrow House, Bodmin: 45; Weidenfeld & Nicolson Ltd: 46; Bridgeman Art Library: 47; Fotomas Index: 50; Bridgeman Art Library: 51; Weidenfeld & Nicolson Ltd: 53; National Portrait Gallery, London: 54; Bridgeman Art Library: 55; Weidenfeld & Nicolson Ltd: 56; Mary Evans Picture Library: 57; Weidenfeld & Nicolson Ltd: 58a; HT Archives: 58b; Weidenfeld & Nicolson Ltd: 58c; Museum of Oxford/courtesy Lord Dartmouth: 59; Tate Gallery, London: 60; Ashmolean Museum, Oxford: 61; Weidenfeld & Nicolson Ltd: 62; private collection, England, on permanent loan to Fitzwilliam Museum, Cambridge: 63; David Souden: 64; Weidenfeld & Nicolson Ltd: 66; Mary Evans Picture Library: 70; Fotomas Index: 72; Weidenfeld & Nicolson Ltd: 73; National Portrait Gallery, London: 74 and 75; David Souden: 77a; National Portrait Gallery, London: 77b; Weidenfeld & Nicolson Ltd: 79; Ashmolean Museum, Oxford: 80 and 81; Weidenfeld & Nicolson Ltd: 82; by kind permission of Lord Saye: 83; Mary Evans Picture Library: 85; Ashmolean Museum, Oxford: 87; Mary Evans Picture Library: 88; National Portrait Gallery, London: 89; National Portrait Gallery, London: 90a; The National Trust Photographic Library: 90b; HT Archives: 92a and 92b; Fotomas Index: 93; National Portrait Gallery, London: 95a, 95b and 96; Weidenfeld & Nicolson Ltd: 97; Northampton Chronicle & Echo: 98; HT Archives: 101; Weidenfeld & Nicolson Ltd: 102; A. F. Kersting: 104; Fotomas Index: 107; Mary Evans Picture Library: 110; David Souden: 111; The National Trust Photographic Library/John Bethell: 112; Weidenfeld & Nicolson Ltd: 113; Fotomas Index: 114, 115 and 116; Weidenfeld & Nicolson Ltd: 118; Fotomas Index: 121; National Portrait Gallery, London: 122; Ashmolean Museum, Oxford/HT Archives: 126; by gracious permission of Her Majesty the Queen: 129; Weidenfeld & Nicolson Ltd: 131; Scottish National Portrait Gallery/courtesy the Earl of Rosebery: 132, 134, 137, 138, 139; Weidenfeld & Nicolson Ltd: 140; Mansell Collection: 142, 143 and 146; Weidenfeld & Nicolson Ltd: 147; Fotomas Index: 149a; National Portrait Gallery, London: 149b; National Portrait Gallery, London: 151; Suffolk Record Office: 152; National Portrait Gallery, London: 154; by courtesy of the Board of Trustees of the Victoria & Albert Museum: 156; National Portrait Gallery, London: 157; Fotomas Index: 159; Museum of London: 160; National Portrait Gallery, London: 161; Weidenfeld & Nicolson Ltd: 162; by gracious permission of Her Majesty the Queen: 163; National Portrait Gallery, London: 164, 165 and 166; Weidenfeld & Nicolson Ltd: 167; HT Archives: 170; H. Rex Cathcart: 172; Weidenfeld & Nicolson Ltd: 174 and 176; HT Archives: 179; Mansell Collection: 18O; Walker Art Gallery, Liverpool.